The Indomitable Frank Whitcombe

How a Genial Giant from Cardiff became a Rugby League Legend in Yorkshire and Australia

Martin Whitcombe and Bill Bridge

ST DAVID'S PRESS
Cardiff

Published in Wales by St. David's Press, an imprint of

Ashley Drake Publishing Ltd
PO Box 733
Cardiff
CF14 7ZY

www.st-davids-press.wales

First Impression – 2016

ISBN
978-1-902719-47-4

British Library Cataloguing-in-Publication Data.
A CIP catalogue for this book is available from the British Library.

Typeset by Replika Press Pvt Ltd, India
Printed by Akcent Media, Czech Republic

CONTENTS

Foreword by Jim Mills   v

Acknowledgements   vi

Preface by Fran Cotton   vii

Introduction   viii

 1. A Family at Play   1

 2. Army Games   6

 3. A Broughton Ranger   14

 4. Wearing the Three Feathers   18

 5. Enter Harry Hornby   23

 6. Odsal Here we Come   29

 7. War-time Glory and Gloom   36

 8. Building the Dream   44

 9. Rising to the Challenge   52

10. Winning the Peace   63

11. The Indomitables Depart   72

12. Across Australia   87

13. Let the Action Commence   98

14. The First Test   117

15. The Ashes Retained   123

16. Mud-baths in New Zealand   138

17. Back to Bradford   149

18. Hard Men   159

19. The Road to Wembley   164

20. The Lance Todd Hero   174

21. Bowing out   184

22. Goodbye to a Rugby Giant   197

23. The Whitcombe Sporting Dynasty   204

Appendix 1: The Rugby Career of Frank Whitcombe   228

Appendix 2: 'Australasian Tour 1946'   236

Bibliography   246

For my brother Simon and my father Frank Whitcombe Jnr

FOREWORD

When Frank Whitcombe's grandson Martin asked me to write a few words about Frank, I was only too pleased to have a little input for a man I have admired tremendously since coming into the rugby league game.

Frank died at the age of 44 so I never met him, but he is someone who I feel walked the same path as myself. My old friend Trevor Foster was forever talking to me about his great friend and team-mate and the more I heard about Frank the closer I felt to this legend of our game.

Jim Mills (RFL Archives)

Firstly, the Whitcombes lived a stone's throw from my family in the Grangetown area of Cardiff. Frank lived in Wedmore Road while we were in Gloucester Street just a few minutes' walk away. My brother David was born in that house and my grandparents lived in Ninian Park Road just around the corner.

Frank was born in 1913 and I arrived in 1944, years apart, but the way our lives took the same path is something special to me. We both played for Cardiff RFC and for Bradford Northern RLFC; we both played at Wembley in Challenge Cup finals; and we both played for Wales and Great Britain. We were both prop forwards and when our playing careers were over we both went into the licensed trade.

Many people who played with Frank have told me what a wonderful forward he was, a very strong, powerful prop who also had a fair turn of speed for such a big man. Trevor Foster, I know, thought the world of him.

The only thing I am sad about is that I never met the great man; I am sure we would have become great friends. I am sure, too, that this book on Frank and the 'Indomitables' will be a great success. I am so proud to have walked the same path as this wonderful man.

Jim Mills
Bradford Northern, Wales and Great Britain

ACKNOWLEDGEMENTS

I am grateful to the following people for their help in producing this book: Brian Whitcombe, Mollie Whitcombe, Natasha Whitcombe, James Whitcombe, Carron Whitcombe, Dawn Walters, John Walters, David Lee, Diane Lee, Tony Walters, Tracy Walters, Dai Richards (Rugby Relics), Frank Mugglestone, Keith Jones, Tony Orford, Joan Warburton, Neil Warburton, Neil Fox MBE, Gary Etherington, Harry Jepson OBE, Charlie Ebbage, Graham Morris, Peter Jackson, Jim Mills, Fran Cotton, Maurice Bamford, Phil Davies, Simon Foster, Trevor Foster OBE, Professor Tony Collins, Ian Jackson (Swinton), Martin Bass, Dr Kathryn Hughes, John Downes, John Mason (Bradford Bulls Foundation), Stuart Farmer (Leicester Tigers), Sam Morton, Howard Evans, Pat Bennett, Sandra Bennett, Paul Bekon and Joe Jones (London Welsh), Claire Bridge, Les Hoole, Andy Shackleton, Alan Brookes (Featherstone Rovers), Lee Robinson (Wakefield Trinity), Mike Rylance (Wakefield Trinity), Jeff Smith (Castleford), Phil Caplan (Leeds), Les Williams (Llanelli RFC), Harry Edgar (Rugby League Journal), Anne Greenwood, Philip Laird (Australian Railway Association), Bill Phippen (Australia), John Pitchford (Keighley), Harry Waring (Dewsbury), Bill Le Couteur (New Zealand), Dr Jim Golby, Les Smith, Ian Jackson (Swinton), Mary Webster (nee Grainge), Larry Writer (Australia), Kevin Hutchinson, Laura Hutchinson, Tim Adams, Richard Overall (RMS Rangitiki), Rob Porteous (RFL), Phil Bennett OBE, Chris Fowke (Army Rugby Union), Geraint Ashton Jones (Royal Navy Rugby Union), Geoff Mason (Royal Navy), Ron Taylor, Ralph Caulton (New Zealand All Black), Gary Slater, Peter Crowther, Neil Dowson, Mike Nicholas (Warrington Wolves), Huddersfield University Rugby Football League archive, Bill Kirkbride, John Kaye (Wakefield RFC and Yorkshire), Phil Horrocks-Taylor (Middlesbrough, Yorkshire and England), Keith Wilkinson (Bradford RFC), Mike Dixon, Leslie, 'Legs' Bentley, Archie Rika Rane, Len Haley, Billy Boston MBE, Tom Fattorini, Eorl Crabtree, Matt Kelly, Jeremy Crabtree, Arran Crabtree, Bev Risman OBE, Jed Stone OBE (Hampshire Rugby Union), Ian Tabor (Cardiff RFC), Stephen Winterburn, Richard Thorpe, Marc Selby (Wigan), Dick Williams (Gloucester Rugby Heritage), Stephen Berg (New Zealand Rugby Museum), John Waind (Wakefield RFC and Yorkshire), Ian Gibson (Leicester Tigers and Yorkshire), David Duckworth, Dave Sherwood (Hull Kingston Rovers), Tony Capstick, Dave Smith (Royal Air Force Rugby Union), Alden Phillips (Keighley RUFC), Roger Harrison, Alex Murphy OBE, Stuart Duffy, Pat and Richard Emanuel, Denise French (National Museum of Australia),Terry Williams (Rugby League Central, Sydney), Mark Ring and Mark Jones (Wales and Grange Albion Baseball Club), Ian McIntosh (Natal Sharks), David Lightfowler and Mark Heap. I would also like to say a special thanks to Neville Chadwick Photography for their assistance with a number of images in this book and to David Ingham for the use of his painting on the cover.

Martin Whitcombe

PREFACE

Some of my favourite childhood memories were of chatting with my dad and asking about his rugby experiences. He was a professional rugby league player with St Helens and Warrington, before and after the Second World War. Both clubs had very successful periods at this time, leaving him with an array of medals which I loved looking at.

My favourite was the solid gold Championship winning medal for the 1947-8 season, when Warrington beat Bradford Northern at Maine Road, Manchester. At that time, Bradford were a star-studded team but one man always came out in our conversations and that was Northern's giant open-side prop forward, Frank Whitcombe.

Fran Cotton

Dad always enthused, not only about his scrummaging and play in the loose, but also that he was very light on his feet for a huge man and surprisingly a good place kicker and an excellent tactical kicker of the ball. This was unheard of back then and even now is rare to see such skills from a prop forward.

Frank Whitcombe became a Welsh international and a Great Britain tourist. He is widely regarded as an all-time great of rugby league.

Some years later when I had switched my affections to rugby union, I noticed when reading the paper about the County Championship the name F. Whitcombe in the team playing prop for Yorkshire. I immediately put two and two together and realised this must be the son of the legendary Frank Whitcombe.

Then, after my own playing days were over, I spotted the name Martin Whitcombe playing for Yorkshire Schools. At the time I was coaching at Sale and decided to follow this up when Martin was in the Yorkshire team playing North Midlands in the County Championship semi-final at Moseley.

I was standing behind the posts when suddenly this burly Yorkshire prop bustled over, underneath the cross-bar to score. Martin then signed for Sale and had a terrific career, also playing for the North of England and England B.

The Whitcombe dynasty is remarkable for the fact that they all played top-class rugby and all played their rugby at prop forward. There may be even more to this story with the next generation.

Fran Cotton
Sale, England and British Lions

INTRODUCTION

As part of their celebrations on being named European Capital of Sport in 2014, the City of Cardiff organised a gathering to mark the success of sporting heroes from the city from the last century, with British and Empire heavyweight champion Jack Petersen and the brothers George and Frank Whitcombe among them.

A special event was organised on April 8 2014 in their hometown of Grangetown when Councillor Peter Bradbury, cabinet member for Community Development, Co-operative and Social Enterprise, launched the 'Local Heroes' project and explained its purpose in Cardiff's year as European Capital of Sport.

James Whitcombe, Frank's great-grandson, takes the Rugby League Challenge Cup back to 52 Wedmore Road, Grangetown, Cardiff.

"We want all our young sportsmen and women in Cardiff to know that our current set of superstars – Gareth Bale, Sam Warburton, Elinor Barker and Geraint Thomas – are merely giants standing on the shoulders of sporting colossuses from previous generations in the city," he said, sowing the seed of an idea which has become this book.

Among those heroes were many who took the road from Cardiff to play rugby league in the North of England following the great schism in the union code in 1895. Among the first were Wharton "Wattie" Davies and Dai Fitzgerald, both Cardiff boys, who signed for Batley, were in the team which won the Challenge Cup in its inaugural season, 1896-7, and took the trophy again in the 1900-1 campaign.

Among many others to 'go north' from Cardiff were inductees into the Rugby League Hall of Fame Jim Sullivan and Billy Boston plus other greats including 'Johnny' Freeman, Clive Sullivan, Colin Dixon and Jim Mills. Frank Whitcombe was another and this is his story.

Martin Whitcombe
January 2016

1

A FAMILY AT PLAY

At first sight, Frederick William Whitcombe was a man typical of his times: a hard-working, hard-playing Welshman, given to enjoying a drink or two and even a scrap or two as a bare-knuckle boxer in the smoke-filled halls of Cardiff as Britain entered a new century.

He worked as a blacksmith's striker in the Cardiff Dry Docks – an area of that prosperous city known as Tiger Bay – but the Whitcombes, Fred and Gertrude, were far from wealthy.

Gertrude knew that if she did not meet her husband as he emerged, weary, grimy and thirsty, from his forge on a Friday afternoon he would, along with his workmates, head for the bars and boozers of Cardiff and spend most of his wages slaking his thirst and enjoying himself. It was her duty to relieve him of his money before others did.

Fredrick Whitcombe, the founder of a rugby dynasty.

In his fighting days he would regularly come across Police Constable Tommy Foster, one of whose duties was to break up the illegal fist-fights which Fred would use to supplement his income. Tommy's grandson Trevor would later figure prominently in the life of one of Fred and Gertrude's 10 children, all born at 52 Wedmore Road in the Grangetown area of Cardiff.

Of those 10, Teddy, the eldest boy, was a successful baseball player – Cardiff being, along with Newport and Liverpool, a major centre for the game which provided footballers and rugby players with a summer activity to keep them in good physical condition – and a leading

Fredrick John (Teddy) Whitcombe, baseball player and football player at Grange Albion.

George Whitcombe in his days at Port Vale FC.

footballer for Grange Albion, one of the most respected of amateur clubs in the city.

Another brother, George, was even more successful as a dual-code sportsman. Born in 1902, he too played for Grange Albion and also for Bargoed, but was good enough to earn a professional contract with Cardiff City in the First Division of the Football League.

A half-back, George played for Cardiff for three seasons, including that of 1923-4 when City finished as runners-up in the title race, before being sold to Stockport County. After only 15 games for Stockport, George left following a dispute over wages and moved on to Second Division Port Vale in August 1926.

One of the highlights of his career in the Midlands was a fourth-round FA Cup-tie against the mighty Arsenal. The pair drew 2-2 at the Old Recreation Ground before Vale were beaten 1-0 at Highbury in the replay. Arsenal went on to reach the final where they were beaten by George's first club, Cardiff City, at Wembley – the only time the FA Cup has been won by a non-English team.

George played a total of 51 games for Port Vale before moving on to Notts County where he made just seven appearances, including a County Cup encounter with Frickley Colliery during which he was sent off for the only time in his career.

George Whitcombe might have epitomised the journeyman professional footballer but he was anything but average at baseball, playing five times for his country against England and being honoured with the captaincy of his national team.

Staying with Grange Albion throughout his baseball career, he helped the club win the Welsh Baseball Union Cup three times between 1921 and 1932. He also won the Dewar Shield, awarded to the Welsh League Champions, five times over the same period. When he retired, Grange Albion made him a life member of the club.

George Whitcombe sends news from Stockport, to say he's made the first team.

With his boxing father and role-model brothers like Teddy and George, it was hardly surprising that another son of Fred and Gertrude Whitcombe would follow the family's sporting tradition. But they and Frank William Whitcombe – born in May 1913 – could hardly have imagined that he would have been the man to found a special rugby-playing dynasty.

Frank's childhood was spent at Ninian Park Council School in Grangetown, where he was introduced to rugby and was soon a regular at full-back for the school team. His spare time was divided between kicking a rugby ball with his friends on the Sevenoaks playing field and selling Gertrude's home-brewed beer and, in the summer, sloe gin to the neighbours. A wife and mother had to help with the family income during the hard times in working-class Cardiff.

When he reached 14, the young Whitcombe had to find work and he took his first job as a delivery boy for McNeil's 'The Coal', before becoming a van boy with the Great Western Railway.

England captain Louis Page shakes hands with his Welsh opposite number George Whitcombe, May 17 1930. Page also played football for Manchester United & England.

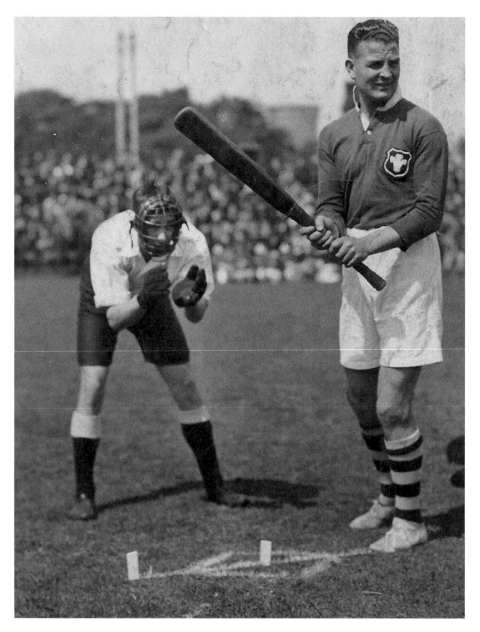

George Whitcombe batting for Wales against England, at the Old Recreation Ground, home of his then football team Port Vale F.C., May 17 1930.

Rugby was still his game of choice and at 17, thanks to encouragement from his brother George, he began playing senior rugby with the Cardiff club, one of the great institutions of the Welsh game, quickly earning recognition

Frank Whitcombe is pictured on the extreme right of the second row in this photograph of the Ninian Park School team in 1922.

as a young full-back of promise. Young Whitcombe's cousin, Frank Trott, was also a full-back at Cardiff and would later play eight times for Wales.

But the Thirties were as grim in Cardiff as they were all over Europe and North America, with poverty the scourge of the working class and unemployment a cloud which had no silver lining.

Four months after joining Cardiff and enduring a period out of work, young Whitcombe took the step which was to change his life, provide him with the first strides on a march which would take him to fame and prosperity and make the name of Whitcombe synonymous, for generations of Yorkshire folk, with the name of Bradford Northern and the game of rugby league football.

2

ARMY GAMES

On January 17 1931, Frank Whitcombe began a new life as a motor driver in the Army, Sapper No 1869154 in the 38th Field Company, Royal Engineers, giving the recruitment officer a false date of birth; a misdemeanour which was far from being a rare occurrence during the days of hunger marches, soup kitchens and heart-wrenching poverty for millions.

Fortunately for Frank, apart from landing a full-time job with further career opportunities aplenty, he had become a member of an outstanding sporting unit. In his first year as a soldier with the 38th Field Company, he won the Royal Engineers' Athletics Challenge Cup, Boxing Cup and Rugby Cup and he made the positional change which was to make his name as a rugby player.

38th Field Company Royal Engineers, Aldershot in 1931-2. Frank Whitcombe is in the second row, fifth from left.

It was no small challenge to turn from full-back to prop forward, but young Whitcombe was already a grown man, albeit one with surprisingly small feet which enabled him to side-step at will, a brilliant pair of hands, the unquenchable belief in his own strength and ability to be expected of the son of a bare-knuckle fighter, and a sense of humour which not only enabled him to always look on the bright side of life but also provided his team-mates with encouragement whenever things were going against them

He showed his potential in a Colchester Garrison Cup first round match when his company – whose team was chosen from between 80 and 150 men – took on the 2nd Battalion the Bedfordshire and Hertfordshire Regiment, who had between 300 and 1,300 men from whom to pick their line-up.

Jim Croston with the Challenge Cup plinth after Wakefield Trinity's victory over Wigan in the 1946 cup final.

The 38th Field Company won the game 14-3 and an observer reported in the *Eastern Counties Advertiser*: "Sapper Whitcombe played a fine game for the Royal Engineers forwards, who excelled at dribbling movements." Whitcombe also scored two of his team's three tries.

It was fortunate that, as he began to learn his new craft in the underworld of the front-row of the scrum, the battleground of the line-out and the mayhem of rucks and mauls, young Frank had some wonderful tutors, among them the Ireland No 8 forward Hal Withers, Scottish winger John Crawford and an outstanding centre from Wigan in Jim Croston.

Croston played twice for the Army in the 1933 Inter-Services Championship and his performances were noticed by a former Army officer Capt James Pickles, who happened to be the secretary of Castleford RLFC.

Croston accepted Castleford's offer to turn professional, bought himself out of the Army and began a hugely-successful career in the 13-a-side code. He kept in touch with young Whitcombe, and his progress in rugby league was a key influence on the latter's thinking, as he rapidly developed in his new position at prop.

After a successful first season in the front row, Whitcombe joined the Aldershot Services club, whose fixtures list included several first-class clubs and he quickly widened his experience playing against the likes of Bristol, United Services and Plymouth Albion.

There was also a major change in his life away from the rugby field and his Army duties as, on July 25 1933, he returned to Cardiff to marry Doris

May Bryan, who had also grown up in Grangetown with a sporting father, Alfie Bryan, a noted boxing trainer who had worked with 'Peerless' Jim Driscoll, the pride of Wales.

Alfie encouraged his new son-in-law to try the Noble Art, and the big lad with the big heart duly won his first 11 bouts, making a favourable impression. He was, however, totally unimpressed with the other side of the boxing coin when he was beaten in his 12th fight and decided on the spot that 11 good wins were not worth one good hiding. He hung up his gloves.

Back to rugby, Whitcombe earned his first selection for the Army during the 1933-4 season, confirming that he was becoming a force in the game; it was rare for a soldier with the rank of Sapper to earn a place in a team whose players were, almost to a man, officers or non-commissioned officers.

So quickly did he make his mark, he would represent the Army on 27 occasions during the next 18 months, at a time when they played most of the leading clubs in England and Wales. He figured in one match, a 14-3 defeat at Bristol, about which the *Western Daily Press* commented: "Most of the Army attacks came from the vigorous work of their forwards. Outstanding

The Duke of York meets the Army team at Twickenham, March 2 1935. Frank Whitcombe is fourth from the left.

were Douglas Kendrew whose form, however, hardly reached international class, Reginald Hobbs and Sapper Frank Whitcombe."

In February 1935 he played for the Army when they beat the Territorial Army 18-5 at Taunton, in a match which served as trial before the selection of the Army XV for the Inter-Services tournament.

His name was in the team selected to face the Royal Navy at Twickenham and as well as congratulations from his team-mates and fellow Royal Engineers, there came more tangible reward with promotion from Sapper to Lance Corporal.

There was also the pleasure of three days away, from his 12-men-to-a-dormitory barracks at Gosport, to prepare for the match against the Navy. The Metropole Hotel in London was a touch of luxury for the boy from the mean streets of Grangetown where, in the previous October, his wife Doris had given birth to their first child, a son, Brian.

Frank learned of his selection in a letter from Major R S Walker, honorary secretary of the Army Rugby Union based at the War Office on Whitehall. The letter stated that players were to provide their own white shorts with the Army supplying shirts and socks, and that there would be two days of practice at the Royal Military Academy in Woolwich before the big day at Twickenham.

All players were allocated two tickets for the game and two complimentary tickets for the dance, to which attendance was compulsory, after the game. The team were told: "Drinks must be paid for by players and all extras must be paid for before leaving the hotel."

Unusually, Major Walker added a hand-written footnote to his letter to Lance Corporal Whitcombe. It read: "Now look here Whitcombe; just you get those boots of yours fixed up. No comment was made last Saturday but they were noticed. If you turn up at Twickenham like that you may not go on to the field. So see to it."

Boots duly replaced, Frank Whitcombe then played his part in a famous 11-8 victory over the Navy.

A newspaper report of the match was a paean of praise for the winners: "Never was there a rugby match more sporting and emphatically never one much harder. This was a glorious victory, and a surprising one considering that the winners played throughout the game with six forwards.

"Bernard Cowey, the Army's Welsh international right-wing, went off the field crocked after just six minutes then a greater misfortune befell them as prop forward Douglas Kendrew, the pack leader, also had to retire with a shoulder injury.

"Kendrew had been a British Lion on the 1930 tour of Australia and was also the current England captain; his loss left the Army team in a desperate situation.

"Playing conditions were ideal and it was, especially in the first half, one of the most exciting matches witnessed between these two Services. Mistakes, of course, were made on both sides and the quality of rugby never reached the highest standard but nothing could have surpassed the wonderful fight which the six Army forwards put up.

"The six played magnificently, packing 3-3 to hold their own surprisingly well in the scrums, but in the loose, where matters were more even, the Army carried out many storming rushes. It would be unfair to praise one; the six great fellows were all wonderful.

"The Army also had the advantage of having more thrustful half-backs than the Navy, in Dean and Cole. Dean's effective breakaways from the base of the scrum were always a menace, while Cole's absence from first-class rugby for nearly two years has not impaired his eye for an opening although his hands were not as good as usual.

"All the Army three-quarters played well, and it was a great afternoon for England international wing Novis who recovered from a recent injury to win his 10th Inter-Services cap and was an inspiration to his side, scoring one try, and making another for Hobbs.

"Sayers converted one try and what a roar went up when he landed a penalty goal close to half-time to give his team the lead. Lane and Hammond scored tries for the Navy, Gosling converting one and the Army held their lead, throughout a second half full of attack and counter-attack, for a glorious victory."

Frank Whitcombe's immediate opponent in the match was John 'Tubby' Linton, from Malpas in Newport. A strict naval officer and renowned perfectionist, Linton later gave up playing rugby for fear of injuries affecting his performance at sea.

During the Second World War he became a submarine commander and was responsible for the sinking of 81,000 tons of enemy shipping. In an attack on Maddalena Harbour in Italy, on March 23 1943, he was killed in action and was later awarded a posthumous Victoria Cross.

Douglas Kendrew would later rise to the rank of Major General, be awarded the Distinguished Service Order four times and serve in Korea and Cyprus, where he survived an assassination attempt by the EOKA rebels who were seeking independence for their country.

In 1963, he was appointed Governor of Western Australia and was so highly regarded in that role that his term of office was extended twice, before his eventual retirement in 1974.

Even without Kendrew and Cowey, the Army were favourites when they faced the RAF in the decisive match of the tournament – the RAF having already lost to the Navy – but they were beaten by more tactically aware opponents who were given great service by Beamish, the best forward on the field, and fly-half Walker.

The RAF went ahead with a penalty goal but the Army responded with a try in the corner from Novis then, early in the second half, Walker kicked through a startled defence to create the try which gave his side a 6-3 victory and ensured the tournament ended in a three-way tie.

Headingley's George Augustus Walker, 'Gus' to his friends, who later became an Air Chief Marshal, was capped by England and gave great service to Bomber Command during the Second World War, despite being severely wounded several times.

In peacetime, Walker was an RAF representative on the RFU committee for 16 years, was President of the Union for the 1965-6 season, and from November 1968 until July 1970 he was Air Aide de Camp to the Queen.

Bernard Cowey may not have influenced the Army's performance on the pitch, but it was at his invitation that Frank Whitcombe joined London Welsh at the beginning of the 1934-5 season, playing for them when he was not turning out for the Army and rapidly making a serious impression.

Frank made his London Welsh debut on November 17 1934, against Newport at Herne Hill, then played against Neath and Swansea on the club's Christmas tour and at Gloucester, Newport and Pontypool on their Easter tour. He also played home matches against Newport and Northampton and away, on the club's visit to Leicester.

His final appearances for London Welsh in that first season were in the prestigious Middlesex Sevens at Twickenham on April 27, where he helped the Welsh reach the final, in which they were beaten 10-3 by Harlequins. One of Whitcombe's team-mates that day was Geoffrey Rees-Jones.

Rees-Jones scored two tries for Wales in their historic 1935 victory over the All Blacks and

OFFICIAL

PROGRAMME
1935

6 D.

MIDDLESEX COUNTY R·F·U

7

**A·SIDE
FINALS**

TWICKENHAM
SATURDAY · APRIL 27 · AT 1·40 P M

(By special permission of the Rugby Football Union.)

The official programme for the 1935 Middlesex Sevens at Twickenham.

The Rest team which played against Wales, May 4 1935, Frank Whitcombe is sitting on the front row left.
The team was as follows: Tommy Stone (Cardiff), Alan Edwards (Aberavon), Randall Lewis (Aberavon), Jack Thomas (Aberavon), Trefor Jenkins (Treorchy), Ben Southway (Blaina), Eddie Youatt (Neath), Mog Rees (Neath), Frank Whitcombe (London Welsh), Illtyd Williams (Bridgend), L M Proctor (Maesteg), Will Mabbett (London Welsh), Walter Vickery (Aberavon), T Sayers (Abertillery), Arthur Childs (Abertillery)

later he became a founder member of No. 1 Commando and a pioneer in the training of Special Forces during the Second World War.

Whitcombe's next game was the following Saturday when he returned to Cardiff to appear in a match between Wales and the Rest, organised to benefit the King George V Silver Jubilee Trust at the Arms Park, a fixture which caused one of those controversies that the game seems to so often generate.

Another game had been organised for that day, between Wales Secondary Schools and the Rest, at Aberdare. Half-backs Hayden Tanner and Willie Davies, cousins and students at Gowerton County School in Swansea, were selected for Wales in both games, Tanner as captain of the Wales Schools team.

Eventually it was decided that the pair should play at Cardiff, the Welsh Rugby Union insisting they should perform in the senior game so that selectors could assess the potential of two such gifted talents, with a view to them playing international rugby.

Famously, the two schoolboys played for Swansea at St. Helen's, in the team which beat the All Blacks in 1935, with Tanner also starring at fly-half the same season when Wales also managed to overcome the New Zealand tourists.

For the record, Wales beat the Rest 13-5 with tries from Gwyn Moore, Elfed Jones and Ike Jones, with Tommy Owen James adding two conversions. For the Rest, Frank's London Welsh team-mate Will Mabbett scored a try, which Lloyd Williams converted.

Of those in action that day in Cardiff, several would take the same road as Frank Whitcombe and 'go north'. Willie Davies, the teenage genius at fly-half, would join Bradford Northern, win the Lance Todd trophy at Wembley and play alongside Whitcombe for the Odsal club, Wales and Great Britain.

On the wing for Wales was Arthur Bassett, another star bound for rugby league, earning a place in the game's history when he scored a hat-trick of tries as Great Britain retained the Ashes in Brisbane in 1946.

Alongside Frank in the Rest team was winger Alan Edwards, also a future Bradford and Wales team-mate and a man who became one of only five men to win all six of rugby league's six major trophies – the Yorkshire League and Cup, the Lancashire League and Cup, the Championship and the Challenge Cup.

In the back row for the Rest that day in Cardiff was Arthur Childs, who would soon leave Abertillery for Halifax where he quickly became established in the Thrum Hall club's side.

Exactly 29 years later his son Rodney, then playing for Halifax RUFC at Ovenden Park, would play alongside Frank Whitcombe's younger son, Frank junior, in the front row for the North Eastern Counties in their fixture with Wilson Whineray's 1964 All Blacks, at the Great Yorkshire Showground in Harrogate.

3

A BROUGHTON RANGER

By now Frank Whitcombe had himself been spotted by the rugby league scouts in south Wales, who kept the clubs in the North of England aware of the upcoming players who might make the grade as professionals.

The first offer came from Wigan in the summer of 1935 but Frank, despite the best efforts of his brother George to persuade him otherwise, rejected their advances.

When a second contact was made on September 18, this time by Broughton Rangers, he decided to take up the offer, took the train from Euston to Manchester Piccadilly station and signed the forms. The signing was a shock to the men responsible for selecting the Combined Services team to face the All Blacks, as they had named Whitcombe in their pack for a trial match against a London Counties XV.

Rangers had finished in mid-table at the end of the 1934-5 season and had decided to invest in new players in order to draw the crowds, which would bring in the money for the club to progress further.

Among their signings before they landed Frank Whitcombe, were scrum-half Ernie Thompson from Huddersfield, who would become club captain and also play for England, international stand-off Jack Garvey from St Helens, Wales and Llanelli full-back Bryn Howells and Frank Hillman, who had played alongside Whitcombe for Aldershot Services.

Frank's four-year stint in the Army, which had helped him develop into one of the outstanding young players in the country, now came to an end. Of the £100 (plus two bespoke suits) which Rangers had paid him to turn professional, he needed to spend £90 to buy himself out of the Army, so actually 'went north' for just £10.

On bidding the 21-year-old Lance Corporal Whitcombe goodbye, his commanding officer described him as "a cheerful and hard-working man, a capable motor driver and an exceptionally good rugby footballer".

Whitcombe, his wife Doris and son Brian began their new life at 5 Cawdor Road in Fallowfield, a modest suburb of Manchester, where they were joined by Bryn Howells, a former steel-worker from Hendy who was one of those unfortunate players who, for all their talent – and Howell had

Broughton Rangers during Frank's first season, 1935-6, with the players wearing the club's new blue and white quartered shirts.
Back row L-R: Captain Stuart Hampson MC, JP, (Director), Dr J Wishart (Director), Ted Smith (Trainer), W Barnes, George Mills, Dick Manning, Bert Cambridge, Frank Whitcombe, Bill Morgan, Alf Scott (Masseur), Bert Atkinson (Director), and George Wilson (Vice Chairman).
Second row L-R: Bryn Howells, George Bunter, Jack Garvey (captain), Jim Cumberbatch, Glyn Jones, and Billy Stott.
Front row L-R: Tom Kenny, Ernie Thompson and ball boys.

that in abundance as a great catcher and kicker of a ball – did not gain the recognition they deserved.

In Wales Howell was understudy to the great Vivian Jenkins and, unfortunately, when he turned to rugby league he found his way to international honours blocked by another superstar, Jim Sullivan.

He was similarly unfortunate in his other sporting sphere – cricket. Initially a professional with Gorseinon, near Swansea, he played in the Lancashire League and was offered terms by Lancashire County Cricket Club, but his dreams of playing the first-class game ended with the outbreak of the Second World War.

An unusual clause in several of the Broughton Rangers players' contracts was that they were to expected to work at Belle Vue Zoological Gardens in Manchester, part of the leisure complex which also included Rangers' ground and was, for many years, an attraction for pleasure seekers from all over the North of England.

The money earned looking after the animals was a useful addition to the £3-a-week the men drew for playing rugby league football.

After playing his first game of rugby league for the Rangers 'A' team at Hull, Frank Whitcombe made his debut for Rangers in their home fixture against neighbours Swinton – then a power in the game – on October 19

1935 when the club's directors had the satisfaction of seeing their new-look side triumph 9-0.

They had made three changes in the backs, two at half-back and two in the pack, leaving out several highly-experienced players and pitching Whitcombe and scrum-half Joe Luckey into their first games. In terrible weather, Frank played a key part in Rangers' first try, making a telling break against a formidable defence and passing to stand-off Tom Kenney to score.

Billy Stott then ran half the length of the field against a strong wind, chipped over Swinton's full-back and touched down in the corner. Another try by Kenney sealed a memorable victory for Rangers and Whitcombe – "strong in the pack and conspicuous in the loose" according to one observer – had made a great impression in his first game of rugby league.

After a run of brilliant victories in the New Year, Rangers finished sixth in the table for the 1935-6 season, their best performance in 20 years, and the investment in new players had proved successful.

But not everything went as smoothly off the field. One lunchtime, Frank - ever the joker and never one to turn down a pint or five - and his team-mates retired to the local public house for a drink and, on returning to work at the zoo, decided to set free the collection of zebras.

The players laughed until their ribs ached but the management were not impressed: that was the end of the Rangers players earning extra income from looking after the animals. Eager to make up the lost income from the Zoo, Frank decided to make use of the heavy-goods driving licence he had earned in the Army and take up a demanding new job as a wagon driver, with the work hard and the hours long.

But his contribution to Rangers' success on the field continued, not least in a memorable 13-0 victory over Wally Prigg's touring Australians on a foggy Christmas Day in 1937.

A correspondent wrote of the game: "The Australian team was as near as possible to a Test 13, but had travelled through thick fog on the bus and had to feel their way to the playing area. Fortunately the fog cleared slightly to allow the game to be played.

"Rangers won the ball in four successive scrums and the Kangaroos were called upon to defend stoutly, their backs tackling well. For 10 minutes the Australians were scarcely out of their own half, and a penalty in front of the posts gave

Wally Prigg, captain of the 1936-7 Australian touring team.

Howell an easy shot but he failed. The Australians were then awarded a penalty for obstruction but McKinnon also failed.

"Seeing the action became difficult after 20 minutes but Rangers continued to attack and Mills landed a penalty goal. Howells was then successful but failed with his third kick, and Hazelton raised the Australian morale with a great run.

"In the second half the Australians gave the ball more air, but lost Herb Narvo who was sent off for striking an opponent and

Frank Whitcombe, left, joins a Broughton Rangers team mate trying to halt the famous New Zealand fullback George Nepia, then playing for Halifax.

from the penalty landed by Howell, followed quickly by another goal, put Rangers clear and Smith scored a try in the last minute to ensure Rangers would win, Howell adding the two points".

By the end of the 1936-7 season, many of the leading clubs in the game had taken notice of the improvement at Broughton Rangers and Jim Sullivan, who wrote a weekly column in the *News of the World* as well as figuring on the field for Wigan, knew what was going on.

"I believe Tom Spedding, the Broughton Rangers' secretary, has told the *World* he has not been approached for the services of Whitcombe, their grand front-row forward," wrote Sullivan.

"I have no reason to doubt Tom's word but I do know there are more than a few clubs a trifle interested. I have asked my own club Wigan several times to sign Frank but the price is the snag and is what frightened away a Yorkshire club last season. One of Rangers' neighbours – you don't need many guesses here – wanted Whitcombe but thought the price prohibitive."

"I remember Frank Whitcombe's brother, George, playing for Cardiff City, surely something unique for two brothers to become first class in different codes. There was a time you know when I nearly became a soccer player, the late Herbert Chapman, whose judgement was so seldom wrong, thought he saw in me the makings of a decent soccer player, and he made strong efforts to persuade me to sign for Huddersfield Town".

4

WEARING THE THREE FEATHERS

The progress made by Frank Whitcombe in his new career had also been observed by the Welsh selectors and he made his international debut on Saturday November 5 1938, in a 17-9 victory over England at Stebonheath Park, Llanelli.

Wales were a power in international rugby league at that time, having won the European Championship for the previous three years with victories over England and France. Rugby league across the Channel had improved significantly since 1931 when the French Rugby Union had been ejected from the Five Nations Championship amid allegations of professionalism and suspicions of administrative deficiencies.

Many union players, finding themselves with only club rugby to play, turned to rugby league which soon became the more popular of the two codes in the French rugby heartland in the south of the country which led to the emergence of France at international level and the creation of the European Championship.

The prominence of rugby league in France did not last long however. During the Second World War, the country was divided between the German-occupied north and the French-run Vichy Government in the south. The rugby union clubs opted to co-operate with the Nazi's puppet French Government and their influence soon became apparent when rugby league was prohibited in southern France.

Players returned to the union game and the financial assets of all league clubs and administrations were seized, never to be returned. The ban on the playing of rugby league was lifted after the war but officialdom ruled that the game could not be called rugby; from April 24 1949 until June 26 1991, rugby league in France had to re-style itself 'Jeu a Treize' – 'game of 13'.

There were issues, too, for those Welsh players who had left rugby union forever to play rugby league, which meant leaving home, family and friends for a new life in strange, sometimes alien surroundings. One thing is certain however, they may have left their homeland but they never lost the passion to play for their beloved Wales.

Trevor Foster, a major force at Bradford Northern for most of his life, remembered: "Wales is a very proud nation with a particular regard for sporting prowess, especially in rugby, and we as players always found there was a special atmosphere in the Welsh dressing room.

"It was never quite the same for the Great Britain team; we always felt we owed something to the good Lord for allowing us to wear the three feathers. We always wanted to wear the famous scarlet jersey for everyone back home, and particularly so against England."

When Frank made his debut for Wales, with Emrys Hughes (Huddersfield) the other prop and Con Murphy (Leeds) at hooker, he was the only player on either side to represent Broughton Rangers. Playing at Centre for England however was Jim Croston, his old team-mate from Royal Engineers days, who was making his fourth international appearance. The two had travelled a long road since their time in the Army together.

The great Jim Sullivan of Wales ...

Jim 'Buller' Sullivan was outstanding in another win for Wales but the game – played in a dense sea fret – failed in its wider role; to show the 18,000 crowd how exciting the game of rugby league could be when played by the best of exponents.

Sullivan was the unchallenged star of the rugby league world. Born on December 21 1903, he was brought up on Portmanmoor Road, in the Splott district of Cardiff and began playing rugby union for St Albans Old Boys at the age of 15. By the time he was 17 he had played 38 games for Cardiff, including one against the Barbarians.

Selection for the Barbarians to play against Newport on December 28 1920 brought him the honour of being the youngest ever to play for the illustrious club, at the age of 17 years and 26 days.

He was also an exceptional baseball player, appearing for Splott YMCA, and he was capped by Wales against England in July 1921. A month later he turned professional as a rugby player with Wigan for a signing fee of £750, and eight days after his 18th birthday he made his debut for Wales

... and Wigan, here holding the Lancashire Cup.

at Taff Vale Park, Pontypridd, where the home side were beaten 21-16 by the Australians.

Sullivan played for Wales in every game, bar one, from that day until he retired and was described by Eddie Waring, as one of "the greatest Welshmen ever to be signed."

Surprising aspects of the fourth successive win for Wales against England were that the home side were second best at the scrum and played the entire second half without their second-row Harold Thomas who had suffered a fractured pelvis.

Sullivan repelled England with a series of massive kicks in the opening spell then Wales took charge with tries from Alan Edwards and Des Case, who both crossed in the corner, Sullivan adding the goals with superlative kicks from the touchline then landing a penalty just before the break.

Gus Risman crossed early in the second half for Wales before the Widnes pair of Tommy McCue and Tommy Shannon combined for the latter to touch down for England. Billy Belshaw kicked the goal and added a penalty goal but a drop goal from Risman sealed the Welsh victory and a final penalty from Belshaw was incidental.

The Wales Team in Bordeaux, April 16 1939. Frank Whitcombe is back row, fifth from left.
Jim Sullivan (Wigan) captain, Des Case (Bradford Northern), Dennis Madden (Leeds), Gus Risman,(Salford), Alan Edwards (Salford), Oliver Morris (Hunslet), Cliff Evans (Leeds), Dai Prosser (Leeds), Jim Regan (Huddersfield), Frank Whitcombe (Bradford Northern), Harold Thomas (Salford), Emrys Hughes (Huddersfield), Gwyn Williams (Wigan). Referee, J W Webb.

A second cap for Wales came Frank Whitcombe's way with the trip to face France at the splendid new Parc Lescure Stadium in Bordeaux on April 16 1939. The arena was built for the 1938 FIFA World Cup and the last football match to be played there had been the third-fourth place play-off game between Brazil and Sweden.

In a match for which Wales were clear favourites to win and retain their European crown, Whitcombe's direct opponent was the redoubtable Henri Gibert, known in French rugby league as 'The Bear'.

Wales made three changes to the side that had beaten England. Cliff Evans moved to outside-half, for the injured Dai Jenkins, where he would be partnered by Oliver Morris, while Dai Prosser was preferred to Emrys Hughes at prop.

Further alterations were necessary when the party reached Bordeaux; Jim Regan replacing Con Murphy at hooker and Gwyn Williams stepping in for Alex Givvons at loose forward after injuries to the two first-choice men.

To the surprise of almost everyone but themselves, the French played well above expectations and deservedly won the match 16-10 to claim their first European Championship, just five years after the competition had been founded.

The French team in Bordeaux, April 16 1939.
François Noguères (XIII Catalan), Raphael Sarris (Toulouse), Max Rousié (Roanne) captain, Jean Dauger (Roanne), Etienne Cougnenc (Villeneuve), Jep Desclaux (Bordeaux), Pierre Brinsolles (Villeneuve), Henri Gibert (Roanne), Henri Durand (Villeneuve), André Bruzy (XIII Catalan), Antoine Blain (Côte Basque), Louis Brané (Toulouse), Maurice Bruneteaud (Villeneuve).

Five of the French team – Françoise Noguères, Max Rousié, Jep Desclaux, Pierre Brinsolles and Antoine Blain – had been capped by their country at rugby union before France were dismissed from the Five Nations Championship. Desclaux was the captain of France when he signed up to play rugby league for Bordeaux but had reverted to the union game during the war.

Another Frenchman on duty that day in April was the teenager Jean Dauger, who would later be trapped in a wrangle between the two codes. He turned to union after the war – by which time France had regained their place in the Five Nations – and there was much discussion in French rugby as to whether he should be picked to play for France due to his previous links with rugby league.

Finally, when he was in his thirties, the French selectors bowed to public opinion and named him in their side to play against Scotland in 1953. The Scots were not happy to see Dauger on their field, protesting that they were playing against an 'ex-professional'. Such was the furore France never picked him again.

5

ENTER HARRY HORNBY

Most clubs had played just three Championship matches of the 1939-40 season before the fateful day, September 3 1939, when the British ultimatum to Hitler expired and war was declared. As a result of these changed national circumstances the Rugby Football League agreed to abandon the fixture list and create two separate leagues for Yorkshire and Lancashire for the duration of the war, with the winners of each league playing off against each other to decide the Championship.

The Rugby Football League's Emergency Committee also introduced measures to enable players to play for whichever club they liked as a guest, if either their club did not have a game or the player was surplus to requirements for a particular match.

Bradford Northern had prepared well for the crisis with coach Dai Rees adopting a policy of picking players who wanted to appear for Northern, secure in the knowledge that the squad was strong enough to guarantee regular winning pay, rather than having a team full of 'guests'.

Regular Northern players who were employed in the war effort or returning to the city on leave were encouraged to play as often as they could.

The man behind the clarity of the plan was Harry Hornby, who had become managing director of the club in 1936 after a brief spell on the board at Halifax.

Born on June 10 1883, Harry was the son of Joe and Ada Hornby, who lived on St John's Terrace in the West Bowling suburb of Bradford. On leaving school he went into the family scrap

Mr & Mrs Harry Hornby.

Dai Rees, one of Harry Hornby's best signings.

metal business and married Gertrude Mabel Schutt from Pudsey in 1907, the same year that Bradford Northern left their Park Avenue ground and moved first to Greenfield Stadium then to Birch Lane in the heart of West Bowling the following year.

They finally moved to the new Odsal Stadium, playing their first home game against Huddersfield on September 1 1934, when Northern were beaten 31-16 but attracted a crowd of over 20,000.

Having taken over the reins of his father's business, Harry Hornby decided to use his entrepreneurial abilities to revive Bradford Northern and his first signing was Dai Rees, the former Halifax, Wales and Great Britain forward, as coach.

Rees had been the outstanding player when Halifax beat York 22-8 in the 1934 Challenge Cup final and had carried the experience he had gained as a player into his second career as an astute tactician, superb motivator and great believer in building team spirit.

Rees and his platoon of scouts would provide Hornby with the background on many imaginative signings for the club, among them Newport's second-row Trevor Foster who joined Bradford in 1938.

According to Odsal folklore, Harry drove his Buick to Wales with a bulging wallet in his pocket determined to come home with his man. Foster did not take the bait immediately but Harry was persistent and in the end the deal was done.

Another major coup was the signing of Ernest Ward from Dewsbury Boys Club for £50 on his 16th birthday. He would become one of the greats of the game and Rees soon identified him as a future captain of the club.

Northern's pay structure then was £8-a-man for a win and £4 for losing; an away draw qualified for winning pay, a home draw for losing pay. But Ernest Ward was special and had a unique addendum to his contract which guaranteed him a fixed payment up to a maximum of 13 weeks if he was unable to play having been injured while on duty with Northern's first team.

Centre Tom Winnard, an excellent goal-kicker, had signed from St Helens for a then club record fee of £385 in 1933 then George Carmichael, an outstanding full-back with Hull Kingston Rovers, moved to Odsal, as did Ted Spillane, a half-back from New Zealand.

To strengthen the pack, England prop Len Higson, second row Frank Murray and local Police Boys Club loose-forward Billy Hutchinson were signed, as were hooker Vincent Dilorenzo from Warrington and the hard-as-teak Edwin 'Sandy' Orford, originally from Crumlin in South Wales.

The Orford family had moved to Yorkshire in 1921 when the master of the house was appointed shaft sinker at Walton Colliery, near Wakefield. The young Orford also went into the mining trade, working as a pony driver at the age of 14 alongside Castleford's second-row forward Ken Jubb. At 16 Orford was in Dewsbury's first team and soon came to the attention of Dai Rees.

Northern then signed Bill Smith, the captain of Ryton RUFC in County Durham, who, at the age of 23, had played for Durham for three seasons and also appeared for a Northumberland and Durham XV against the All Blacks. Standing 5ft 10in and weighing 13st 2lb, Smith had previously played in a trial match for Rochdale Hornets under the name of Jones.

Sandy Orford, proudly wearing his first Welsh cap, England v Wales at Odsal, December 23 1939.

Next to move to Odsal was George Bennett, a stand-off born in Newport on July 8 1913 and a product of the Risca Rugby Union Club. He had 'gone north' to join Wigan and the following article appeared in the *Hull Daily Mail* on April 8 1936: "Wigan created a surprise yesterday when they announced that they had put George Bennett, their Welsh international stand-off on the transfer list. The reason for the decision is not given, nor is the fee. "Bennett is considered to be one of the finest half-backs in the game"

Bennett moved from Wigan to Bradford Northern on December 9 1937 for a club record fee of £1,000. His first game was on Christmas Day against Bramley when Northern won 15-10.

Two years earlier, on January 1 1935 at the Stade Chaban Delmas in Bordeaux, Bennett won the first of his three caps as Wales lost 18-11 to France, becoming the first black player to win a Welsh cap in either code of rugby.

Former All Black tourist, the Maori George Harrison was another recruit for Northern, signing from Wigan on October 22 1937. He made his debut the following day against Huddersfield at Fartown.

Harrison, who was not on the transfer list, was 24, weighed 14st 10lb and stood 6ft 2in. He could play in the second-row or at loose forward and had moved to London from Wigan the previous season.

Then Northern became the first club to sign players from overseas who were still living outside England.

George Harrison, the Maori forward who joined Northern from Wigan, October 22 1937.

They had received cabled confirmation that full-back Graham Gilbert, who had toured Great Britain with the 1935-6 All Blacks, and half-back Robert Hohaia, who had played for the All Blacks when only 18, had accepted terms and would soon be taking a ship for England.

Still not content, Harry Hornby and Dai Rees turned their sights on Broughton Rangers and their much talked-about prop Frank Whitcombe. Hornby made an enquiry as to Whitcombe's availability and was given short shrift by Tom Spedding, his opposite number in Manchester. Undaunted, in December 1938 he sat behind the wheel of his Buick and set off to cross the Pennines.

The transfer talking began on a Wednesday morning and ended on Friday afternoon when Northern agreed to pay £850 – a world record for a front-row forward; Harry Hornby had worked his magic again.

But it would be wrong to think of Hornby as a one-dimensional big spending man; his interests and ambitions spread far beyond the world of rugby league. His pet project was the development of Odsal as a 'community stadium', decades before the term had been invented.

He would take any chance, chase every dream, to reach his ultimate: seeing the ground in use throughout the year and attracting ever bigger crowds.

Odsal Stadium on April 1 1939, when a crowd of 66,308 saw Halifax face Leeds in the Rugby League Challenge Cup semi final.

Ignoring rugby union's intransigent stance against anything even remotely connected with rugby league, he promoted a union seven-a-side tournament at Odsal with Bradford RFC – of whom he was a committee member, and later, a life member – beating Otley in the final. There was also a war-time Yorkshire Substitute Cup final in which Bradford were again triumphant, this time beating Brighouse 22-3 before a crowd of 9,000.

His open-door stance was rewarded when the RFU finally gave permission for rugby union matches to be played involving union and league players, one such going ahead at Odsal when, notably, Bob Weighill, then a serving officer in the Royal Air Force and later secretary of the Rugby Football Union itself, was among the participants.

Brass band concerts and sheep-dog trials were among the off-the-wall ideas Hornby turned into reality. The ground was also used throughout the war as base for an Air Raid Reporting Centre.

Never missing an opportunity to make money for the business of running Odsal, Hornby even applied to Bradford City Council for half of Dai Rees' salary to be paid from local government funds on the grounds that he was effectively acting as caretaker of Odsal as well as coach to Bradford Northern: the council rejected Hornby's suggestion.

His greatest ambition – rugby league trophies aside – had been to introduce speedway to Odsal and he was on the verge of launching the new sport when war broke out.

Undaunted, he bided his time and when peace was restored in 1945 he called in Johnnie Hoskins, who always claimed to have invented speedway, to manage the new Bradford team.

For several years Odsal attracted huge crowds to watch top grade speedway and the brilliant rugby Bradford Northern were producing. But still Harry Hornby was not satisfied.

He underwrote improvements to the floodlighting system used for speedway so that evening rugby could be played and half-a-century ahead of its time he introduced floodlit cricket.

He also brought the world-famous Harlem Globetrotters basketball team to Bradford but his proudest moment came in May 1954 when the Rugby League Challenge Cup final between Warrington and Halifax ended in a draw at Wembley with the replay being set for Odsal.

On that amazing afternoon a world record crowd of 102,569 swarmed over the shale bankings of the stadium, but it was a figure which many who were present on the day would contend to their dying breath was far below the actual attendance.

But all things have an end and Harry Hornby's golden era at Odsal was halted in 1958 when, at the age of 75, the great man retired and sold his 1,009 shares in Bradford Northern.

His horn-rimmed spectacles, bushy eye-brows and trade-mark Homburg hat were now heading for the cruise ships of the world, and the pleasures of sailing Lake Windermere at sunset. The replacements for his passion for Odsal and rugby league.

Harry Hornby died in Morecambe – Bradford-on-Sea – on March 13 1971, survived by his wife Gertrude with whom he had no children. He was buried five days later at Hale Carr Cemetery in nearby Heysham.

Trevor Foster had played throughout Northern's great years and later, along with other former players Joe Phillips and 'Sandy' Orford, helped rebuild the club when the glory days appeared to be over for ever, paid the perfect tribute: "Harry Hornby made Bradford Northern and Odsal Stadium. He had a knack of bringing the best out of people, a marvellous foresight and an aptitude for publicity which really put Northern and rugby league on the map."

Sandy Orford, back row centre, with his fellow directors when Bradford Northern were re-formed in 1964. Another former player, New Zealander Joe Phillips, is third from left on the front row.
The Directors: Chairman Mr Joe Phillips, Vice Chairman Mr Frank Hillam, Directors Mr P.J. (Phil) Lloyd, Mr J.W. Pell, Mr R.L. Johnson, Mr W.G.C. (Geoff) Cooper, Mr G. Brown, Mr J. Cameron, Mr H. (Harry) Womersley, Mr J. (Jack) Fricker, Mr M. (Maurice) Lambert, Mr E.J. (Sandy) Orford.

6

ODSAL HERE WE COME

Frank Whitcombe played his last game for Broughton Rangers – a 22-6 defeat at St Helens – on December 18 1938, before having to quickly find new accommodation for his growing family which now included Frank junior – born on July 21 1936, in the Wibsey district of Bradford close to Odsal – in time to celebrate Christmas before making his debut for Northern against Bramley on Boxing Day.

The transfer was confirmed in the *Yorkshire Evening Post* on Christmas Eve 1938: "By the signing of Frank Whitcombe from Broughton Rangers, Bradford Northern have made a move which, it is expected, will do much towards increasing their scrummaging power.

"Whitcombe is one of the most powerful forwards in the game, weighing about 15st, and Con Murphy, the Leeds hooker, who had Whitcombe at his side in the Welsh team that played England at Llanelli on November 5, says that Whitcombe is a man and a half in his strength to support the hooker. Whitcombe, who is 24, 'came north' via Cardiff RFC two years ago to sign for Broughton, he plays on the referee's side of the front row of the scrummage, he was capped for the first time last month".

Before the game Frank was introduced to fellow-Welshman Trevor Foster and the two gelled perfectly, beginning a close friendship which would last a lifetime.

Northern won 25-7 before a crowd of 11,500 with Foster scoring three of their seven tries. Others to touch down were Charles Freeman, Leslie Grainge, George Bennett and Len Higson while Graham Gilbert added two goals. Whitcombe made a splendid impression, tackling superbly and still going as strongly at the final whistle as he had been at the first.

As was normal in those days, the return game over the Christmas period was played the following day and Frank made an impact on his team-mates when he arrived at the team bus. As he climbed the steps he banged his fist

Donald Ward joined his brother, Ernest at Bradford Northern March 25 1939, after playing in France.

Harold Edwards, moved to Odsal from Wigan in November 1937.

on the window and shouted: "I have not come here to draw losing pay!"

The message hit home: Northern won 11-5 at Bramley and the big man had announced his arrival in terms everyone at the club understood.

But the club was not complacent – Harry Hornby was not the kind of man to stand still – and the recruitment of outstanding players continued. In the New Year, Northern signed Welsh international prop Harold Edwards from Wigan, Ernest Ward's brother Donald, who had been attached to the Paris Celtic club as player-coach, and 19-year-old Des Case from Newport RFC.

In 1939 Hornby was back on to road to the Valleys, first signing Emlyn Walters from Glynneath, a winger with remarkable speed, then the player who was to become the jewel in Northern's crown. Dai Rees, of whom it was said had more spies than Winston Churchill, took a call from his brother Len in Wales, during which it was suggested that Willie Davies, then first choice for Wales at fly-half, was available at a price of £1,500.

William Thomas Harcourt Davies was born on August 23 1913 in Penclawdd, where his parents ran the Ship and Castle public house. On September 28 1935, while still at Gowerton School, Willie Davies and Hayden Tanner played at half-back for Swansea when they became the first non-international team to beat the All Blacks.

Former Pontypridd captain, Emlyn Walters, became a great crowd favourite after joining Northern, on July 10 1939.

After winning six caps for Wales, Davies made his last appearance as a union player, for London Welsh against Pontypool, scoring a try in a 12-6 victory on April 11 1939. On joining Northern he became a teacher at Bingley Grammar School

His signing was a bargain – and it was a statement of intent from Bradford Northern: they would compete with anyone in the transfer market if it brought success on the field.

Davies played his first game at Odsal on August 26 1939, the opening game of the new season, and Northern recorded a 29-10 victory with Davies and fellow-debutant Emlyn Walters, who scored three tries, leaving the crowd in raptures at the quality of their performances.

Willie Davies (centre) meets Harry Hornby (left) and Dai Rees at Odsal, July 17 1939.

Whitcombe immediately appointed himself the club 'minder' for Davies and he stuck faithfully to his role for the rest of their time together, in club matches, internationals and on the unforgiving pitches of Australia.

Frank Whitcombe's son Brian remembers: "Dad was great friends with Willie Davies but apart from their friendship Frank knew that Willie was such a good footballer he was more than likely to get winning pay with Willie in the team. So heaven help anyone who touched Willie Davies."

At this time Bradford Northern had 1,000 members, the biggest membership in the game, but Harry Hornby wanted to double that figure. To help reach that target he allowed members to pay for membership on a weekly basis, handing over the cash at the turnstiles, a scheme many other clubs would copy.

Dewsbury's unique war time match.

Graham Gilbert returned to his native New Zealand on the outbreak of war. He played 27 times for the All Blacks including four Tests.

But more serious things were afoot, war with Germany being declared on September 3 of that year. The New Zealand tourists had arrived in England on August 29 but five days later the tour was cancelled and the unfortunate players were told that no immediate passage home was available but that they had to be ready to travel at 48 hours' notice. The only games they played were a 19-3 NZ victory against St Helens the day before war was declared, and against Dewsbury, six days later, when NZ won 22-10.

The first impact of war on Bradford Northern was the decision of their captain and full-back Graham Gilbert to return home to New Zealand.

The threat of air-raids also brought regulations restricting the size of crowds permitted at rugby league games. Headingley had a limit of 8,000 imposed while grounds capable of holding much bigger crowds – like Odsal – were restricted to 15,000 and clubs in 'danger zones' such as Hull FC needed police approval to play their games.

The Rugby Football League also introduced rules which gave freedom of movement to players, with men free to play as 'guests' for a club. Bradford Northern were the first club to make use of this freedom, completing negotiations to secure the services of Stan Brogden, a former Odsal player who had moved to Hull.

Dai Rees had come to the conclusion that the war would be the biggest challenge to Northern becoming a power in the game, particularly if they were forced to fill their team with guest players. For the duration of hostilities Rees managed to use guests only when there was no alternative and when the player or players were of the highest calibre.

Examples of Northern using guests came when Wigan's Jim Sullivan played for them against Halifax in May 1942 and kicked six goals in a 21-16 defeat, and the appearance of Keighley's Ken Davies in the League Championship play-off final against Dewsbury at Headingley when Northern lost 13-0.

Davies, from Blaengarw, a mining village in South Wales, had signed for Keighley from Bridgend RFC when faced with a simple choice: go down the mine or 'go north'.

Ken Davies home on leave.

Jim Sullivan summed up the mood of the rugby league community when he wrote: "I hear that the Salford v Leigh game yesterday may spell the end of our game until next season.

"So great is the uncertainty nowadays that no-one is in a position to say whether this is the case or not and it is most unlikely that the evening matches arranged in midweek will be played.

"There must be no question of players being absent from important war work for any match and since the main idea is to keep the game going and provide some relaxation as a guard against war strain, clubs should regard the winning of games as of secondary importance. Juniors should be included in place of missing stars and results be allowed to take care of themselves."

Sullivan ended his column by remarking, perhaps mischievously: "I hear that Welsh international forward Frank Whitcombe has registered to serve in the Royal Navy".

'Big Jim' was spot on, but Whitcombe's circumstances had changed. He had become a long-distance lorry driver for the Heckmondwike-based company of Harold Wood Ltd. The haulage business, located near to Bradford, had transported bulk liquids – such as aviation fuel – on government contracts to RAF bases from the outbreak of war and so Whitcombe was now in a reserved occupation and would not now be joining the Royal Navy.

The new job also involved delivering toluene to be used in the preparation of explosives at munition dumps all over the country. Frank would often drive through the black-out and on many occasions took shelter under his truck when air-raids were in progress.

On the rugby field, Frank Whitcombe had a day to remember on October 23 1939, when Bradford Northern travelled to Hull Kingston Rovers and he scored three tries in a 23-18 victory for his side.

Despite the war, rugby league went on with the game's governing body continuing the selection process for the planned tour of Australia due to start in April 1940. In the early days of the Second World War – the period known as the 'phoney war' – there was still optimism that the conflict would be over by Christmas.

The first trial game for the planned tour was a match between England and Wales at Odsal on December 23 1939 and Trevor Foster was picked to make his first appearance for his country. He would recall: "I remember well being welcomed into the dressing room by Frank, who introduced me to his great pal, the Welsh captain and my hero Jim Sullivan.

"Jim Sullivan led by example; he was arguably the greatest full-back of all time and as a captain he had a great aura. He did not allow us to put on the famous jersey until just before we left the dressing room for the national anthem.

"I remember his words clearly. After a brief talk about our tactics for the game he said: 'You boys must give every last ounce of your effort today. When you come in here after the match I want to see your tongues hanging out. You will give everything for your jersey. Now pull your jersey on!'

"Jim was very kind to me that day and left a strong impression. He told the other players, and especially Frank, to look after the young Foster and see that he has a good game on his debut."

Foster did indeed have a good game, scoring a try as Wales won 16-9 before a crowd of 15,257.

He was picked in the next trial, a meeting of the Yorkshire and Lancashire Leagues at Craven Park in Barrow on March 23 1940, where 8,683 saw the visitors prevail 13-10.

The final trial was scheduled to be a match between teams drawn from those who had toured Australia in 1936 and a 'Probables' selection for the 1940 tour, as the Rugby Football League clung to the hope that their tour could go ahead. Bad weather twice forced the postponement of the game and by the time it was played – May 4 – the departure date for the tour had already passed.

The 'Probables' led 21-5 at half-time and held on to a final margin of 29-21 after losing centre Jim Croston, one of the outstanding players of the first period, to injury at half-time. Other 'Probables' to impress were half-backs Dai Jenkins and Willie Davies and forwards Frank Whitcombe, Hudson Irving and Trevor Foster, who was again among the try-scorers.

Frank Whitcombe (dark shirt) playing for Wales against England at Odsal, in Jim Sullivan's last game for his country, December 23 1939.

Eventually the inevitable decision was made to cancel the tour and it was to be six long years before the likes of Frank Whitcombe and Willie Davies would have the opportunity to take on the Kangaroos on the hard fields of Australia.

But both of them could look back with pride on their efforts in the 1939-40 season. Whitcombe had picked up winners' medals in the Yorkshire League and the Championship itself, the latter after a two-legged final with Swinton.

The first leg was played at Station Road where Northern achieved what no other club had managed to do during the season, a victory, when they won 21-13, giving them a precious eight-point advantage to take into the home leg.

Swinton took an early lead but could not press home their advantage in the way their supporters had expected, although they were still ahead until a minute before the interval. In the second period Bradford's forwards, led by Whitcombe, Foster and Bill Smith dominated and silenced the home crowd.

The visitors built on the 10-8 half-time lead earned by tries from Harrison and Smith, both converted by Carmichael. Further touch downs came from Whitcombe and Davies with Carmichael adding a further goal before Swinton's late rally, which produced a try for Shaw with Hodgson adding the two points.

The second leg of the final ended in a comfortable 16-9 win for Bradford and an aggregate score of 37-22, after a match marred by the dismissals of Jenkins and Bowyer.

Northern had to play Foster on the wing after the sending off of Jenkins but with Whitcombe and Higson outstanding were still able to control the forward tussle, the former scoring a try to go with others from Winnard (2) and Ward, with Carmichael and Winnard each landing a goal. For Swinton, Williams crossed with Hodgson adding two penalties and a drop goal.

Northern's success in the two-legged final earned them their first major trophy since they had won the Challenge Cup 34 years previously and the joy their triumphs had brought to their supporters was underlined in a celebratory article.

"For the first time in our history Bradford Northern are the champions of the 13-a-side Rugby Football League.

"What troublesome days there have been for the club since we left Park Avenue, then, at Greenfield, Birch Lane and now Odsal. There have been times when the club was not expected to last the day. The last gasp has almost gone many a time but by some means, often unknown, sometimes not wanting to be known, it always survived.

"There are many who, in various ways, take credit for having kept the club alive; it seems hardly possible to count them."

7

WAR-TIME GLORY AND GLOOM

Instead of touring Australia with Great Britain in the summer of 1940 Frank Whitcombe, like many other men in reserved occupations, joined one of the civil defence units.

Back in uniform, he found himself serving as a Sergeant Major under Lieutenant Teddy 'Two Pips' Lightfoot in the Wibsey branch of the Home Guard, whose headquarters, sociably enough, was the Park Hotel on Reevy Road in Wibsey.

Some rugby league clubs had decided to close for the duration, but the board at Odsal had decided to carry on.

The war had already made its impact at Odsal with scrum-half Ken Burns, who had played his last game for Bradford Northern in a 22-18 defeat at Halifax on November 11 1939, one of those fortunate Expeditionary Force soldiers evacuated from the beaches of Dunkirk after the 'phoney war' had exploded into the real thing. He was later posted to North Africa.

Ken Burns was among those evacuated at Dunkirk.

As the 1940-1 season began, news arrived at Odsal of the first Bradford Northern player to be killed. Welsh winger Charles Freeman had played 28 games for the club between 1938 and 1940, scoring six tries, one of them on the day Frank Whitcombe had made his Boxing Day debut against Bramley. Called up as a reservist, he died accidentally while serving as a private in the 2nd Battalion the South Wales Borderers on October 14 1940.

The *Sunderland Echo* published details of Charles Freeman's death. "When Private Leonard John Chalcroft was charged at Omagh County Court yesterday with the wilful murder of Private Charles Freeman, a native of Bradford, at Trillick it was stated that the Attorney General had instructed that no further evidence should be given and the case against John Chalcroft was dismissed.

"At the inquest last week a verdict was returned that Freeman was shot by Chalcroft on sentry in the execution of his duty."

Northern lost another player for the duration in England winger Leslie Grainge who played 140 games for the club and was their second highest try-scorer in the 1938-9 season. His last game for Northern was a 13-8 defeat at Swinton when he was 29 and still had years of playing ahead of him.

He was drafted into the Royal Navy in September 1940, serving first on a minesweeper then becoming a submariner at HMS Dolphin, the spiritual home of the submarine service. When the war ended he was 34 and his playing career was over. He, like so many in various sports, had given the best years of his life to the war effort.

Northern began the new 1940-41 season in great style, winning their first nine games, but then came a couple of setbacks, including a 2-2 draw at Huddersfield on November 29, a day when England met Wales and Bradford were without Whitcombe and Trevor Foster, who were wearing the scarlet jersey, and John Moore who was in England colours.

The following week they were beaten 8-5 at York but they then went on a winning streak of 13 successive victories until April 2 1941. In that period they won the Yorkshire League and earned a place in the Championship final. Their great run continued with a Yorkshire Cup final triumph over Dewsbury at Huddersfield on April 5.

The *Yorkshire Evening Post* reported: "It would be difficult to imagine a keener or more exciting Yorkshire Cup final than that waged between Bradford Northern and Dewsbury at Huddersfield last night.

"There was a grand, pre-war sized crowd and they were entertained by a match of fluctuating fortunes with perhaps the biggest sensation being a miss by Jim Sullivan in front of the posts which would have given Dewsbury the lead at half-time, instead of which Bradford were able to claim the advantage."

Northern went on to win 15-5 with two tries from Trevor Foster.

Jim Sullivan was clearly impressed as he wrote: "Can Bradford Northern, once the Cinderellas of rugby league football, reap the reward of their remarkable enterprise since they moved from humble Birch Lane to palatial Odsal by winning all four cups this season?

"Northern have in the bag the Yorkshire League and Cup and yesterday they started upon their effort to achieve the hat-trick when they visited Wigan in the first leg of the Championship final.

"Their prospects of carrying this off, too, you can glean yourselves by looking at the result of yesterday's game at Central Park. Whoever leads in this meeting will start the return match at Odsal tomorrow with an advantage. That is the game which will decide the Championship.

"A year ago Northern won the title by winning both their matches against Swinton. Strangely enough, they embark on their Challenge Cup programme next Saturday by entertaining Swinton who have staged a revival – as have several other Lancashire clubs – just for the purpose of taking part in our biggest competition.

"If they dispose of Swinton, who have not had the advantage of playing together for some weeks, they are at home again the following week in the third round to Featherstone Rovers, Castleford or St Helens. In my opinion they will reach the semi-finals, in which home and away matches will be played on May 3 and 10.

"What an attraction it would be for Whitehaven folk if Northern are in possession of all four cups when they travel to Cumberland on May 24 for their charity match with Wigan.

"Since I played at full-back for Dewsbury against Northern in the Yorkshire Cup final at Fartown last week, I can give you first-class information on this startling Bradford rise to fame.

"First of all let me answer those few killjoys who question the advisability of continuing competitive rugby league in these times.

"On successive Saturdays, Bradford Northern played the semi-final and final of the Yorkshire Cup on the Huddersfield ground and there was a total crowd of 25,500 and gate receipts of £1,527. Make no mistake about it, the go-ahead spirit of Bradford Northern in the board room is emulated on the field.

"The Dewsbury side, including nine recognised stars from Lancashire, were no mean opponents and had I not hit the post with a penalty kick, when I should have landed it safely between the posts with my eyes closed, we should have led by a point at half-way.

"I think even Northern supporters would agree that we were hardly 10 points inferior. I consider that the turning point was two penalty goals by George Carmichael at a vital stage of the match.

"While fully aware of the high quality of Northern's backs, notably Carmichael, Ernie Ward, Emlyn Walters and Gus Risman, it is my firm opinion that the untiring energy, speed and total fitness of the forwards form the main strength of the successful Odsal combination.

"All six are terrors in the loose with Trevor Foster and Frank Whitcombe, the Welsh internationals, and John Moore, the Hull-born loose-forward, among the best I have seen for many a long day.

"Len Higson and Bill Smith are practically at the same level but the surprise packet is Cliff Carter, who has taken over the hooking duties from

Vincent Dilorenzo. Carter is normally the Leeds reserve hooker and the Headingley club have no qualms about allowing Northern to play him."

To defend their Championship title Northern would have to play Wigan over two legs and they started in fine style with a 17-6 triumph at Central Park on April 12, scoring tries through Emlyn Walters (two), Gus Risman, Walter Best and Len Higson, with their sole goal coming from Ernest Ward.

For the return match at Odsal two days later, which drew a crowd of 20,505, Northern were unchanged and the margin was equally emphatic with Tom Winnard (2), Gus Risman (2), Emlyn Walters and John Moore all touching down in a 28-9 triumph in which the only blemish was the sending off of hookers Cliff Carter and Joe Egan just after half-time.

John 'Jackie' Moore perished during the Battle of the Java Sea in 1942.

Again Jim Sullivan was impressed: "Last week I asked can Bradford Northern win all four cups. Since then they have added the Championship to their Yorkshire League and Cup success and are installed as firm favourites for the Challenge Cup.

"I am writing of course before I know the result of their second round tie against Swinton at Odsal yesterday but if the Lancashire club have fared any better than Wigan did in their two Championship final matches – in which Northern scored 45 points to 15 – I shall be as surprised as you.

"The Bradford team is probably the greatest to have represented the Odsal club and when it is remembered that they would have been even stronger with Willie Davies in their team the chances are they would have been all-conquering in peace-time football.

"From a financial point of view Northern must be regarded as a wonderful asset; look at the figures and see for yourself the magic of Harry Hornby's boys: Yorkshire Cup semi-final at Huddersfield 10,500 (£588); Yorkshire Cup final at Huddersfield 13,316 (£939); Championship final at Wigan 12,000 (£642); Championship final at Odsal 20,205 (£1,148).

"In a nutshell a total attendance of 56,000 with gate receipts of £3,317. To these remarkable war-time figures we have to add those from yesterday's cup-tie with Swinton and if Northern are safely through to the third round they are at home again to Castleford and we can expect all war-time records to be broken.

"One sterling member of the Bradford Northern side I feel sorry for is Wilf McWatt, the popular Hull Kingston Rover who has been a fine connecting link at stand-off half. He has been prevented from sharing the final triumph of his club first by injury and now because he has been called up by the Royal Navy."

McWatt, who was on loan from Hull KR, played 19 matches for Northern in that season and he was soon to be joined at his naval training centre by John Moore, the club's other Hull-raised forward.

As Sullivan expected, Northern beat Swinton and Castleford and, with three trophies already in the cabinet, faced Leeds over two legs in the Challenge Cup semi-final.

The first meeting at Headingley on May 3 ended in a 10-10 draw, Northern's points coming from tries by Gus Risman and Tom Winnard and goals by Risman and Ernest Ward but there were hints in their performance to suggest that at last they were running out of steam after a demanding season.

Those suspicions were proved to be correct in the second leg at Odsal just five days later when Leeds pulled off the surprise of the season, winning 12-2 with George Carmichael being the loser's only scorer with a goal.

Leeds would go on to win the Challenge Cup – ironically at Odsal – but Northern could reflect with great satisfaction on winning five trophies in two seasons.

They were also discovering the cruelties of the war which raged all the while. When Singapore surrendered on February 15 1942, military policeman Harry Thorpe, who had played his last game as Northern's hooker at Halifax on October 22 1938, became a prisoner at the notorious Changi camp before being sent to work as a slave labourer building railways for the Japanese in Thailand. Amazingly he survived the ordeal and returned to Yorkshire when hostilities ceased.

Then Northern heard that their superb loose-forward John Moore had been killed in action on February 27 1942. Moore had played 188 games for the club between 1935 and 1941, scoring 19 tries. He was a key individual in the teams which won

Military Policeman, Harry Thorpe, was captured in Singapore in 1942 and survived the notorious Japanese railways in Thailand.

two Championships and the Yorkshire Cup and his final appearance came in the 12-2 setback against Leeds in the Challenge Cup semi-final. He won an England cap when he played in the 8-5 win against Wales at Oldham in November 1940.

He perished when his ship HMS Electra was sunk while covering the withdrawal of the badly damaged HMS Exeter during the Battle of the Java Sea.

The *Gloucester Citizen* reported on March 27 1942: "HMS Electra, which led the allied fleet of destroyers in the Battle of the Java Sea a month ago, went down with her Ensign flying.

"Survivors, who were rescued by an American submarine, which was itself repeatedly attacked by the Japanese, are now in Australia. They say that the Japanese blazed away at Electra from 2,000 yards but their gunnery was so poor they took half an hour to sink her.

"When the Japanese appeared on the horizon and opened fire the destroyers turned away behind a smoke screen then counter attacked and again retired. As they turned away, Electra, which had been leading, became the last in line and three salvoes from the Asagumo struck her, wrecking the boiler room and bringing her to a standstill.

"When the forward guns had been knocked out and there was no ammunition left for the after guns the ship was abandoned. The life-boats were smashed but a few rafts were left. Most of the casualties were caused by shrapnel when the men were in the water."

Of the ship's company of 173 men, 54 were picked up by US submarine S38 but sadly John Moore was not among them. The survivors later boarded a ship bound for England but she was torpedoed by a Japanese submarine and sank. All on board perished.

Harry Hornby wrote: "Jackie Moore gained something more valuable than international honours – he won a reputation for being fine and fair, both on and off the field. Always a 100 per cent team man, his memory will be kept evergreen, as will his example be cited as a pattern to those youngsters who follow on."

Another loss for Northern and its wider family was that of full-back Private Rowland Eastwood who was killed in action. The *Yorkshire Post* recorded on September 17 1943: "Private Eastwood was serving with the Central Mediterranean Force. Today would have been his 34th birthday.

"His wife has been told that he was killed by machine gun fire while on a special patrol in search of important information. He was killed at the side of his officer after they had got the information through."

There was a touch of lightness to lift the gloom when Northern's match programme on October 7 1944 carried part of a letter to his father from a

Private Turnbull, of Marshlands, who was serving with the 14th Army in Burma.

"Whilst we were going along on patrol we came across a clearing marked out for rugby football, complete with goal-posts," he wrote.
"Imagine if you can the delight and surprise of those of us who hailed from the West Riding when we saw a large notice marked 'Odsal Stadium'.

"Soon the whole company were made aware of what and where Odsal Stadium was and later we formed a team. Of course it was called Bradford Northern."

It was in 1942 that Frank Whitcombe became an adopted Yorkshireman, representing the County in a match against Lancashire played at Dewsbury on March 28, the home side coming out on top 13-2.

The *Yorkshire Post* reported: "Yorkshire made the most of their chances in the last representative match of the season and beat Lancashire at Dewsbury where there was a crowd of 4,000.

"Yorkshire's forwards, the more experienced of the packs, gave their side a grand lead in open play where Hudson Irving and Ted Tattersfield were strong and tireless workers. Yorkshire's backs rarely slipped into complete attacking action because of the keen marking of some of Lancashire's youngsters.

"Stan Brogden was given little rope at standoff, despite the enthusiastic efforts of Dai Jenkins at scrum-half. The result was that the three-quarter line, in which Russell Pepperell was a keen and able centre, was unable to develop the soaring promise revealed by Eric Batten who scored a couple of excellent tries.

"His first was a beauty. He beat three men with an inside side-step, but the best try was that scored by Irving after a long passing movement in which Pepperell handled the ball twice and in which Tattersfield was in the right place at the right time to give the try-scoring pass. A couple of goals by Ernest Ward completed Yorkshire's scoring.

"Lancashire had struck the first blow when Billy Belshaw kicked a penalty goal and their backs, among whom Jack Cunliffe ran well, would have built on that score had their finishing been better."

There was increasing concern at the number of rugby league players being taken from the game by military service and former Bradford Northern and England winger Ernest Pollard wrote a letter to John Wilson, the secretary of the RFL, putting forward a plan to make up for the losses.

The letter was later reported in the *Yorkshire Evening Post*: "Ernest Pollard feels there will be a shortage of men to take the place of the stars who shone so brightly before 1939 and suggests that the RFL should get to work to

WAR-TIME GLORY AND GLOOM

provide training centres in Yorkshire and Lancashire at which youngsters could be given the best tuition.

"He would put an experienced rugby league man in charge of each training centre and he would pay a salary of £200 or £250 to the men appointed. The men would look for a supply of players, by some scheme to be devised, which could be allocated to different clubs."

There was a report on Northern's two Kiwi players George Harrison and Robert Hohaia in the *Yorkshire Evening Post* on October 24 1942. "Robert Hohaia, the Maori half-back who played for Bradford Northern before the war, is a prisoner of war in Italy and George Harrison, Northern's Maori forward, has been wounded in the thigh and foot and is reported to be on his way home."

8

BUILDING THE DREAM

With the war in progress there were restrictions which prevented Harry Hornby and his fellow directors developing the club and the ground as they would have wished but there was no doubting their ambition, which was detailed in a message from the board to Bradford Northern's supporters.

"It must be obvious to any thinking man that the directors and all connected with the management of this club have made great efforts and sacrifices to put Bradford Northern where they are today and our anxiety now is to consolidate our gains and hold on to them until such times as we can make full use of them again.

"Never mind what anyone says or does, it is our intention to give you the best we can for as long as we can and I am sure our lads are out to win every time and to serve up attractive football. It is often said that a country gets the government it deserves and that also applies to rugby league. If you think our lads deserve your support do all you can to support them.

"The rugby league football world is looking on to see how Bradford Northern is going to tackle their problems and we are looking forward to you giving your answer in no unmistakable terms. We have the chance now to establish Bradford once again as a major rugby centre and our advice is that you grasp it with both hands."

The directors had the statistics to back their argument: their records showed that in war-time rugby only three visiting clubs had won at Odsal – Dewsbury, Halifax and Huddersfield twice.

Frank Whitcombe had been a key figure in the team which had risen to such heights and he was so influential on and off the field that he was allowed by coach Dai Rees to train to his own schedule. That involved running up and down the cinder bank at the Rooley Avenue end of Odsal for hour after hour, building the stamina which enabled him to play at full power for 80 minutes every time he took the field.

His lorry-driving job also helped him build his strength; loading his wagon by hand was good for upper-body strength and Rees acknowledged that giving his leading prop forward freedom to work himself into tip-top shape worked perfectly. "Frank always knew best how to train himself," he said. "Never to do too much and risk a breakdown but always to be as fit as he could be at his weight."

Whitcombe's strength was legendary; his signature tackle was to pick up an opposing forward, throw him over his shoulder and send the unfortunate player head first to the ground. Today it would be penalised as a spear tackle; rugby league was a different game then.

In the gym at Odsal there were three parallel lines marked on the floor. One was to mark half-way, the other two to the left and right to mark the feet positions for the one-on-one scrum pushing exercise, a routine at which Whitcombe was unbeatable.

One day Northern's raw young forward Frank Mugglestone challenged Whitcombe to a pushing match and as they settled to their task the youngster cleverly locked his legs in such a way that his opponent was unable to shift him.

Mugglestone was known to all the players at Odsal as the 'Kid' and having successfully matched the master of the scrum test he was now sure he would have earned new respect and a new nickname. No chance; throughout his career at Odsal he would continue to be known to all as the 'Kid'.

The only war-time season when Northern failed to win any silverware was that of 1942-3 when they were disqualified after playing in

Frank Whitcombe loading wool bales alone, a great way of building up strength.

To use the words of Frank Whitcombe 'why use a crane when you can use your hands'.

the final of the Emergency Championship, having already lost 17-4 over two legs in the semi-final of the Yorkshire Cup to Huddersfield.

Northern had finished third in the league and qualified to play at Dewsbury – who were managed by Eddie Waring - in the semi-final. Dewsbury had enjoyed a successful season, winning the Yorkshire Cup and the Challenge Cup and their sights were set on a third trophy.

Their dreams appeared to be shattered as Bradford ground out an 8-3 victory with tries from Trevor Foster and Emlyn Walters and a goal from Ernest Ward. After the game, however, Dewsbury accused Northern of fielding an ineligible player in Sandy Orford, who had earlier been transferred from Odsal to Wakefield Trinity.

He was appearing for Northern as a loan player but had not figured in the four games the regulations demanded for a semi-final, having figured against Dewsbury and Keighley in league games and Huddersfield in a non-league encounter.

Dai Rees had picked him for the semi-final in good faith but Dewsbury's complaint was upheld by the Rugby Football League and it was the Crown Flatt club who faced Halifax in the Championship final in which they triumphed 33-16 over two legs.

Only then was it found that Dewsbury had themselves fielded an ineligible player in the semi-final against Bradford and as the situation descended into farce they were stripped of the title and the Championship declared null and void.

Frank Whitcombe demonstrates his unique tackling style on the unfortunate Jim Featherstone of Warrington in the 1948 Championship final at Maine Road, Manchester.

Sandy Orford, the Bradford man deemed in breach of the rules in that semi-final, became a professional wrestler when his rugby league career was over at the end of the Forties. He fought under the names of 'The Black Angel' and 'The Mask' and was a tough enough opponent to face the six-time world champion Lou Thesz on three occasions, losing two bouts and drawing the other. Yorkshire's Shirley Crabtree – known to all as 'Big Daddy' – fought his first bout against Sandy Orford at St James Hall, Newcastle, on Saturday June 14 1952.

Regulations regarding rugby league players taking part in rugby union matches were eventually relaxed by the Rugby Football Union

Frank Mugglestone (left) and James Kibble (right) holding a bomb from a Wellington bomber, RAF Quastina, Palestine, 1944.

as the demand for entertainment for workers and service personnel increased but prior to the eventual cross-code matches Vivian Jenkins, the former Wales full-back now employed as a sports writer for the *News of the World*, wrote an article in which he named his choice as the union code's 'team of the last decade'.

His selection was: H Owen Smith (England); W Wooller (Wales), R Dick, G Macpherson, I Smith (all Scotland); C Jones (Wales), W Logan (Scotland); H Rew, S Tucker, R Longland (all England), G Beamish (Ireland), J Beattie (Scotland), A Marshall (England), J Siggins, J Russell (both Ireland).

Jim Sullivan, a colleague of Jenkins at the *News of the World*, was promptly challenged by Mr Robert Wooler, a reader from New Wortley in Leeds, to name his own rugby league XV to take on the union line-up in a mythical match. Sullivan accepted the challenge.

Len Higson and Sandy Orford on holiday together in Southport, proudly wearing their Bradford Northern blazers.

"Of course it would not be possible for the teams to get to grips but if I attempt to select my best XV it will lead to interesting discussion between north and south," wrote Sullivan. "I have framed my team on men who I have either played against or watched this season.

"Here it is, although I am well aware it will not please everyone: B Belshaw (Warrington); S Williams (Salford), J Croston (Castleford), G Risman (Salford), E Walters (Bradford Northern); V Hey, D Jenkins (both Leeds); M Hodgson (Swinton), D Cotton (Warrington), F Whitcombe (Bradford Northern), L Thacker (Hull), T Foster (Bradford Northern), J Bowen (Wigan), H Irving (Halifax), J Moore (Bradford Northern).

Sullivan added: "I should imagine that the above team will suit even the anonymous Bradford Northern supporter who wrote to me in abusive terms the other day, accusing me not so much of a Wigan bias but of a Lancashire one. I think my selection gives you a pretty good idea of what I think of Harry Hornby's smart lads."

In October 1943 Harry Hornby completed one of his most successful signings when he persuaded Eric Batten to join Bradford Northern. The *Yorkshire Post* ran this story: "Eric Batten, the international winger, has gone from Hunslet to Bradford Northern at a substantial transfer fee, part of which is to be paid at the end of the war.

"Batten might have gone to Leeds, who had come to an agreement with Hunslet a few weeks ago, but the player declined to sign. He played for Leeds last season when Hunslet were out of action and he has not returned to Parkside this season. Batten's first game in Northern's colours will be against Dewsbury in the first round of the Yorkshire Cup.

"Because of his strength and speed, Batten, 27, is bound to increase the power of Bradford's wartime team, but managing director Harry Hornby makes it clear that the acquisition of Batten is just one step in the direction of giving Bradford Northern the best possible team for post-war football."

Northern's Eric Batten, leaps over his brother Bob, with the style he inherited from his father Billy Batten. May 3 1947.

Also in 1943 the cross-code gates were opened and fixtures between international players and modest club performers were played all over the country with gate receipts going to charities.

Frank Whitcombe's charity rugby union team. Len Higson is on the extreme left on the back row, next to Donald Ward with Vic Darlison fourth from the left.

Frank Whitcombe had his own rugby union fund-raising team, with the Red Cross the usual beneficiary. One match was played against English Electric RUFC at the Phoenix Park ground in Bradford, the day after Northern had played at Barrow.

English Electric employed 5,000 staff in the city who made generators for the Royal Navy. Among the workers was Frank's fellow Welshman and Northern star Emlyn Walters.

Charles Atkinson, who was 13 at the time, remembered that January Sunday in 1944. "Many of my friends at Hanson High School went along to watch the match. It was a chance to meet Frank Whitcombe. He and his team-mates at Bradford Northern were our heroes, every boy wanted to be Eric Batten in the backs and our enforcer Frank Whitcombe in the pack."

On February 26 1944, Wales and England shared the honours in a 9-9 draw at Wigan, which attracted a crowd of 16,028. Playing for Wales that day were Frank Whitcombe, Trevor Foster, Willie Davies and Emlyn Walters, while far away in Edinburgh, Ernest Ward, a Private in the Lancashire Fusiliers, was appearing at full-back in a rugby union services England XV against Scotland at Murrayfield.

The programme for Northern's home game against Leeds on March 6 1944, illustrated the pride felt by everyone at Odsal in having their players figuring in international matches.

"One of the selections with regard to the England v Wales game at Wigan last Saturday which would have given universal satisfaction wherever rugby football is played was that of Trevor Foster as captain of Wales.

"Good luck lads, all of you, from all of us at Odsal. You have gained these well-deserved honours by unquestionable merit and we trust you will always carry them with fitting dignity. You have brought honour also to your club and management. Your club-mates are justifiably proud of their association with you."

Still the war went on and one Bradford Northern player was decorated for bravery, as the *Yorkshire Post* recorded: "When about 250 other ranks were decorated by the King at a recent investiture at Buckingham Palace a number of officers attended, at their own request, to receive their medals with the men who had won decorations alongside them in the field and in the air.

"Many North countrymen were decorated, among them two brothers, one in the Army the other in the Royal Air Force. They were Lieutenant Roy Dennis, Durham Light Infantry, whose home is in Manchester, who won the Military Medal when he was a Lance Sergeant in the Coldstream Guards. Before the war Lieutenant Dennis played for several seasons with Bradford Northern.

"Pilot Officer Roy Dennis, of RAF Bomber Command, who lives in Featherstone, received the Distinguished Flying Medal."

Sadly, Roy Dennis was killed two weeks later when his Wellington bomber stalled and crashed after take-off at RAF Turweston in Buckinghamshire. Of the crew only the rear-gunner survived.

9

RISING TO THE CHALLENGE

When Bradford Northern embarked on the 1943-4 season their target was to win the Rugby Football League Challenge Cup, not least because their neighbours and greatest rivals Leeds had won the trophy in 1941 and 1942, and had been beaten in the 1943 final by Dewsbury.

They further strengthened their already powerful squad when they signed Jack Kitching, a former Bradford RFC and Yorkshire winger. He was in the Navy when he signed but made his debut for Northern on February 5 1944 in a 44-5 home win over York, scoring two tries.

Alf Marklew joined Northern from Barrow a week later. Originally a guest player, he made his debut as a registered Odsal player in a 13-13 draw with York on February 12.

Jack Kitching, former Bradford RFC and Yorkshire winger.

Spurred on by success in the Yorkshire Cup and a winning run in the Championship, Northern powered their way into the semi-finals of the Challenge Cup in which they emerged successful over two legs by a 9-5 margin against Halifax.

The *Yorkshire Post* reported the first leg of the semi-final which was played on April 10 1944: "Bradford Northern had reason to feel they had done well in keeping Halifax to a lead of three points at Thrum Hall where there were 10,350 spectators to see the home side win 5-2.

"The honours in this lively game went to the forwards, who broke up so quickly and battled so keenly so as to severely limit the scope of the three-quarters.

"Halifax gained the lead after 13 minutes when Jack Dixon broke away to send Tommy McCue over but after that all their attacking efforts were met by a tenacious defence and they had to look to Herbert Lockwood for points from a penalty goal.

"Northern's opportunities for attractive back play were equally few, Eric Batten, like Arthur Bassett on the Halifax wing, had scarcely an opening but Walter Best, Northern's other wing, showed speed in a fine effort in the second half.

"Northern's goal was kicked by George Carmichael in the first half and it followed a move in which the Bradford men got very near a try after Donald Ward had broken through and Jack Kitching had given him support.

"Billy Hutchinson did some fine work in the loose for Northern; Halifax had good foragers in Jack Dixon, Arthur Childs and Chris Brereton and their lead might have been bigger had their backs been able to play up to the work of the men in front of them."

Two days later on Easter Monday, Northern won the second leg 7-0 before a crowd of 27,000 and again the *Yorkshire Post*'s man was at the game.

"The second leg of Bradford Northern's semi-final with Halifax produced one of the sternest games seen at Odsal in war-time football.

"Northern were much the more aggressive side but Halifax maintained a superb defence that was not penetrated until late in the second half.

"For Halifax, Jack Dixon the loose forward, gave a grand display, as did Hudson Irving while Jack Goodall and George Todd at half-back were cleverer than the Bradford pair.

"Fortunately for Bradford their forwards were very assertive with Frank Whitcombe, Herbert Smith and Trevor Foster to the fore.

"In the first half Ernest Ward kicked two penalty goals and after the interval Batten obtained a try to set up the final against Wigan, again over two legs."

One Halifax player had more reason than his team-mates to regret losing. Friend Taylor, who had moved to Halifax from Oldham but continued to live in his home town, was later fined £3 for unlawful use of motor fuel in travelling to the match in Bradford on Easter Monday and fined another £1 for not signing a declaration of the journey.

His driver, Charles Dearnley, of Chadderton, pleaded guilty to unlawful use of motor fuel and failing to declare the journey. He was fined £10. War-time restrictions were strict indeed

Wigan at that time had the jinx on Bradford. Northern's only victory at Wigan, in a history going back to 1895, was by 17-6 in the first leg of the Championship play-off on April 12 1941.

The first leg of the final was played at Wigan on April 15 1944 where a crowd of 22,000 turned up to watch a classic, which was reported by the *Yorkshire Post*: "Not since Park Avenue was a stronghold of what was then the Northern Union has the Rugby League Challenge Cup been taken to Bradford.

"This season Bradford Northern, who wear the old Bradford colours, are favourites for the trophy. They went to Central Park on Saturday and kept

Frank Whitcombe (right) and Trevor Foster (centre) holding the line.

Wigan's lead for the first stage in the two-part tie down to three points; their followers will reckon Northern are good enough to put things right at Odsal next Saturday.

"It was a hard match at Wigan, with the defence much stronger than attack, the one complete passing movement gave Wigan their first-half try but the success of it carried attacking inspiration for neither the home side nor their opponents.

"Northern, with mastery in the scrummage for the second half, dwelt for long periods on Wigan's 25-yard line without being able to open a way to the try line. Donald Ward went near to scoring then Willie Davies and Ernest Ward almost pierced the defence, and then came the thrill of the second half when Eric Batten went tearing down the touchline.

"He cleared one defender with a leap, which raised vivid memories of a similar effort made by his father when Hull were in the final at Headingley 22 years ago, but Jack Bowen, Wigan's loose-forward, reached the important spot in time to complete the tackle to save a try.

"Jim Featherstone's try for Wigan was made when Hector Gee, the Australian scrum-half, flung out a sharp pass to Ernie Ashcroft who put the ball back inside to Jack Blan and Blan let Featherstone have it just at the right time."

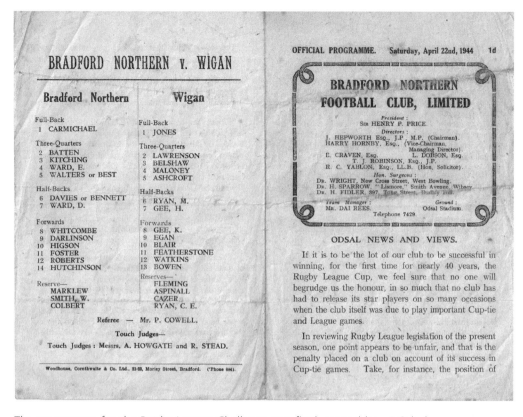

The programme for the Rugby League Challenge cup final, second leg at Odsal.

Seven days later the sides met again at Odsal where Northern had won 18 consecutive matches and the mood among the players was that they would finish the job back home.

They made three changes for the return leg on April 22, Trevor Foster returning to the second row as captain with Jack Kitching and Emlyn Walters being recalled to the backs.

Harry Hornby wrote in the programme: "If it is the lot of our club in winning the Challenge Cup for the first time in nearly 40 years we feel sure that no-one will begrudge us this honour in so much as no club has had to release its star players on so many occasions when the club itself was due to play important cup-ties and league games.

"Within a few hours we shall all know if it is to be our fate to hold the Challenge Cup for the next 12 months or otherwise. That the final match should be between ourselves and Wigan at Odsal Stadium seems to be particularly fitting. Each club has had a hard road to travel to reach the final and we can justly claim to be the league's two leading clubs today."

Frank Whitcombe's official club photograph.

But before the kick-off there was a bad-tempered discussion between the two camps over the colour of the jerseys to be worn in the second leg. Wigan were unhappy that Bradford had worn white jerseys with red, amber and black bands, complaining that they clashed with their traditional cherry and white hoops.

In the first game Wigan had changed to blue jerseys and when the teams took the field at Odsal the Lancastrian side were again wearing blue. Northern were later fined 10 guineas and their coach Dai Rees was reprimanded.

Over 30,000 – a huge gathering for a match played in war-time – had made the trek to Odsal, meaning over 50,000 had attended both legs, and the roars from the crowd intensified after just 11 minutes when Eric Batten picked up a loose ball and raced over Wigan's line to make the two sides level on aggregate.

Ernest Ward's goal-kick was off target and despite Northern's domination of possession they could not break down Wigan's defence again before the interval which came with the sides still locked together.

Wigan started the second period the stronger but a foul on Northern's hooker Vic Darlison gave George Carmichael the opportunity to put his side ahead from 20 yards and he gleefully took his chance.

Sensing victory, Northern redoubled their efforts and had Wigan's defence at full stretch but it was not until the dying minutes of the game that the decisive try was scored. It came when Frank Whitcombe, in a tremendous feat of strength and determination, battered his way over the line from close range to score the points which secured the Challenge Cup by a margin of 8-3.

The crowd were delirious with joy as Trevor Foster climbed the steps to receive the trophy and hold it high for his players and their adoring public to see; the Challenge Cup was back in Bradford for the first time since 1906 and the club had reached new heights.

Their goal when the 1944-5 season kicked-off was to repeat that success. The competition was again played over two legs with Northern reaching the final after seeing off St Helens (away 15-8, home 34-13), Wakefield Trinity (home 18-8, away 3-10) and Keighley (away 0-5, home 35-3).

With Northern heading the Championship table and Huddersfield languishing in mid-table, the Odsal club were clear favourites to win the two-legged final, but they went into the match without full-back George

Carmichael, Ernest Ward moving to full-back and winger Alan Edwards filling the vacancy in midfield.

On Monday April 30 1945, the *Yorkshire Post*'s report on the first leg read: "Huddersfield will take a lead of three points to Odsal for the second part of the Rugby League Challenge Cup final next Saturday.

"They gained it with the only try scored at Fartown on Saturday where each side scored a couple of goals and they are built to fight sternly in defence of it on Bradford Northern's ground. Their forward strength in the loose is considerable; they proved that in their semi-final games against Halifax and they emphasized it against Northern at Fartown.

"Northern, the Cup-holders, had a scrummage advantage on Saturday but they lacked midfield drive. Alan Edwards was not as happy at centre as he would have been on the wing and Jack Kitching was without the lead to which he has responded so well in recent times with the

The programme for the Rugby League Challenge cup final, first leg at Huddersfield.

result that the fast Bradford wings rarely had running chances.

"There was no-one in the Bradford midfield as aggressive in attack as Huddersfield's Randall Lewis who partnered the sound Alex Fiddes in the centre. Of course, if George Carmichael is fit for the second game Northern will be able to move Ernest Ward back to the centre and Edwards to the wing. Then their back division may present Huddersfield with a different sort of problem.

"But Huddersfield's tacklers were sound enough at Fartown, where George Bennett, the off-half, came nearest to a try for Northern with a dash on the short side of a scrummage. Only once did Eric Batten look like being brought into the game as a scoring power and Edwards kicked too often.

"Huddersfield took the lead in the 11th minute of a game in which no man spared himself in conditions which were not good. There was more than a reminder of winter in the weather, the ball was not easy to hold and the wind was full of trouble.

"But Lewis knew what he was doing when he made a drive that carried a Huddersfield passing movement to within a few yards of the line. The ball went loose and Grahame, in the right supporting position, snapped it up and whipped it out to Ossie Peake on the wing and his inside side-step left the last defender helpless and he touched down. Jeff Bawden's left boot added the goal points.

"Ernest Ward kicked a good penalty for Northern and Bawden one for Huddersfield before half-time and Ward landed another goal in a second half in which Bradford had more of the attack but the home defence never faltered.

"Young Bill Leake at full-back made a few slips on a trying afternoon, and in the Huddersfield pack were such stalwarts as Jack Miller, Joe Bradbury, Les Baxter and Alex Givvons to match the strenuous efforts of Frank Whitcombe, Len Higson and Billy Hutchinson and Jack Miller was as good as the best on the field."

When Huddersfield arrived at Odsal on May 5 1945 they knew they were facing a team unbeaten in their last 34 home matches and there was an air of expectancy in the programme.

"To all our friends who have come considerable distances to see the Cup final may we extend a hearty welcome and express the hope that, with a silver lining of peace breaking through the dark clouds which have disrupted our way of living for six dreary years, they will have the anticipation and realisation of witnessing rugby league football matches of an attractive nature at Odsal Stadium."

The Second World War ended in Europe on May 8 and the final made news in France with French journalist Maurice Blein writing a report on the second leg in his newspaper *France Soir* together with an assessment of the respective merits of the league and union games.

A crowd of 17,000 turned up expecting Northern to pull back the deficit. Both teams knew that a score would swing the tie their way but heavy

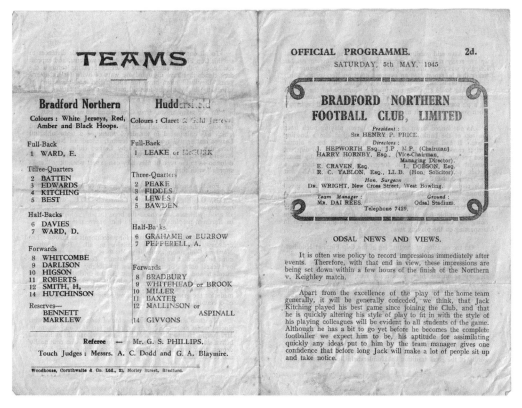

The programme for the Rugby League Challenge cup final, second leg at Odsal.

rain had left the playing surface muddy and the continual drizzle did not make for an expansive game. As a result there were many handling errors in a scoreless first half in which neither team could make progress on the mud-laden pitch and the defences were well on top.

In the second half Northern gained the advantage when Willie Davies beat two men to put winger Eric Batten in for a try which was improved by Ernest Ward to give the home side a 5-0 lead, putting them 9-7 ahead on aggregate.

The stage was set for Northern to take control but instead it was Huddersfield who showed the strength of character to get back into the game. As Northern grew more anxious and their passing more ambitious the visitors intercepted and Jeff Bawden scored the decisive try to end the Bradford club's hopes of retaining the trophy, with Huddersfield winning the second leg 6-5 and recording a 13-9 overall victory.

But the Northern players did not have long to ponder their defeat. They had overcome great rivals Wigan 18-15 in the semi-final of the Championship

Walter Best (left) and Billy Hutchinson tackle Huddersfield's Alex Givvons. Northern's Laurie Roberts and Donald Ward look on. The Challenge Cup final, Odsal, May 5 1945.

and earned themselves a place in the final against Halifax, the first leg being scheduled for May 19 with the return match to follow just two days later.

The *Yorkshire Post* told its readers: "Bradford Northern are seven points down as a result of the first part of the Championship final played at Thrum Hall on Saturday.

"Many of us at the game thought we saw in the play of both teams more than a reminder of the fact that Whitsuntide is a time for cricket, not football. The season has spread out too far although that was not obvious in the mighty drive with which Halifax opened the game as they threw their experienced, strong forward to the Bradford line.

"They turned readily to their backs who, with a sharp move, swung the attack the other way. Harry Millington, a second row running like a back, went through an opening, Tommy McCue was there for the pass and he scored under the cross-bar for Hubert Lockwood to kick the goal.

"The thrills of the opening minutes were not maintained as Northern struggled against a tricky wind. Ernest Ward kicked a splendid goal against it and that was the extent of the scoring in a first half in which both sides failed by faulty handling to profit from good approach work.

"The second half brought two penalty goals for Halifax. Lockwood was the kicker and on each occasion he measured the wind and distance with considerable skill. Northern might have had a try early on had Jack Kitching taken a pass from George Bennett who had opened up the defence. George Todd cut loose similarly for Halifax only to finish with a forward pass with the line just five yards away."

Victory by 9-2 gave Halifax hope of taking the title as they made the short journey to Odsal two days later but they came up against a Bradford Northern determined to ensure their season did not end with a second defeat in a two-legged final.

The *Yorkshire Post* reported: "Bradford Northern earned the Rugby League Championship when they beat Halifax 24-11 – six tries and three goals to one try and four goals – at Odsal yesterday.

"They finished six points up over the two games and the strength and pace of their attack in the first half will be remembered. They struck again and again to gain a mastery they never lost, though there was a point in the second half when Halifax rallied magnificently and were within scoring distance of the lead.

"Halifax started in a fashion which suggested they could build on the seven-point lead taken from Thrum Hall. Tommy McCue was here, there and everywhere and Northern were stretched in defence until Walter Best, on the left wing, snapped up a loose ball outside his own 25. He shot away, beat Hubert Lockwood when the odds seemed to be on the Halifax full-back putting him into touch and he finished a thrilling run with a try to which Ernest Ward added the goal.

"Before Halifax had settled, Northern were in again with another thrilling try after an attacking position had been gained by a spectacular piece of work by Eric Batten, who threw off three or four would-be tacklers and cleared Mel Meak with a hurdler's leap. The ball went out to Best who passed inside for Alf Marklew to score and put Halifax behind on aggregate.

"The Halifax tackling was not good at this point, Jack Kitching cut through for a grand try then linked with Billy Hutchinson and Batten to put Alan Edwards in for another, Ernest Ward adding the goal. Donald Ward went over for a try and against those 19 well-earned points Halifax could show only two penalty goals by Hubert Lockwood but Lockwood landed another goal early in the second half then Tommy McCue crossed, and there were now only three points in it on aggregate.

"In a thrilling climax Halifax continued to battle onward. Northern responded with a penalty from Ernest Ward, and a try made by Kitching for Donald Ward then another score from McCue whipped up Halifax but their only reward was a further goal for Lockwood."

After the disappointment of the Challenge Cup final, Northern took the Championship by a 26-20 aggregate score and finished off another memorable season during which Eric Batten equalled the club record for tries in a campaign, matching the 35 scored by Emlyn Walters in the 1940-1 season.

10

WINNING THE PEACE

The war was over and the best team Bradford Northern had ever assembled were about to find out how good they were. Dai Rees had adopted a strategy of building a team during the war years which would dominate the game when peace returned: now his planning would be put to the test.

An early indication that Northern would make a good impression on the 1945-6 season and those to follow came when they reached the final of the Yorkshire Cup. They faced Wakefield Trinity at Thrum Hall on November 3 and a crowd of 24,292 turned up to watch a match played in wet, misty conditions.

The first half was dominated by the defences with Wakefield scoring a penalty goal to lead at half-time. Only two minutes after the players had left the field, the crowd were amazed to see the Bradford side reappear and take their places ready for the start of the second period.

It was a typical stroke of genius from Dai Rees. When the Wakefield men strolled on to the field and started to take up their positions the referee blew his whistle to restart play. Not fully organised, Trinity had left a large unmarked area in front of their posts.

Donald Ward kicked the ball deep – a rare occurrence in a game where possession was everything – and his forwards, led by Alf Marklew, raced in pursuit, to the alarm of Wakefield centre Johnny Jones and full-back Billy Teall, who fumbled the ball deep in their own half.

Through the centre came the 17st 9lb Frank Whitcombe at full gallop, hacking the ball past the two stricken defenders then hurling himself forward in a crash dive to touch down for the only try of the game, to which George Carmichael added the goal. The game then reverted to the pattern of the first half, with Northern being happy to grind out a 5-2 victory.

Wakefield's manager was Jim Croston, Frank Whitcombe's long-standing friend from their days together in the Royal Engineers in 1931. Croston said after the final defeat: "We all make mistakes and our mistake today has cost us heavily. But team spirit is high and with that spirit we should be able to bring something home to Wakefield this year."

He was right: on May 4 1946 the Challenge Cup final returned to Wembley for the first time since the end of the war and Trinity beat Wigan 13-12.

During the summer of 1945 the Australian government had made it clear to their counterparts in London that they were eager for a rugby league team representing Great Britain to tour their country to lift the morale of their people who were struggling to come to terms with their losses during the war and the fear they had endured of invasion by the Japanese.

Things initially moved quickly and in September the *Hull Daily Mail* had concrete information: "Mr John Wilson, the secretary of the Rugby Football League, has learned from a Reuter's message from Sydney that Dr Herbert Evatt, the Australian Minister for External Affairs, has left by air for England bearing an invitation for a side to go to Australia at the end of next season.

"We had an invitation from Australia 12 months ago to send out a side as soon as possible after the war," said Mr Wilson. "But naturally there were difficulties in the way of accepting it, transport being one.

"Normally for an Australian tour the team leaves England in April and arrives in Sydney in May; whether or not there can be any variation in the mode of travel – by air for instance – remains to be seen.

"The availability of players is another concern. Most of those up to the standard to make an Australian tour are in the services and they might not be allowed the time away. Nevertheless, an invitation would be welcomed by the management committee and discussed as soon as possible."

Dr Evatt made a personal plea for the tour of Australia to go ahead, which was reported in the *Western Morning News* of October 11. "Relationships between the Mother Country and Australia are more important than winning or losing matches," he said when he addressed the Rugby Football League Council in Manchester.

He urged the Council to send the party, and not worry about its strength as the Australians would not be up to their usual standard. He added that Great Britain had held the Ashes for 25 years and it was time for Australia to regain them.

Transport and the release of service men to undertake the tour were vital questions but Dr Evatt was sure they could answered. The Council decided to report to their clubs and that another meeting would be convened as soon as possible to reach a decision.

They released a brief statement on October 24: "Following Dr H V Evatt's recent appeal, the Rugby Football League Council today decided to send a touring team to Australia next April."

It was a momentous decision and one which would have enormous impact on the lives of the players fortunate enough to be invited to join the demanding tour.

With the decision made, the creation of a selection process had suddenly become crucial and the return to the international scene of France after the war offered new opportunity. But before travelling to France, the cream of British rugby league was named for a Wales v England game on November 24 at the St. Helen's ground in Swansea.

Frank Whitcombe was in the Wales team, along with his friend Willie Davies who was making his first appearance on the field in Swansea since turning professional. A crowd of 30,000 saw Wales triumph 11-3.

Then it was time for Paris. The Rugby League XIII team left Leeds on a Thursday and crossed the Channel the following day to ensure their arrival would not be delayed should ferry crossings be cancelled due to bad weather on the Saturday morning.

The *Yorkshire Post*'s man on the ferry reported on the Friday: "Six members of the Rugby League Council met members of the French Council today for the first time since 1939 and agreed terms under which English teams will visit Toulouse and Albi in March, Roanne and Lyons in April and Perpignan and Carcassonne before the end of the season.

The Hotel Lutetia in Paris, the base for the Rugby League XIII in 1946, previously the headquarters of German Army Intelligence during the Second World War.

"The team had a splendid Channel crossing. Frank Whitcombe, the burly Bradford Northern forward, was the life and soul of the party and there was a great welcome for them when they reached Paris where, among others, Paul Barrière, the former resistance fighter and now vice-president of the French Rugby League, greeted them.

"It is bitterly cold here in Paris and reports from the Parc des Princes where the game will be played, indicate that the pitch, though hard, will be playable. The cold weather has kept ticket sales down but Fernand Queheillard, the secretary of the French RFL, is satisfied that if the day is reasonable there will be a crowd of around 20,000.

"The French had expected their opponents would turn out in white jerseys but John Wilson told them his team would wear the same maroon kit they had worn in Swansea. That meant a colour clash with the red jerseys the French had planned to wear. A search of Paris, where sports

The Rugby League XIII: Parc des Princes, Paris, Sunday January 6 1946.
L-R: Ike Owens (Leeds), Bob Robson (Huddersfield), Bob Nicholson (Huddersfield), Ken Gee (Wigan), Joe Egan (Wigan), Frank Whitcombe (Bradford Northern), Tommy McCue (Widnes), Willie Davies (Bradford Northern), Alan Edwards (Salford), Ernest Ward (Bradford Northern), Eric Batten (Bradford Northern), Martin Ryan (Wigan), Gus Risman (Salford & Captain).

gear is in as short supply as it is in England, failed to provide another set of jerseys so a wire was flashed to Roanne for 13 white jerseys.

"This morning the players were out and about early. They found their way to the shops in search of toys and presents for their families at home and this afternoon they will have a coach tour of the city and their first look at the Parc des Princes where history will be made tomorrow."

"The match was billed as a French RL 13 v an English RL 13 and it was the official relaunching of the rugby league code in France after six years of being banned by the French government. The England-based team took the honours 19-6 with tries from Eric Batten (three), Martin Ryan and Alan Edwards with Gus Risman kicking two goals; the French points came from tries by Jep Maso and their best player Martin Martin.

"The 10,000 crowd were treated to some brilliant passing from both teams and John Wilson, the RFL secretary, was encouraged by the success of the first rugby league game ever to be played on the Parc des Princes pitch, which had been off limits for the game during the war years. The members of the Australian tour sub-committee must have seen much to encourage them to think that they can take out of this side the framework from which they can build the team for Australia.

"Maurice Blein, one of the leading French sports journalists of the time, was impressed by Eric Batten's hat-trick and added: 'It was the football lesson we have been waiting for; our players are badly in need of coaching.'"

After the success of the trip two further trial matches were arranged, the first being played at Wigan on January 30 1946 but rain and hail following on from a fall of snow made the game totally invalid as a preparation for Australian conditions, the Colours beating the Whites 18-3 after they had led at the interval through a try from Joe Egan. After the break the Colours added tries from Ernest Ashcroft (2) and Jeff Bawden with the latter adding a goal. Joe Lewthwaite crossed for the Whites.

Jim Sullivan, writing in the *News of the World*, said: "I am glad the rugby league authorities have decided to play a second Australian tour trial. The conditions at Central Park were so totally unlike what our men will experience in Australia that it did not constitute a fair test of their ability.

"Even at their worst Australian grounds never become so wet and muddy. When the second match comes along at Leeds, I believe the ground will be firm and lend itself to the development of quick movement and pace which our men must possess if they are to be successful on the hard-baked grounds Down Under.

"For the second match it would have been a good idea for the selectors to pick the best two teams available and at half-time introduce a few others but I realise England play France at Swinton only three days later."

A month before the match at Headingley was played, the Rugby Football League announced the two managers for the tour. Wilf Gabbatt from Barrow was appointed business manager with Bramley's Walter Popplewell the team manager.

Popplewell, who had given over 45 years' service to the Bramley club, was joint manager on the 1936 tour of Australia while Gabbatt had held several offices with the Rugby League Council and was chairman of the League in 1933-4.

Each manager was allocated an allowance of £400, twice that given to previous managers. It was also announced that Walter Crockford would travel with the party as the Council representative and would pay his own way.

On the day the second trial match was played at Headingley there was worrying news for the RFL Council when it was learned that all arrangements had been completed in Australia for a tour by Derby County Football Club. The RFL's tour plans were no nearer completion than when they started.

The *Yorkshire Post* reported: "A Reuter's message says that the Derby party of 17 players, two officials and the trainer will arrive in Australia by air on May 15 and will return by sea, sailing on July 1. The Football Association has granted the team the status of a representative England side.

"The RFL was asked last October to send a team to Australia this summer but although vigorous efforts have been made both here and in Australia to arrange transport for 26 people, the RFL have had no encouragement. When John Wilson visited London last week in an effort to fix things up he could get no definite promise.

"In view of the latest news about Derby County, whose tour has been arranged at relatively short notice, the *Yorkshire Post* understands that the RFL will make further representations in London to the authorities controlling transport. As the RFL only entered into an agreement for a tour at the express invitation of Dr Evatt they seem to have a strong case."

There was nothing to cheer the RFL when their second trial match went ahead, the Whites beating the Colours 18-14 in a dull, spiritless game played in a biting wind which forced the referee to play four quarters instead of two halves to allow the players, especially the backs, to warm their frozen fingers.

Tries for the Whites came from Jack Taylor (Wigan, 2), Chris Brereton (Halifax), and Trevor Foster (Bradford Northern) with Jimmy Ledgard (Dewsbury) kicking three goals and Ted Ward (Wigan) one. In reply Trevor Petcher (Barrow, 2), Arthur Bassett (Halifax) and Harry Ogden (Oldham) crossed and Des Clarkson (Hunslet) kicked a goal.

Speculation as to who would be selected for the trip ended on March 11 when the tour sub-committee announced a touring party of 32, comprising

Gus Risman, is the centre of attraction as he raises the Challenge Cup trophy.

26 players, two managers, a representative of the RFL Council and, for the first time, three journalists, Alfred Drewry (*Yorkshire Post*), Eddie Waring (*Sunday Pictorial*) and Ernest Cawthorne (*Manchester Evening News*), the latter being contracted to produce reports from the tour for Bradford's *Telegraph and Argus*. A fourth journalist, Harry Sunderland, would join the party in Australia.

Gus Risman was named as captain and would be making his third trip Down Under, equalling the feat of Jim Sullivan (Wigan), Jonty Parkin (Wakefield Trinity) and Joe Thompson (Leeds). The only other player to have previously toured Australia was the Widnes scrum-half Tommy McCue, who was named vice-captain.

The son of a Latvian seaman, Risman, 35, had just been demobilised from the 1st Airborne Division in which he had reached the rank of Lieutenant. After the tour he continued playing until he was almost 44 and made a total of 873 appearances.

The squad was announced as; full backs: Martin Ryan (Wigan), Joe Jones (Barrow); wings: Eric Batten (Bradford Northern), Joe Lewthwaite (Barrow), Arthur Bassett (Halifax), Albert Johnson (Warrington); centres: Gus Risman (Salford), Bryn Knowleden (Barrow), Ted Ward (Wigan), Jack Kitching, Ernest Ward (both Bradford Northern); stand-offs: Willie Horne (Barrow), Willie Davies (Bradford Northern); scrum-halves: Dai Jenkins (Leeds), Tommy McCue (Widnes).

Front-row: Frank Whitcombe (Bradford Northern), Ken Gee, Joe Egan (both Wigan), Fred Hughes (Workington), George Curran (Salford); second-row: Doug Phillips (Oldham), Bob Nicholson (Huddersfield), Trevor Foster (Bradford Northern), Les White (York); loose-forwards: Ike Owens (Leeds), Harry Murphy (Wakefield Trinity).

There were 15 English and 11 Welsh players in the tour party and although its official title was Great Britain they would be known throughout their time in Australia as England. Bradford Northern had six players in the party, equalling the record held by Huddersfield who had provided six men for the 1914 tour.

Risman said: "I am proud to be chosen as captain of Great Britain for what might be called the Victory Jubilee tour; I have great faith in the blending of youth and experience which the selection committee have given us.

"I feel confident that we shall put up a great fight to retain the Ashes and I know that we have the best wishes of the whole rugby league public behind us."

One concern of the press, and the man on the terraces, was that only 11 forwards had been selected as opposed to the usual dozen, which meant that those making the trip would have a heavier work-load to bear than their predecessors.

Prior to departure, all the players faced a stern medical examination and before going to see the doctor, Frank Whitcombe confided to Trevor Foster that he had developed a knee problem. It was an unusually sombre Whitcombe who was called into the surgery but 20 minutes later he emerged beaming.

"How did you get on with your injured knee?" asked his great friend. "Oh fine," was the response. "When the doctor asked to see my injured knee I showed him the good one."

On March 15 the bulk of the party met up in Leeds to sign their tour contracts. The only men absent were all from Bradford Northern. Kitching and Davies were teaching, Whitcombe was away with his lorry and Ward, who was still in the Army, had not reached Leeds when the roll-call was made.

Risman was the first to sign the contract then watched on, as his men added their signatures to the contracts before they completed their passport forms and were measured for their tour blazers and flannels, for which the RFL had obtained special ration coupons.

The issue of transport had finally been resolved. The party would travel on the aircraft carrier HMS Indomitable – peace-time travel by ocean liners had not yet been resumed – and would leave England on April 3. When their tour was over and they returned with the Ashes they would be forever known as 'The Indomitables'.

There were still grave doubts as to whether those players who were selected, but were still in the armed forces, would be released for the tour by the War Office. The men concerned; Doug Phillips, Les White and Ernest Ward, were all serving in the Army so the RFL sought six months leave of absence for them.

At first the War Office simply turned down the RFL's request regarding Phillips and White and would not make a decision on Ward so the selectors nominated Bob Robson (Huddersfield), Eddie Watkins (Wigan) and Sid Rookes (Hunslet) as their replacements.

In the end, after lobbying by several Yorkshire MPs, the War Office relented and all three first-choice players were able to take their places in the touring party, albeit only after two of them – Ernest Ward (Lancashire Fusiliers) and Phillips (Royal Armoured Corps) – had represented the Army in the 1946 Inter-Services tournament.

The decisive match that season was the Army v the Royal Air Force on March 23 and the following day Wales were to play France at Bordeaux so Phillips had to pull out of that game. Tourists Frank Whitcombe, Trevor Foster, Ted Ward, Dai Jenkins and Fred Hughes – whose son Emlyn would later captain Liverpool and England as a footballer – were all on duty for Wales, who lost 19-7.

At the time of the announcement of the tour party Bradford Northern had been on top of the Championship but losing so many key players for the remaining fixtures dented their hopes and they finally finished fourth in the table and qualified for the play-off final.

They faced top-of-the-table Wigan at Central Park on May 11 and perhaps not surprisingly were beaten 18-4, their points coming from two goals landed by George Carmichael.

11

THE INDOMITABLES DEPART

T he tourists left railway stations at Bradford, Leeds, Barrow and Manchester under instructions to gather in London before travelling as a group the following day to Devonport, where they would board HMS Indomitable.

The *Yorkshire Observer Budget*, published in Bradford, carried an article on the departure of those who left Bradford Exchange Station: "There were conflicting emotions among the four Bradford Northern players and those who saw them off.

"Ernest Ward, Jack Kitching, Frank Whitcombe and Willie Davies were the four who left Bradford – Eric Batten and Trevor Foster would join them en route – and they expressed themselves delighted to be making the trip.

Bradford Exchange, Tourists Ernest Ward, Frank Whitcombe, Willie Davies and Jack Kitching are given a rousing send off by family, friends and Bradford Northern players and officials.

A last word of encouragement from Harry Hornby (third left) and Dai Rees (right) for (from left) Ernest Ward, Willie Davies, Frank Whitcombe and Jack Kitching.

But all also felt a twinge of regret to be parting temporarily from their wives and families who were there to wish them *bon voyage*.

"I'm overjoyed to be making the trip," said Frank Whitcombe, "because I was in line for such a tour when the war broke out and when it had to be cancelled I thought my last chance had gone.

"We all realise it won't be altogether a picnic and that there will be a great deal of hard work for us all, but we are anxious to do all we can to uphold the prestige of the rugby league game and Bradford Northern RLFC."

"Similar sentiments were expressed by the other three and all had good wishes showered on them by the party of friends and relatives from whom they took leave. These included Harry Hornby, Bradford Northern's managing director, Northern's team manager Dai Rees, Harold Edwards, the club's former Welsh international, and Ernest Ward's mother and father.

"The Leeds contingent took with them the Ashes trophy which had been found after being missing for seven years. RFL secretary John Wilson, bidding them goodbye, jovially warned them not to lose the trophy again, in any sense of the word.

"'They should have a jolly good tour,' he said as their train steamed away. 'They will land in Australia at just about the end of their autumn but will find the winter there is rather like pleasant summer weather over here, although the nights are rather cold.'"

The touring party duly met up in London where the players and officials went to their first official engagement. Alfred Drewry described their reception in the *Yorkshire Post*: "With the exception of the four Welshmen who are travelling from their homes direct to Devonport, all of us who comprise the RFL's Tour Party are tonight spending our last night ashore for five weeks.

"The party went to Australia House where, on the roof overlooking central London, we were greeted by John Greasley, the Australian Resident Minister and a keen follower of rugby league, previously having been a prominent member of the Balmain club in Sydney.

"'May I wish you a safe and pleasant journey,' he said. 'In Australia you will get a rousing welcome. The Australian rugby followers will hope that the best team will win and naturally they will expect the home side to prove the best.'

"Gus Risman replied that his team would have something to say about that and when Mr Beasley asked if the tourists liked barracking, which the crowds in his country liked to indulge in, Risman assured him that his team would not be worried, all he and his team were looking forward to was a series of fine struggles.

"Mr Beasley did not see the Ashes trophy which has been held by the RFL since 1922. We have it securely fastened up in a small black box in the possession of Mr Popplewell. No matter what happens to the rest of his luggage the Bramley official will not allow the trophy to go from his care. 'I hope it will be my duty to still be in charge of the trophy in six months' time,' he said.

"It is the first time a rugby league side has visited Australia since 1936 and the first visit by any sporting side to any of the dominions since the war. Mr Beasley mentioned this fact when, in a final message of good wishes, he said that the sporting associations between parts of the empire were the finest links that could be established.

"We spent some happy hours in London tonight. The players told me of the difficulty they have had in getting the necessary travelling kit and of the generous ways the clubs and supporters have helped them.

"The six Bradford Northern players have all had £25 from the club, Les White of York received more than £60 from well-wishers and Fred Hughes, the Workington forward, was presented with £78."

The Tourists visited Australia House in London on April 1 1946, where Mr John Beasley, the Australian Resident Minister (centre) bade them farewell at a rooftop ceremony.

The next day the touring party travelled by train to Plymouth, boarded HMS Indomitable at Devonport and after being welcomed by Captain W G Andrews DSO prepared for the five-week, 12,000 mile voyage.

Bob Sloman, the former Oldham second-row and an Australia tourist in 1924 and 1928, was a visitor to Indomitable prior to departure and gave the tour captain Gus Risman money for a Saturday night toast. Risman said: "Every Saturday night while the party are away there will be a toast to all those left at home."

Alfred Drewry's article on April 3 read: "Although the tourists have welcomed a decision to dispense with all but the lightest of training for the moment they could not resist this morning taking a ball on to the wide open spaces of the flight deck.

"Many Naval ratings looked on but not for long; in a matter of minutes they were joining in a rough-and-tumble loose scrum. Real training will not begin until April 22 when we have passed through Colombo. The players have had a hard season, particularly those who have been playing rugby union in the services.

Journalist Harry Sunderland took this photograph at Frank Whitcombe's request and posted it to his family in Bradford. Sunderland added in his letter, "Frank, I feel sure is going to be one of the greatest successes of the tour, and will be very popular in Australia".

"The tourists sail before dusk this evening on the voyage to Sydney and sailing orders indicate there will be a stop of about 24 hours in each port of call – Gibraltar, Malta, Port Said, Colombo and Fremantle – so there will probably be a chance for the players to get ashore for a short spell at one or two of these places.

"I was mildly surprised when all members of the party turned up for breakfast this morning. Every time one leaves a familiar spot such as a mess room it is at the risk of being lost in the labyrinth of passages and staircases that honeycomb this great ship, so for safety's sake nobody wanders far without company.

"The party has already made progress in mastering the techniques of climbing and descending the ship's steep iron ladders and surmounting the foot barricades which crop up every few yards. Getting over these 2ft high steel walls and getting through doors just 2ft wide is quite a business for the 17st Frank Whitcombe and the 6ft 2in Doug Phillips. They have already learned that the best way to get through is to swing, Tarzan style, by means of the grips bolted to the top of the openings.

"The total number on the Indomitable when she sails will be about 2,000, which includes the ship's company, reliefs for men serving at stations abroad and Australian and New Zealand servicemen on their way home to be demobbed."

Eddie Waring wrote in typically jaunty style for the *Sunday Pictorial*. "Two tons of Britain's best rugby league footballers have been added to the 23,000 tons of this famous aircraft carrier Indomitable.

"The team had quite a send-off from Devonport with the piping of the harbour ships bidding them farewell. History is being made by this mode of travel and though vastly different to the usual methods the boys are settling down well.

"Gus Risman, Dai Jenkins, Eric Batten and Trevor Foster are in the Admiral's Office and Willie Davies, Frank Whitcombe, Jack Kitching and Ernest Ward are in the Air Intelligence Office, practically on the flight deck.

"The 11-strong Welsh group in the party are Gus Risman (from Barry), Trevor Foster (Newport), Arthur Bassett (Kenfig Hill), Ike Owens (Pontycymmer), Doug Phillips (Skewen), Joe Jones (Cilfynydd), Fred Hughes (Llanelli), Frank Whitcombe (Cardiff), Ted Ward (Ammanford), Willie Davies (Penclawdd) and Dai

Eddie Waring.

Fred Hughes, (second from right, front row) leads the Welsh choir entertaining Mr William McKell, Prime Minster of New South Wales.

Jenkins (Treherbert) and they assure me that South Wales folk are greatly interested in their doings.

"The Welsh contingent have asked me to say '*Iechyd da*' to their folks and have formed a Welsh choir which will sing for me on one of my earliest broadcasts."

The Welsh choir sang at a number of concerts, events and sing-songs throughout the tour.

On Sunday April 7 Alfred Drewry reported from the tourists' stop-off in Gibraltar: "The aircraft carrier HMS Indomitable has been anchored beneath the Rock of Gibraltar after a smooth, uneventful passage across the Bay of Biscay. We leave for Malta early today, arriving next Tuesday to drop off 800 Navy ratings.

"None of the touring party has been able to go ashore; we hope for better luck in Malta. Everyone is well and in high spirits and already the sea air and yesterday's sunshine have begun to have magical effects on the English winter complexions.

"The players are also making their own entertainment; Dai Jenkins and Ike Owens have joined the Welsh choir formed by the irrepressible

Fred Hughes. The other members are Trevor Foster, Ted Ward, Joe Jones, the only pianist in the party, and big Doug Phillips and there have already been some rousing sing-songs in the Warrant Officers' Mess where the players are quartered.

"I suggested to Ernest Ward that the Yorkshire reputation for choral singing should be upheld but I must confess that the Jack Kitching, Ernest Ward, Eric Batten, Les White, Harry Murphy and Alfred Drewry ensemble has been beaten for volume if not, we claim, for purity of tone.

"Fred Hughes has been dubbed 'Lucky Fred' after he won the sweepstake on the Lincoln Handicap and also made a fair

Frank Whitcombe, Ted Ward and Arthur Bassett on the flight deck of HMS Indomitable.

Relaxing ashore in Aden, are (back row L-R) Les White, Bob Nicholson, Bryn Knowelden, Willie Horn, and Dai Jenkins (front centre) with crew members beside him.

Indomitable anchored at Valetta Harbour, Malta.

amount of money from a bookmaking venture when the only player to back a winner was Ernest Ward.

"Everyone is highly satisfied with the living conditions and Eric Batten summed up the food situation by saying that when we reach Sydney he expects to weigh two stone more than he does now. Bob Nicholson is also mightily pleased at the prospect of putting on weight: he lost half a stone between August and March after being demobbed from the RAF.

"But Frank Whitcombe is a trifle apprehensive about this life of ease; he weighs 17 stone now and wants to get down to 16 so he is the one exception to the non-training rule."

Two days later the Indomitable arrived in Malta and Alfred Drewry reported from Valletta: "The rugby league tourists, cheerful and already sun-tanned, had their first excursion ashore today in brilliant Mediterranean sunshine. They spent their day sightseeing and buying presents.

"All the players are fit with the exception of Eric Batten who cut a leg at Workington in his last match in England; poison has set in but is not serious.

"The players have made themselves very popular with the ship's company and have accepted two challenges thrown out by the ship's deck-hockey teams, while the genial Captain Andrews has asked them to play a rugby league match in Fremantle.

"The players and management, anxious to show their appreciation of the Navy's hospitality, have fallen in with the idea wholeheartedly. A signal will be sent to the mayor of Fremantle asking to organise a ground for an exhibition match there, probably on April 30, with the proceeds going to Navy charities.

"The players drew their two deck-hockey matches against the electricians' department and against a select side when their team, eager for action of any kind, quickly showed an aptitude for the game and have entered three teams in the ship's knockout tournament – England, Wales and Great Britain.

"The managers' first job on arrival in Australia will be to book a return passage and at an informal meeting the players expressed a wish to travel overland across Canada or the United States. The managers said they would do their best to arrange such a journey.

"The players have bought watches for 30 shillings, silk stockings at five pairs for £1 and fruit from dozens of Maltese traders who sculled round

Mount Lavinia Hotel in Colombo, Ceylon.

HMS Indomitable in small boats at the risk of having the ship's hoses turned on them.

"The weather has continued to be kind and as we cruised along the coast of North Africa yesterday Gus Risman, who served in this part of the world during the war, was able to point out landmarks. This is also familiar territory for the Indomitable; in 1942 she was damaged by a bomb while escorting a convoy to Malta and a year later, while she was supporting the invasion of Sicily, she was torpedoed."

A week later the Indomitable had passed through the Suez Canal and reached Aden. Alfred Drewry's next article read: "The Indomitable, sailing exactly to schedule, arrived in Aden today and despite the sticky heat the rugby league tourists had another jaunt ashore, hunting souvenirs to go with those bought at well-stocked Malta.

"All the players are fit and well. Eric Batten's knee has healed and he can claim the distinction of having swum in the Gulf of Suez. We lost a basketball over the side while the ship was at anchor and Eric went in after it. So did Frank Whitcombe but he had no choice: someone pushed him in!

"Though training does not start officially until we leave Colombo on April 23 the players are getting plenty of exercise."

On Tuesday April 22 the rugby league party went ashore in what was then Ceylon, now Sri Lanka, in holiday mood and on a morning tour of Colombo's suburbs were intrigued by the changing scenes and colours.

Alfred Drewry wrote: "A surfing and swimming expedition to the palm-fringed beach at Mount Lavinia provided a refreshing break for the tourists from the monotony of ship-board life.

"After stewing for seven days and nights in the humid heat of the Red Sea and across the Indian Ocean no-one could resist the call of the big white breakers which crashed invitingly on to the cool, firm golden sand, not even those who saw in a fishing boat the carcass of a young shark which had been caught earlier in the day.

"All the players are well and cheerful but reached Colombo a trifle limp. Time passes slowly, it seems three months rather than three weeks since we left England. We are now counting the days to Australia and football.

"Everyone is weary of the sea and is restlessly eager to get into action, an indication that the long days of rest have served their purpose and that muscles strained and tired by the long season of football in England are now rested.

"We leave Colombo today and as the weather gets cooler the players will get down to light training, mainly exercise and maybe a little with the ball in the hangar. There will be no lack of instructors: Gus Risman, Ernest

Ward, Trevor Foster, Willie Davies, Ike Owens and Doug Phillips were all Physical Training Instructors during war.

"But training will be nothing hectic, certainly nothing as violent as deck-hockey; I suspect that team manager Popplewell was secretly relieved when the second round saw the elimination of the party's three teams in the ship's tournament.

"The next bid for the limelight comes on Saturday in the ship's sports; the tourists should at least win the tug-of-war with this 130 stone team: Doug Phillips, Trevor Foster, Ike Owens, Frank Whitcombe, Harry Murphy, Fred Hughes, Ken Gee and Joe Egan. Willie Davies is the coach."

The Indomitable crossed the Equator on April 25 and Trevor Foster recalled: "Tradition dictates that a visit from the great King Neptune (Captain Andrews) is due. It adds that all the men travelling on the boat should be shaved then dunked into a huge water-bath on deck by the King and his entourage.

"This proved an almost impossible task when Neptune and his crew – all in fancy dress – faced big Frank Whitcombe so Neptune immediately recruited Frank to his team for the purpose of ensuring those who were dunked received a full quota, just short of drowning.

"Frank in turn recruited Doug Phillips and Fred Hughes. All the lads were held under three times then released. Eddie Waring, however, thought he would only report on the antics and not get too involved in the fun since it looked a little risky so he remained fully clothed and at a distance on the bridge.

"He was spotted, marched down and put through his paces. Big Frank made sure Eddie was well looked after and administered six hearty dunks and held him deep under the water before releasing the gasping and panicking Eddie to a huge cheer from all the lads. Eddie had been a great sport and was loved by the players."

On April 29 the Australian public were given their first insight into the Great Britain party when the *Daily News* carried this article: "The English rugby league team which will reach Fremantle tomorrow by aircraft carrier will be a big draw in the Test series against Australia.

"Organisers anticipate upwards of 70,000 at the three Test matches with gate receipts of £6,000 to £7,000 at each. There will be two Tests at Sydney Cricket Ground and one in Brisbane then the tourists will go to New Zealand.

"More than 1,300 seats reserved at £1 each have been set aside for the first match in Sydney and the organisers say they could have sold the whole of the reserved stand seats in 30 minutes. The normal gate when two of Sydney's eight main league teams meet for a Saturday fixture is £2,000.

"Captain of the touring team is 35-year-old Welsh international Gus Risman who is making his third trip to Australia. He was here with the 1932 and 1936 teams and has been a football star since he was 17. Centre three-quarter for Salford, he was appointed player-manager of Workington Town at £1,000 per year just before the tourists left England.

"An outstanding player and the heaviest man in the team is 17st 31-year-old front-row forward Frank Whitcombe while one of the youngest players is full-back Martin Ryan who tips the beam at 12st 7lb. Though comparatively young he is one of the team's most spectacular players.

"Another exciting player is wing three-quarter Eric Batten. To escape defenders he leaps over his opponent's head, a trick he learned from his father who also toured Australia some years ago.

"The team represents many occupations: winger Jim Lewthwaite is a ship-builder, centre Ted Ward is a crane driver, there are two school-teachers, a lorry driver, a book-maker and a coal miner and with the team came a pile of empty suitcases to be filled with Australian food and clothing when the men return to England.

"Having brought sufficient men for two teams, the visitors have agreed to play an exhibition match in Fremantle to which the public are invited. There will be no charge for admission but a collection will be taken for charity."

The first scheduled stop for the tourists in Australia was indeed Fremantle where they were met by journalist Kerwin Maegraith who wrote this article for the *Courier Mail*: "At the shriek of dawn this department boarded HMS Indomitable in the gallant cause of sketching Mr Gus Risman and his Herculean footballers from England.

"Our meeting with England was the greatest moment since Livingstone met Stanley and anyone who thinks he can stop Mr Risman and his fellow-sailors playing football should go over to Italy and keep Vesuvius quiet.

"Don't imagine they turn these footballers out of a mould – like racehorses. They are all shapes and sizes and Mr Risman's team has obviously been selected to suit cartoonists. Not since the Russian ballet came here have such strong, stern men hit our shores.

"Take Frank Whitcombe; he is 17st and runs 100 yards in 11 seconds. Then there is George Curran who is so powerful Herb Narvo would turn in his account to behold him. I asked one forward with cauliflower ears if he would like to be a heavyweight boxer but he said prize-fighting was too cissy.

"When you ask these players if they think they can take the Test matches from Australia they sink into a trance of intense joyfulness. I asked Mr

Batten, from Bradford, 'Do you think you can win? 'I do feel sorry for the other side,' he replied.

"The baby is Martin Ryan, who was born with a football in his hands. Mr Jenkins, who owns a pub in Leeds, thinks the best writer he knows is Walter Popplewell, the tour manager, who signs the cheques for shore leave."

The Indomitable arrived in Freemantle – the port for Perth, just a few miles up the Swan River – in the early hours of April 30.

At 11am they attended a formal welcoming reception hosted by the Mayor, Councillor Gibson, when it was announced that as a gift from the Fremantle Patriotic Fund the two managers and 26 players would have a food parcel sent to their homes in England.

In the afternoon at Fremantle Cricket Ground an exhibition game of rugby league was played, honouring the promise made to the Indomitable's Captain Andrews during the voyage. A decent crowd turned up with see Tommy McCue's Reds beat Gus Risman's Blues 24-5.

The game was covered by Kevin Maegraith for the *Courier Mail* who reported: "What struck me about the English players, both in the game at Fremantle and in their training, was their speed, the way the forwards and backs fanned out, their remarkable lightness of foot and their combination and understanding in spite of the limited opportunity to play together.

"Soon this combination will develop into one of the greatest teams Australia has seen; their first work-out on Australian soil showed they are raring to go.

"Big, beefy, curly-headed Frank Whitcombe, in spite of weighing over 17st, got around the field with pace and was in everything going on in the scrum. Frank was a lorry driver who carried munitions round England all through the Blitz and the battles in the skies over England.

"Managers Walter Popplewell and William Gabbatt are the ideal public relations men for the team and they withstood the heavy barrage of newspaper and publicity men at Freemantle with ready smiles. If the Western Australian hospitality is an indication of what will follow in the East, Gus Risman told me he will demand that his men do their football work first and be entertained afterwards. The favourite pastime here is entertaining Englishmen to grilled steak and eggs.

Frank Whitcombe preparing for training in Freemantle.

"This morning I heard beautiful music coming from the Ward Room and if I could have enlisted the aid of an interpreter it would have been a real concert. Fred Hughes, Willie Davies (a school-teacher who is anxious to see Brisbane's schools), Ernest Ward, a baritone with a rich tone, his namesake Ted and Joe Jones, a typical Welsh tenor, were warbling 'Sospan Fach'.

"It has become sort of a tradition that a rugby league team should include one policeman and this time it is big Arthur Bassett from Derby who is the custodian of the law with Risman's men. Arthur helped to lock up two escaped German prisoners in England; he is a tough nut who will give us some fun as he is a stylish forward.

"Eric Batten's biggest job is going to be to find friends of his dad, Billy Batten, the former rugby league international, while one of the most spectacular backs you could wish to see is the baby of the team Martin Ryan, a miner."

But not quite everything was going to plan for the newly-arrived tourists, as Alfred Drewry told readers of the *Yorkshire Post* from Fremantle: "The rugby league tourists met with the threat of delay when they arrived here in the Indomitable today.

"They found the aircraft carrier Victorious in dock, severely damaged as a result of the buffeting she received crossing the Great Australian Bight. She was on her way to England with 2,000 passengers and if she is unable to continue her journey in the next few days the possibility is that the Indomitable will discharge her passengers, take on those of the Victorious and turn round instead of heading for Sydney. If that happens the tourists may have to wait in Fremantle for the Victorious to be repaired."

Sure enough, on May 3 the tourists left their accommodation on the Indomitable; she duly took on board the passengers from Victorious and headed home. The tour party were left to settle into a training facility of the Royal Australian Navy at Leeuwin where they could continue to work on their fitness whilst passage to Sydney by rail was arranged.

12

ACROSS AUSTRALIA

Though happy to be living again on dry land, things were not ideal for the tourists during their brief spell in Leeuwin, as Alfred Drewry wrote. "The Navy camp is taxed beyond normal capacity so the players help to relieve staff shortages by washing dishes in the mess where they are accommodated in addition to laundering their own clothes.

"There was quite a domestic scene outside the mess after tea today with Doug Phillips and Ike Owens washing dishes and Harry Murphy, Eric Batten and Dai Jenkins hanging out shirts and socks to dry."

On Saturday May 4 the entire party accepted an invitation from the Western Australia National League to watch an Australian Rules football match between the Subiaco and East Fremantle clubs and that evening they were entertained at a trotting meeting under floodlights at Gloucester Park.

It was a day of mixed emotions for Wakefield Trinity's Harry Murphy and Wigan's Ken Gee, Ted Ward, Joe Egan and Martin Ryan who were all missing the Challenge Cup final at faraway Wembley which Trinity won 13-12.

On May 7, the troop train for Sydney left from the 60th Australian Army Camp Hospital at Claremont, a suburb of Perth, but unfortunately for all those on board another 24 hours had been added to the duration of the journey. A combination of coal shortages for the engine, speed restrictions and frequent changes of rail gauges would make their trip across Australia, hot, tedious and downright unpleasant.

The hastily arranged train journey to Sydney would take the tourists from the Indian Ocean to the Pacific Ocean across parts of Australia where the temperature would rise to 122 degrees Fahrenheit during the day, plunging to freezing point at night but berths on the train for Sydney could not be secured until May 7.

Their timetable gives an indication of the times and changes involved: Perth to Kalgoorlie 16 hours, change trains; Kalgoorlie to Port Pirie at least 20 hours; Port Pirie to Adelaide five hours, change trains; Adelaide to Melbourne overnight; Melbourne to Albury four hours, change trains; Albury to Sydney overnight.

Ernest Ward (pointing) and his fellow tourists, as they cross the Nullarbor Plain.

Alfred Drewry shared the party's frustrations: "After their experiences over the last 24 hours in a crowded troop train the tourists have the right to match stories with anyone who made uncomfortable rail journeys during the war.

"Following the issue of blankets, cutlery and tin plates we boarded a train which left Perth yesterday afternoon. The train stopped at 5.30 so we could have a meal of stew and potatoes, which we ate standing on a wayside platform.

"The next meal, consisting of porridge, bacon and tomatoes, did not come until 10.30 this morning when we arrived at an Army Staging Post outside Kalgoorlie to change trains for the journey across 'Never Never Land' which is how the locals describe the seemingly endless Nullarbor Plain. The players had prepared for a food shortage by buying cooked chickens, baked rabbits and fruit.

"Before settling down for the night Ike Owens, Frank Whitcombe, Fred Hughes, Arthur Bassett, Ted Ward and Doug Phillips put on an impromptu concert for the benefit of the Australian journalists. Owens, who has a

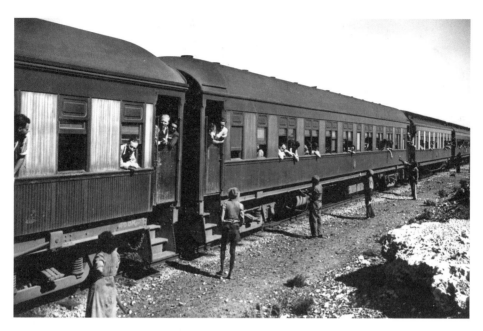

Stopping for food, a break in the long trip across the desert.

pleasant tenor voice, led the way with Welsh songs and the Australians countered with songs from their own land.

"There was no sleeping accommodation on this train and we had to make the best of sleeping on the floor. On the train that takes us from here to Port Pirie, near Adelaide, there are bunks but not sufficient to go round because we are travelling with eight passengers in compartments designed for four. Everyone will be heartily glad when we reach Sydney."

Tom Goodman, of the *Sydney*

Welsh tourists sleeping rough on the train journey. L-R: Ted Ward, Fred Hughes, Frank Whitcombe, Ike Owens, Arthur Bassett and Doug Phillips.

Morning Herald, filed his copy on their journey on Friday May 10: "After two long days and nights on a crowded troop train, on their journey of 2,500 miles from Perth to Sydney, the English rugby league footballers are still travelling through the wide, treeless expanse of the Nullarbor Plain.

"Until the players reach Melbourne on Saturday they will not know the departure time of their connection to Sydney. The team managers Wilf Gabbatt and Walter Popplewell are hopeful that the party will be in their quarters in the Olympic Hotel in Sydney by Sunday.

"The Englishmen and the other 60 civilians travelling on this train, including discharged soldiers, sailors and merchant seamen, who joined the large numbers of service personnel on this trip, are tired and dirty. But they are happier now that the dreariest part of the journey is well advanced; the civilians have experienced Army routine at the various stopping places.

"They were fed yesterday at a staging camp near Kalgoorlie, the famous gold-mining city which was out-of-bounds to all passengers. Kalgoorlie, however, proved to be an oasis in the desert as excellent cold beer was available at the camp and when the passengers transferred to the wider gauge rails, the Army cooks, with their field kitchens on board, served excellent food.

Stopping off at Ararat, 120 miles west of Melbourne, the men on the left of the front and back row are fellow passengers with the Tourists, (back row from left) Ike Owens, Doug Phillips, Frank Whitcombe, Trevor Foster and Ted Ward. Front are Joe Jones and Willie Davies.

"The team's Welsh choir, led by tenors Ted Ward and Ike Owens, has harmonised delightfully in folk songs and hymns which have been supplemented by songs in a lighter vein by the Derby policeman Arthur Bassett.

"Some of the Welsh choruses seem to have staggered the broken-down Aborigines gathered at wayside railway stations begging for food and cigarettes and offering to sell boomerangs. The rousing good humour of the team's comedians Frank Whitcombe and Fred Hughes has had plenty of scope."

For the last leg of the journey, from Melbourne to Sydney, sleeping carriages were provided for the tourists and when they arrived at the city which is the centre of Australian rugby league, Tom Goodman analysed the touring party for *Morning Herald* readers:

"In Fremantle and Perth and on the train journey across Australia I saw a great deal of the English rugby league team, who are now in Sydney; they are a good-looking, happy band and terribly keen to do well on this tour. So far as their football is concerned they remain a 'wait and see' combination.

"Only two, Gus Risman and Tom McCue, have previously played in Australia and some of the others are inexperienced in big football but the team is full of interesting personalities; here are some of them among the many.

"Gus Risman is a gentlemanly fellow who was immensely popular on the tours of 1932 and 1936. He is a stylish centre, one who demands respect on and off the field. On the long train trip, which tested the more temperamental, I saw evidence of the influence of Risman in matters apart from football.

"Willie Davies, the glamour five-eighth, was a member of the famous Welsh rugby union combination of the cousins Hayden Tanner and Davies which began at school and carried on with the Swansea club in 1935 when his team were the only club side to beat J E Manchester's All Blacks and ended when he turned professional in 1939.

"Willie is a schoolmaster and a quiet, thoughtful fellow. If he

Arthur Bassett tests the boomerang he has just bought for 2s (10p) from an Aborigine in the desert.

strikes something like his best form, especially in attack, his team-mates say you will see a bobby-dazzler.

"Martin Ryan, a coal-miner from Wigan, is one of the quieter members of the party. A fresh-faced, wavy-haired lad, he's one of the more earnest players; he is a new discovery as an enterprising full-back.

"Eric Batten is a speedy, resolute winger who resembles his father Billy, of the 1910 side in Australia in looks as well as playing style. Like his dad, he doesn't hesitate to dive over a crouching opponent if that is the only way of getting through. A non-drinker, non-smoker and a crank on physical fitness, this deep-chested athlete will be one of England's hopes.

"Welshman Ike Owens, rated one of the fastest loose-forwards to leave England by his colleagues, is now a stone heavier than when the party left home. He was one of comparatively few non-aircrew members of the Royal Air Force to be awarded the Air Force Medal during the war. A Sergeant Instructor at a famous parachute training centre near Manchester, Ike made 280 parachute jumps.

"Frank Whitcombe is the team's baby-faced 'human tank' and is now approaching 18st. An outstanding humourist with his sense of fun and friendly nature, he is a great asset to a touring combination; moreover he is a tough and intelligent forward. His chief companion in fun is 'Ginger' Hughes, another front-row forward, who has invested proceeds from his book-making business in property.

"English rugby league teams favour playing right and left centre and wing combinations, rather than the Australian system of playing inside and outside centre and the tourists have two ready-made centre and wing combinations available.

Ike Owens and Frank Whitcombe rooming together in good humour.

"One pair is the Bradford Northern partnership of Jack Kitching at right centre and Eric Batten the right-winger; the other is Bradford centre Ernest Ward and Warrington's left-winger Albert Johnson, who have been associated in several important fixtures including England v France at Swinton last year when Johnson scored three tries.

"An early forecast for the three-quarter line for the first Test is Eric Batten, Gus Risman, Ernest Ward and Albert Johnson.

"Risman's outstanding qualities of leadership and his great experience in Test football will be eagerly employed if this 35-year-old Welsh centre shows that he has retained his first-class form. Jack Kitching, a 6ft 2in schoolteacher who runs with his shoulders hunched, helped Batten to be a terrific try-scorer in England and himself contributed a goodly number.

"Ernest Ward, who, with club, services and international fixtures, played as often as three or four times a week during the English season, is the ideal weight for a centre at 13st 12lb while Albert Johnson is regarded as an attractive winger with a neat side-step and deceptive swerve, and the team's other left-winger Arthur Bassett is solid and experienced.

"Young right-winger Jim Lewthwaite rivals Eric Batten for the honour of being England's fastest winger while Ted Ward and Bryn Knowleden are centres whose early form will have to be compared to that of the others.

Sydney Harbour Bridge on a misty morning.

Training at the Sydney Cricket Ground – from left, Ken Gee, Frank Whitcombe, George Curran and Bob Nicholson.

"The front row is solid with Joe Egan and Frank Whitcombe seeming certain to be in the Tests with one from Ken Gee, Fred Hughes and Bob Nicholson filling the other berth. The hard heads of the team look to Nicholson to be one of the successes of the tour in the front or second row.

"Trevor Foster, Doug Phillips and Ike Owens would measure up in weight and size to England's great trio from the 1936 pack, Hodgson, Arkwright and Beverley and Owens especially has great speed. Harry Murphy and Les White are splendid youngsters to have in reserve."

To the delight of the touring party their train finally pulled into Sydney's Central Station at 1.10pm on Sunday May 12, five interminable days after leaving Perth. The following day the *Sydney Morning Herald* ran this story:

"The English rugby league players, who arrived in Sydney yesterday afternoon after their gruelling trip from Perth, will begin training at Sydney Cricket Ground this afternoon. Some of the players are carrying too much weight – a result of all the good food they enjoyed in Fremantle – and some of their heavy baggage has gone astray, forcing some of the men to wear borrowed clothing last night.

"The players are confident that the tour, which will open in Junee on May 22, will produce record revenues and consequently record bonuses. The tourists' management will receive 60 per cent of the gate takings, less tax, and the party's expenses. One third of its profits will be divided among the players.

"The record tour bonus for an English team in Australia was the £120 per man on the 1928 tour; on the last pre-war tour in 1936 the players received £100 per man. These tourists were paid £1 17s 6d (£1.75) per day while they were on HMS Indomitable and will receive £2 10s (£2.50) while in Australia. Their wives in England will receive £3 per week with 5s (25p) per week for each child.

"The New South Wales players toned up physically, and as a result of their two matches against Queensland will have a decided advantage in their first match against England in Sydney on June 1.

"The tourists' team manager Walter Popplewell and captain Gus Risman will concentrate on getting their side into the best possible condition for the first Test against Australia on Monday June 1.

Frank Farrell (second left) lines up a tackle playing for New South Wales against Queensland in the first Test trial.

"Risman said: 'When we reached Australia, we were upset about the weight we had lost on the voyage, now it is the other way round; some of our players have put on too much weight since reaching Fremantle. We are in arrears with our training but we are not worrying.'

"Front-row forward Frank Whitcombe, the team's heaviest man, ruefully confessed to weighing 17st 12lb, nearly a stone heavier than when he left England. 'Oh boy, that's going to take some shifting,' he wailed.

"Risman pointed out: 'Never has a touring team come to Sydney in such uncomfortable circumstances. The players had a sweltering time coming through the Red Sea, were freshened up at Fremantle but then experienced the exacting train journey. Thankfully their good humour triumphed over the discomforts, despite some bungling on train arrangements, especially in Melbourne.

"Ernest Cawthorne wrote in the *Telegraph and Argus* of May 14: "The people of Sydney have taken the touring team to their hearts. The warmth of the reception has been touching and hospitality and friendly greetings have come from all manner of people, including many former Yorkshire

A sight for sore eyes, turkey dinner at the Australian Hotel, Sydney from left: Bryn Knowelden, Bob Nicholson, Jimmy Lewthwaite, Willie Horn and Les White.

and Lancashire folk who go to incredible pains to contact us for news of home towns.

"The serious business of the tour is at hand; today our players had their first real training for more than a week and if they thought it was going to be a quiet sort of affair the boys had a shock. Several hundred people turned out and expressed great admiration, not only at the physical condition of the men after a long and difficult journey but at the manner in which they kicked and handled the ball."

On Wednesday May 15, Alfred Drewry assessed the physical state of the tourists: "They have recovered so well after their troop-train trip across Australia that, after two days of hard training, fears that they might be out of condition for their opening game next Wednesday have almost disappeared.

"One or two of the bigger men have some superfluous weight to work off, but others told me after

The tourists had not had meals like this for seven years, Arthur Bassett and Joe Jones.

today's workout they were ready for immediate action. Eric Batten, Jack Kitching, Jim Lewthwaite, Albert Johnson, Ike Owens and Bob Nicholson are delighted with the fine turf and clear atmosphere of Australia and Batten expects to be two or three yards faster than he ever was in England. The team for the first match will be chosen on Saturday.

"The managers have a busy day tomorrow. In the morning they will be received by the New South Wales Premier William McKell, and then in the afternoon will confer with the Australian RL Board of Control on the poaching question. The managers have the power to act for the RFL Council."

13

LET THE ACTION COMMENCE

The tour opener was played against Southern Districts at Junee on May 22 and ended with a 36-4 margin in favour of the tourists – for whom Frank Whitcombe did not play - but already the progress of the tour was being clouded by stories of English-based players signing contracts with Australian clubs.

Ever resourceful, Whitcombe wrote an open letter to Dai Rees, his coach at Bradford Northern, which was published in the *Yorkshire Post* on the day of the game in Junee. In his missive, Whitcombe refers only to players by their Christian names but the men are his five colleagues from Odsal, Trevor Foster, Ernest Ward, Eric Batten, Willie Davies and Jack Kitching.

Tourists on parade at the Sydney Cricket Ground, L-R: Jack Kitching, Ernest Ward, Harry Murphy, Les White, Frank Whitcombe, Fred Hughes and Arthur Bassett.

"All this paper talk about our boys staying here is only Press stuff," wrote Whitcombe. "Eric and Jack went with me to train at one of the clubs here in Sydney and the next thing we knew from all the papers was that Jack and Eric were going to stay here."

Whitcombe also passed on news of Northern's tourists. "Willie has put on 6lb and is very fit indeed. He is training well but was left out of the team which went to Junee. Trevor, Ernest and Eric played, with Jack and myself as reserves. Trevor had a good game and so did Eric and Ernest, who is back to his old form, the complete centre.

"He has been training really hard and his speed has improved. Trevor is also on the top of his form while Willie is just the same, come-day, go-day chap and is really enjoying himself. I would like to have seen Willie paired with Tom McCue at Junee because he is playing top-class football. He is partnered with Dai Jenkins at Canberra in the next game."

The town of Junee had a population of 4,500 but there was a crowd of 6,135 for the first game of the tour, all cheering wildly as the Great Britain team walked on to the pitch.

The local newspaper described the atmosphere: "Today is Junee's greatest day; Wednesday May 22 1946 will be recorded with pride in the history of Southern New South Wales because it marks the occasion of the visit of the English rugby league team and the resumption of international sport after six years of conflict.

"Thousands of spectators gathered from hundreds of miles around Junee, some of them ardent football fans, others who were caught up in the glamour of a visit of an English touring side, while a percentage would not know a leather rugby ball from a paddy melon."

At lunchtime the following day thousands again turned out at Junee station to applaud their guests before they left for the 10-hour return journey to Sydney.

At the dinner after the game in Junee, Mr Harry Flegg, the President of the New South Wales RFL, made a significant speech, which was reported in the *Telegraph and Argus* by Ernest Cawthorne: "Mr Flegg confirmed that offers had been made by some Australian clubs to a few visiting players to return to Australia after their tour. He added that a few would probably accept the offers.

"I have interviewed many of the team and learned that tentative offers have been made to

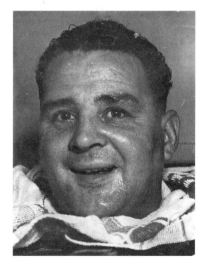

Frank Whitcombe sweats off a few pounds at Langridges gym, Sydney.

two or three of them but their contracts are such that they must return to England before they can come to terms with any club here.

"The players are reluctant to discuss who has been approached but some of the terms are said to be highly attractive."

The second game – against Southern Tablelands in Canberra – would be, a now lighter Frank Whitcombe's first of the tour, having lost some of his excess weight by sitting in the sweat box at Langridge's Gym in Sydney.

The *Canberra Times* previewed the match on Tuesday May 28: "The Governor General, the Duke of Gloucester, with an official party, will attend the football match between England and Southern Tablelands at the Manuka Oval tomorrow.

"The game has aroused interest throughout the region and officials have arranged for the issue of a souvenir programme. A marquee will be erected by the Department of the Interior for use by the visitors as a dressing room. The tourists will make their headquarters at the Hotel Kingston where they will be given dinner in the evening before returning to Sydney on the night train."

Frank Whitcombe (left) meets the Australian Prime Minster Mr Ben Chifley in Canberra.

Frank Whitcombe (left) prepares to meet the Duke of Gloucester, the Australian Governor General, at Canberra.

Great Britain recorded a 45-12 victory but suffered a major setback when young forward Harry Murphy dislocated a collar-bone.

The *Canberra Times* reported: "Murphy's loss is serious because the Englishmen have only brought 11 forwards and Murphy will probably be out of action for at least a month. The mishap occurred immediately after Murphy had scored a try and he was showing good form. 'The hard ground did it,' said Murphy with a wry smile afterwards.

"Murphy said he was tackled cleanly and his collar-bone was dislocated when he hit the ground. After treatment at Canberra Hospital he returned to Sydney with his team-mates. Other players also sustained injuries on the hard ground: right-winger Jim Lewthwaite was limping badly with a bruised calf, scrum-half Dai Jenkins had a swollen knee and centre Ted Ward received a kick near the knee early in the game and was not able to shake it off.

"Doug Phillips, the only player to figure in the tourists' opening two fixtures, said the pitch at Canberra was much harder than that at Junee.

"It was not a thorough try-out for the English forwards; when they had their full set they packed tightly and George Curran won 17 of the 23 scrums in the first half, although he did incur some penalties for striking too soon.

"The big fellows, Frank Whitcombe and Fred Hughes, worked soundly and are bound to be improved by the match while Les White in the second row showed that he is one of the best conditioned forwards. His partner Doug Phillips gave a sound display but Murphy looked to be England's best forward until he had to leave the field."

Great Britain's first major test of the tour was the first of their two meetings with New South Wales in Sydney, and Ernest Cawthorne told readers of the *Telegraph and Argus*: "There are two changes from the side which beat Junee so easily. Frank Whitcombe takes the place of Bob Nicholson and Les White deputises for Doug Phillips. Nicholson is recovering from a bout of pleurisy.

"Phillips is one of several who sustained bruises and abrasions in yesterday's match at Canberra but he will be fit in a day or two. The injury to Harry Murphy is not serious; he saw a specialist today and his dislocated

Frank Whitcombe gets his pass away in the first of two games against New South Wales in Sydney.

collar-bone was put in place again. He is expected to be fit in two to three weeks."

A crowd of 51,634 gathered for Great Britain's first big match of the tour in Sydney, and Ernest Cawthorne reported for the *Telegraph and Argus*: "After being 10 points down soon after the interval, Great Britain rallied splendidly and beat New South Wales 14-10.

"They should have won by a wider margin against the team considered likely to provide the nucleus of the Australian side for the opening Test; they missed two first-rate chances in the first half and although beset by injuries fielded the better back division.

"Between the forwards there was little to choose and a gruelling struggle went on from first to last. Ken Gee and Frank Whitcombe did especially well with Trevor Foster a splendid worker in the tight and Ike Owens a fast and ready opportunist.

"New South Wales took the lead after half an hour when mishandling by Ernest Ward and Albert Johnson on the tourists' 25 allowed Joe Jorgenson to break away and swift handling by Noel White and Pat Devery sent in Arthur Clues for a try which Jorgenson improved. Just before half-time Jorgenson increased the lead with a penalty goal.

"Lionel Cooper crossed in the corner two minutes into the second half, making the lead 10 points, but then came the Great Britain rally.

"Winning scrum after scrum they made steady headway and Owens took a pass from Tom McCue to score a try to which Gus Risman added the goal, following up with two precious penalties. New South Wales defended desperately as the attacks increased and eventually neat passing between McCue and Ernest Ward resulted in Eric Batten going over in the corner and Risman completing the scoring with the goal."

Afterwards, as the *Sydney Morning Herald* reported, New South Wales coach Rick Johnson and captain Joe Jorgenson were enthusiastic about Australia's chances of winning the Ashes.

"Our Test players are developing according to plan and in due course we will be right up to the standard needed for the Tests," said Johnson. "The New South Wales team did very well and I am satisfied with their efforts, although there were weaknesses which will be eradicated.

"All the talk about England running all over us seems to be astray now, just as I thought. The result today means little; if Harry Bath had not

Joe Jorgenson, captain of Australia, in the first Test.

Harry Bath missed the Test series through injury.

been injured we would have won. I still think we will win the Ashes."

Jorgenson agreed with Johnson. "Harry Bath's injury did not help our forwards but they did really well. The side will be better for the experience and I think we will win next Saturday."

In the aftermath of the match it was revealed that Bob Nicholson and Harry Murphy could be ruled out of action for the rest of the tour. Nicholson had had a recurrence of his pleurisy and remained bed-bound while Murphy's displaced collar-bone was still in splints.

The morning after their victory over New South Wales the tourists were on their 51-mile journey to Wollongong to face a South Coast representative side that afternoon.

Arthur Bassett is tackled during the match against South Coast at Wollongong, with Frank Whitcombe in support, where the tourists suffered their first defeat.

The local newspaper reported: "The match between South Coast and England makes history from both the Wollongong and English viewpoints for the home side are certain that records for attendance will go by the board.

"For the touring team it will establish a precedent by being the first match in the British Empire in which a team from the Mother Country has played on a Sunday. That may seem unusual here, where Sunday matches are played almost everywhere, but in the United Kingdom they are taboo.

"The NSW RFL has delayed selection of the team to play England next Saturday until after today's match. Normally it would have been chosen last night but today a double-decker bus-load of Sydney officials will make the trip".

The tourists suffered the first defeat of their tour against South Coast, where there was a record crowd of 13,300 and the injuries were mounting as Ernest Cawthorne wrote on Sunday evening: "Great Britain lost 15-12 and finished with only 10 players, having lost Joe Jones with a twisted ankle, Trevor Foster with a knee injury and Fred Hughes with a strained ankle; Eric Batten was also limping badly.

"These misfortunes apart, the tourists were far from convincing; the forwards lacked fire and the heeling from the scrum was so slow Tommy McCue was often smothered before he could get the ball away.

"There was a lack of punch at centre although Jack Kitching several times made valiant efforts to get Eric Batten away and Arthur Bassett ran strongly at times but against deadly, first-time tackling none of the tourists' outsides could claim ascendancy over the opposition.

"Eric Batten and Frank Whitcombe scored the tourists' tries, Willie Horne adding three goals; for South Coast Tom Ezart, Charlie Hazelton and Jack Russell touched down and Ezart kicked three goals.

"Great Britain now have nine players injured but Bob Nicholson and Doug Phillips should be fit in a day or two and the leg injuries to Willie Davies and Dai Jenkins are responding to treatment."

The return match with New South Wales the following Saturday was always going to be an explosive affair and the home side brought in eight new players for the game for which all 13 of the NSW side were playing for places in the first Test but in the end the tourists were too strong, winning by an emphatic 21-7 margin.

One newspaper reported: "Scrums and rucks were hectic, punches were thrown and collected, dumps were harder than Hades hobs and cautions so frequent they were ignored."

The *Sunday Mail* commented: "England's forwards were the outstanding characters in the defeat of New South Wales. It was stunning football all

Frank Whitcombe putting Arthur Clues in a stranglehold, during the second match against New South Wales.

the time, desperately exciting in the closing stages and so explosive on occasion that it became well-nigh out of control.

"But England's forwards were the smashing personalities, they backed up terrifically, exhibited an astounding faculty for being on the spot and three men completed every tackle. They presented a white wall of protection for Martin Ryan, usually a full-back, who stood in at scrum-half for the regular half-backs Dai Jenkins and Tommy McCue, two of those on the injured list.

"Suffering from a leg strain through the week, McCue told tour manager Walter Popplewell he was willing to play, being worried about the jumbling up of the touring side. But the manager resolved not to play McCue and expose him to the possibility of a more serious injury. Ryan was grand at half-back and Gus Risman gave a brilliant display out of position at full-back.

"He put amazing side on the ball when he kicked, caught the ball with the utmost sangfroid and was as cool as an animated figure on ice but the moods of the others boiled, cautions were distributed freely and men on both sides seethed in the melees.

"That's the way big football has been played in the past between Australians and Englishmen, tremendously tough but no squealing when it's over.

"England's loose-forward Ike Owens played a classic game and so did Doug Phillips, Joe Egan, Frank Whitcombe, Les White and Ken Gee. Arthur Bassett was champion on England's wing and the other winger, Albert Johnson, hurtled and raced and crashed dangerously for every one of the 80 minutes and was as lively as if he were controlled by wires.

"Centres Ernest Ward and Jack Kitching hacked the Australian attacks in halves before the ball reached the flanks; Kitching had a glorious day. New South Wales pursued Ward from first minute to last and second-row Arthur Clues whirled him into touch in the second half and Ward suffered such intense

Frank 'Bumper' Farrell, one of the enforcers in the Australian pack.

pain from thumping down on an elbow nerve that he had to leave the field.

Frank Whitcombe watches Les White move the ball against New South Wales.

Lionel Cooper scored for Australia in the first Test.

"So glittering was the English backing up that eight of them were once in an overlap attack against four NSW defenders and the first strategy Australia will have to devise for the initial Test match is to stop the colossal runs of Ike Owens.

"But we give 'Bumper' Farrell a decent smack between the shoulder blades for his solid ruck work. If all the Australian forwards had been as honest in the tough stuff as 'Bumper' we would have few local worries.

"Sel Lisle was sharp-minded behind the NSW team, Eric Bennett, with his snap kicks, often had England's backs on their heels but the wingers Lionel Cooper and Edgar Newham, did not have a hope, so little did they see of the ball.

"Scorers for England were Jack Kitching, Ike Owens and Joe Egan with tries and Gus Risman (5) and Frank Whitcombe with goals. For NSW Lionel Cooper crossed and Joe Jorgenson kicked a goal."

Arthur Clues' New South Wales jersey, which he gave to Frank Whitcombe.

Gus Risman wrote in the *Evening Chronicle* after the game: "We defeated New South Wales alright but only after a hectic battle in which players were dumped indiscriminately, whether they had the ball or not.

"The Aussie barrackers leave no doubt as which side they want to win; Ted Ward told me afterwards that his role of spectator was the most unnerving thing that had ever happened to him. He sweated it out but only Trevor Foster and Fred Hughes kept him from getting involved in a free-for-all. All this hot Welsh blood!

"Frank Whitcombe and Ken Gee were in their element and did some glorious work in the melees and our manager Mr Gabbatt did some spotting on the touchline, pointing out various Aussie offenders for physical reprimands. We look forward to the Tests with confidence after this game." One of the most physical of the NSW pack, Arthur Clues, gave Frank Whitcombe his jersey after the game.

There was no time for the tourists to bask in the glory of their success over NSW as they had to leave Sydney on Tuesday June 11 for the seven-

Captain Gus Risman takes a photograph at the summit of Mount Canabolas, in the Central Tablelands region. In his lens are, from left, Ken Gee, Ted Ward, Frank Whitcombe, Les White, Harry Turner and George Curran.

hour train journey to Orange where they were to face Western Districts the following day.

The tourists enjoyed a civic dinner at the Canobolas Hotel and in his speech Gus Risman recalled making his first appearance on Australian soil 14 years previously in Orange when he scored a hat-trick of tries.

The following morning the players were taken to see Mount Canobolas, an extinct volcano, before going to a food farm. The *Molong Express* reported: "Frank Whitcombe, the giant English forward, ate four Granny Smith's apples and led the field in the Devonshire tea treat.

"On the return trip to Orange Whitcombe said he would have just a light luncheon; he ordered pork which was served with apple sauce then had the only sweet available – apple pie and cream. He said he would not be having another apple until he returned to England but he was looking forward to letting his hair down when the Queensland strawberries become available."

Ike Owens, Joe Egan and Frank Whitcombe, with 13 month old James Alison in Orange.

The Great Britain party were then taken to the ground for the match, which drew a crowd of 8,000 and Eddie Waring reported: "England's old heads and crafty moves defeated the Western Districts 33-2 at Orange.

"This was apparent in the second half when England's moves began to mature, first Tommy McCue and Willie Horne worked exquisite reverse inside passes then Ted Ward dummied perfectly. Ernest Ward allowed Horne to run round him for the expected pass, Horne went round but Ward turned quickly, dummied and scored a try between the posts.

"But the first half and the first quarter of the second were different. Then the whole-hearted tackling of the Western players was an effective counter to the English attacks. England had their chances in the first half but poor supporting work cost them points and for the Western side Pat Reynolds proved a good captain but the man of the match for them was full-back Oriel Kennerson."

Unwittingly, the Australian RFL Board of Control's representatives were snubbed by the locals at the after-match dinner in Orange. The Western District officials were so eager to thank the tourists for visiting their region they omitted to offer thanks to the Board who had made the visit possible in the first place. Of the 28 speeches made over the two days the only toast omitted was to the Board of Control and at the end of the 25th oration the Board's Johnny Quinlan walked out of the hall.

The tourists left not long after him, to board the train for Sydney, but found there was no sleeping accommodation on board so on arrival at 7.30 in the morning they jumped into taxis for the drive to the Olympic Hotel where they promptly went to bed.

There were only five days to go before the first Test but before then they faced another train journey, this time to Newcastle for what they knew would be another tough encounter.

Great Britain's injury worries were not easing and Tom Goodman wrote: "Final selection for England's team for the first Test on Monday will not be considered before Sunday, the team manager Walter Popplewell said.

The Olympic Hotel, the Tourists base in Sydney, as the sun rises the players head for bed after a sleepless overnight journey.

"It is doubtful whether Bob Nicholson or Harry Murphy, two of the youngest forwards, will be able to play again on the tour and at least four of the likely Test pack will have to play against Newcastle tomorrow.

"Ted Ward, a centre, will play at loose-forward to allow Ike Owens to have a rest. The men who will not play in Newcastle are Gus Risman, Albert Johnson, Eric Batten, Ernest Ward, Willie Horne and Tom McCue among the backs and Ike Owens and probably Les White of the forwards.

"It is a pity that Joe Jones's knee problem will prevent him playing at full-back, otherwise Martin Ryan or Jack Kitching would have been rested and a more thorough deduction on Test team possibilities might have been made. Jones is the only back on the injured list.

"Dai Jenkins will have his first match since he injured his knee in Canberra, having been training for the last few days. He is short of match fitness and seems unlikely to force his way into the Test team.

"It would not be a surprise if Martin Ryan were played in the Test at half-back, as in the game against New South Wales last Saturday, with Gus Risman at full-back and Ernest Ward partnering Jack Kitching in the centre. But the chances are that the rugged, experienced McCue, despite being below his best at Wollongong and Orange, will retain his place as England's first-choice half-back."

A 'Special Correspondent' filed the following report from Newcastle where a crowd of 17,234 assembled: "The Newcastle Rugby League whitewashed a most questionable incident this afternoon when, after an inquiry, they merely cautioned English forward Doug Phillips who was sent off in the second half of the match against Newcastle.

"The Englishmen, beaten 18-13, tried hard under a severe battering by the Newcastle boys who won deservedly. There was never any doubt about the result in the second half.

"The incident which led to the sending off of Phillips was a regular 'Donnybrook' in which 10 players became embroiled in a corner of the field of play only yards from Newcastle's goal-line. A few minutes earlier Phillips had been cautioned when he knocked out Pittman, who was left sprawling on the field in agony; that was apparently the flame that set the powder on fire.

"A ruck occurred which developed into a scramble of flying fists. In the centre of the mix-up Newcastle's Maddison could be seen bobbing up and down like a cork in the ocean as punches and boots were let loose.

"Doug Phillips took a leading part in the fracas, ably assisted by Ken Gee, whose only fault was that he did not punch straight. The referee Mr Lewis violently blew his whistle; perhaps the shock of the shrill blast pulled the players apart. They had lost control of themselves and had the referee wasted only a few seconds the affair might have developed into one of the greatest blots on Australian rugby league history.

"The Newcastle Rugby League held an inquiry straight after the match and dismissed the incident as though it were only a drop of dill water by handing out a caution to Phillips.

"At least 20 warnings were given to players during the match – Phillips and Frank Whitcombe were each cautioned three times – while schoolteacher Willie Davies, of all people, was cautioned for answering back at the referee.

"Unfortunately England lost their full-back Martin Ryan, who retired hurt shortly before the end of the first half. He had a groin strain, an old injury, but there can be no doubt that Newcastle won the game on merit."

The next game – the first Test – was just two days away and the tourists were in a desperate situation. The match was to be played on Bank Holiday Monday and such was the intensity of anticipation in Sydney, the gates at the Cricket Ground were closed behind a full house at 11.30, two-and-a-half hours before kick-off.

Les White (left) and Frank Whitcombe lift Dai Jenkins in training.

The Australian coach Rick Johnston, who was also chairman of selectors, was confident despite the tourists' two victories over New South Wales. "I have prepared them for a Test match and if they play as instructed I have no doubt about the result," he said.

"If we are beaten it will be because Risman's men are superior. I have some surprises in store for the Englishmen!"

Since he had started coaching Australia he'd received a welter of advice from well-wishers. "It goes right over my shoulders," he added. "I have my own ideas on how to win the Ashes."

After a brisk run-out on Saturday morning Johnston said goodbye to his team until Monday afternoon, asking his men to take things easy over the weekend and try and stay in bed as long as possible on Monday morning.

Frank Whitcombe, hard at work in training.

Frank Whitcombe tackles Johnny Grice, in the tourists' defeat against Queensland.

The Australian selectors declared their Test hand first, picking a side made up of 10 players from New South Wales and just three from Queensland.

Roy Westaway, the Queensland prop who played in the first two Tests.

The NSW contingent included the captain, centre Joe Jorgenson, wingers Lionel Cooper – later to join Huddersfield – and Edgar Newham, prop Frank 'Bumper' Farrell, second-row Arthur Clues and loose-forward Noel Mulligan.

The Queenslanders were scrum-half Johnny Grice, second-rower Reg Kay – the Australian Army heavyweight boxing champion - and prop Roy Westaway.

Not all the Australian public agreed with the selection, one aggrieved observer being moved to write to the chairman of selectors:

Sir,

As a great follower of rugby league football I see with disgust the selectors' injustice to Australia's No 1 second-row forward Herb Narvo.

Surely the selectors have the eyes to see that this great forward is playing as well as ever. I have yet to see a forward play better this season.

I was at the match last year between Newtown and St George and I have no doubt that this game is the reason why the selectors are continually overlooking this great forward.

Also, tell me a better full-back playing today that Tommy Kirk.

T F Brown

The match referred to by Mr Brown was played on July 28 1945, and was marred by an infamous incident when St George prop Bill McRitchie had his ear severed.

Although his guilt was never proved, the prime suspect for the offence was Newtown's prop Frank Farrell. Herb Narvo, the St George forward, confronted Farrell in the changing rooms after the game and the two had come to blows.

Great Britain's team for the Test was announced on the Sunday evening before the match and included four Bradford Northern players – Eric Batten, Ernest Ward, Jack Kitching and Frank Whitcombe.

Heading for another training session in Sydney are baggage man Harry Turner, George Curran, Willie Horn, Jimmy Lewthwaite, Frank Whitcombe, and Joe Egan. Front, Albert Johnson and Tommy McCue

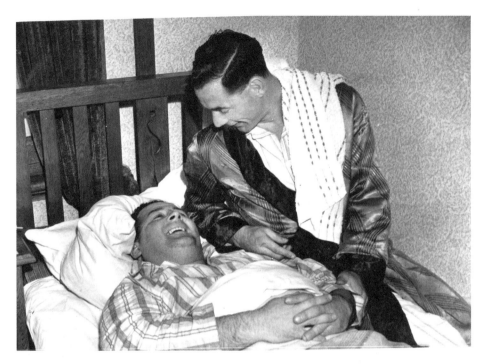

Morning of the first Test and roommates Frank Whitcombe and Ernest Ward share a joke.

The latter was described in the match programme: "A remarkable player for his size, he works hard in the rucks and scrums, is a really shrewd 80-minute player and is sure to be one of Australia's hazards during the Tests."

14

THE FIRST TEST

The Test was played on Monday June 17 and drew a crowd of 64,526 to the Sydney Cricket Ground to witness an 8-8 draw. The following day the Daily Advertiser proclaimed: "The match was marked by poor goal-kicking on both sides. The Australian captain Joe Jorgenson could land only one goal from seven attempts and Gus Risman, his English counterpart, failed with eight of his nine attempts.

Captain Gus Risman leads his team on to the pitch for the game against New South Wales in Sydney. Frank Whitcombe is fifth from the right.

"Apart from the incident in which Jack Kitching was sent off for punching, the game, though particularly hard-fought, was clean.

"Pat Devery was caught flat-footed far too often and was knocked over before he could get rid of the ball, Joe Jorgenson did not show much enterprise, Ron Bailey was solid and scored an excellent try but was never outstanding and Edgar Newham did not have much opportunity but usually made ground.

"Lionel Cooper scored one of the most spectacular tries of the season from near his own 25-yard line when he outpaced the Englishmen, including the full-back Gus Risman, to score in the corner. Dave Parkinson, who came into first-class football very late, did everything that was asked of him and refused to be overawed by the big occasion; he handled perfectly and tackled with certainty throughout.

"Australia's forwards, without exception, rose to the occasion and were right on the spot when it came to solid, dour defending on their goal-line.

"The English, to a man, played well with Frank Whitcombe and Ike Owens, as usual, outstanding and with hooker Joe Egan more in the picture than previously on the tour. Second-row Les White was moved to

Frank Whitcombe 'tackles' Roy Westaway in one of the brutal exchanges of the first Test in Sydney.

the wing for the second half and acquitted himself well; Tommy McCue at half-back mixed his game cleverly, on some occasions running freely, on others cross-kicking to the touch lines.

"Willie Horne combined excellently with McCue and in the centre Ernest Ward made many piercing runs.

"England should have scored within two minutes of the kick-off but made amends three minutes later when Horne picked up after Johnny Grice had stumbled at the base of a scrum and dived the two yards to the line.

"It was a fairly easy kick but Risman missed it then missed three more reasonable opportunities to extend the lead before Egan spun out of a tackle and raced for the corner, only for several Australians to smother him just short of the line and Whitcombe was similarly held when a try seemed certain.

"Jorgenson kicked a penalty to reduce the deficit and for a period the Australians were deep in English territory but when the visitors attacked again Parkinson made a splendid tackle, bringing down Kitching at the last second.

"Parkinson then fumbled after a long kicking duel but Jorgenson was on hand with a clearing kick. Kitching tackled him heavily from behind

Frank Whitcombe breaks the Australian defence to score Great Britain's second try in the 1st Test at Sydney, as Willie Horne (left) looks on and Albert Johnson (arms raised) celebrates.

Les White moved to the wing and played a fine game after Jack Kitching's dismissal, here he closes in for a tackle.

and when he hit the ground the Englishman threw a neat right-handed punch. Referee Tom McMahon was on the spot and gave the Englishman his marching orders without a warning.

"Soon afterwards the Englishmen scored their second try, Whitcombe crossing in the corner after Ernest Ward and Albert Johnson had handled, the referee not seeing a clear knock-on by Ward. Risman again missed the kick.

"The Australian forwards defended solidly until Newham got away and reached the half-way line before being tackled. Bailey wove his way through but lacked support then Roy Westaway, who otherwise had a poor game, barged his way over from 15 yards.

"The Englishmen were equal to the occasion and the game went back to the Australian 25-yard line when Eric Batten made a long, tricky run in which he beat several Australians before being halted by Parkinson. Whitcombe again went close after Ward and Johnson had created the opening and half-time came with England leading 6-2.

Referee Tom McMahon blows his whistle as the tourists' winger Albert Johnson lies flat on the ground.

"At the start of the second half Jorgenson missed a penalty chance and Risman failed with his seventh successive kick at goal then Cooper brought the crowd to its feet when he made a brilliant run up the touchline, fending off several tacklers before he was thrown into touch.

"Parkinson made a solid tackle to halt Batten then knocked out McCue with another; the scrum-half leaving the action for several minutes during which Australia scored their first try after Frank Farrell had fed Jorgenson who in turn released Ron Bailey who galloped to the corner from half-way.

"The battle continued to flow, Jorgenson missing another kick and Risman at last landing one and then came the try of the game. Australia's backs passed swiftly to release Cooper, who swerved and dodged two Englishmen before rounding Risman to level the scores at 8-8.

"There were only a few minutes left when, to deafening roars, the referee caught an English forward off-side and awarded Australia a penalty almost in front of the posts and just 25 yards out. Jorgenson was very deliberate in placing the ball and measuring his run but he put the kick wide and there were no further scores."

The sending off of Kitching aroused its share of controversy. Australian journalist Bill Corbett was vociferous in his defence of the Englishman: "If there was justification in the sending off Jack Kitching yesterday far more drastic action should have been taken against the Australians.

"Easily the worst example came when Albert Johnson nearly had his head torn off, another time an Australian hurtled into Johnson and crashed him on the back of his head when he was nowhere near the ball.

"Jack Kitching should not have been sent off. I think referee McMahon made his decision in a moment of tension and excitement. Kitching did not punch; he pressed down on Joe Jorgenson, who he had tackled, in an effort to regain his feet.

"I know Jack Kitching, I have been with him since he and his comrades arrived in Fremantle. I could not wish to meet a calmer more gentlemanly character than Kitching. He is a schoolteacher and an easy, good-natured personality. He was on the verge of tears as he left the field; he had not previously even been cautioned in 15 years of football.

"Kitching said to me: 'I merely pushed Jorgenson away with my open hand. Jorgenson and I were on the ground struggling when I felt a pain in my ribs. I was bitten but Jorgenson might not have been to blame. Joe Jorgenson and I are good friends and I do want any more to do with this.'"

Kitching was summoned to appear before the NSW RL Judiciary Committee chaired by Major A Frizelle, a dentist, and was given a caution and banned from the next Test. Major Frizelle said he had examined Kitching after the game and did not think the wounds on his side were teeth marks.

Referee McMahon told the committee that he had a good view of the incident and did not think it was possible for Jorgenson to have bitten Kitching, whilst Walter Popplewell, the tour manager, said: "We will not be making an official complaint. We think it is better to let the matter rest."

Jorgenson, who was not called before the committee, had the last word: "I heard at the ground there was talk of a biting incident. I know nothing of any such incident and any suggestion that I bit Kitching is ridiculous. His position in the tackle would have made that impossible. I believe my record for clean play equals that of anyone in the game."

Frank 'Bumper' Farrell had his own memories of his Test debut as Larry Writer recounted in his biography of Farrell. "Early in the first half one of England's schoolteachers, Jack Kitching, was sent off for punching Joe Jorgenson and Frank Whitcombe was lucky not to follow him when he 'king hit' (knocked out) 'Bumper'.

"This led to the famous incident when a groggy and prostrate 'Bumper' lashed out at a St John's Ambulance man who had run on to the field to treat him. 'Bumper' had never received medical treatment on the field and he was not about to start now; he dragged himself to his feet and re-entered the fray."

15

THE ASHES RETAINED

The players, on the brink of exhaustion following their demanding workload – in which Frank Whitcombe had shouldered more than his share of the burden – boarded the train to Tamworth, where they would face Northern New South Wales before heading for Queensland and the build-up to the second Test in Brisbane.

Before they left Sydney tour manager Walter Popplewell disclosed that, despite the team's desperate situation due to injuries, no players would be coming out from England to lighten the load even though he had requested the despatch of two more forwards, having pointed out that Ken Gee, Frank Whitcombe and Doug Phillips had played in four games in 10 days.

Eddie Waring reported from Tamworth: "Dai Jenkins played so brilliantly in helping the tourists to achieve their biggest win so far in Australia – by 61-5 – he will have to be considered for the Second Test match.

Tough mid week games, Arthur Bassett is helped from the field by Dai Jenkins and Ken Gee with Les White smiling in support.

"The little Welshman, making a splendid return to his old form, opened out to Willie Davies in grand style and made the first two tries with long passes. He had good scrum service from George Curran and made full use of it.

"The tourists overwhelmed their opponents; Joe Egan (3), Bryn Knowleden (2), Arthur Bassett (2), Willie Davies, Doug Phillips, Ike Owens and Joe Jones scored tries and Ted Ward kicked 11 goals. The English forwards have been so over-worked in the last few weeks that Joe Egan played in the second row with George Curran at hooker. Salford supporters would not know Curran these days as he now scales 15st.

"At half-time England had scored 38 points without response; they had played brilliant football with Egan in great form. Forwards handled almost as much as the backs and, as usual, Ike Owens initiated many attacks."

Following their success, the tourists left by train for Queensland – the 'Garden of Australia' – and their journey was not without incident, as the following article shows: "The English footballers nearly lost their playing gear at Wallangarra after their all-night journey from Tamworth to the Queensland border; two thieves began to operate on the locks of the trunks containing the equipment but they were outsmarted by the baggage man Harry Turner.

"When the train drew in at Wallangarra Mr Turner went to the baggage van to check that the bags were intact and caught the two thieves working on the locks, one of which had already been removed. At the sight of him the thieves ran off.

"Mr Turner, who also looks after the aches and pains of the team, has proved such an efficient 'Man Friday' to the players he has been engaged to look after them on the last three tours of Australia."

After changing trains twice the team arrived in Brisbane on Thursday evening and Frank Whitcombe shared a five-man room at their hotel with fellow-Welshmen Ike Owens, Ted Ward, Doug Phillips and Arthur Bassett.

Two days later the opposition was the Queensland State XV and Alfred Drewry wrote this scene-setter: "Frank Whitcombe, Doug Phillips and Ken Gee will play their sixth game in 15 days when the tourists meet Queensland.

"Whitcombe is the luckiest as well as the toughest and hardest-worked member of the party; this will be his ninth successive appearance and he has not a single bruise to show for it unlike the others who all have abrasions of one kind or another. Ernest Ward has a knee injury and Tommy McCue shoulder trouble, legacies of the Test, but both are expected to be alright in a few days.

"The tourists will face a strong side, including 10 Test players, but they are aware that New South Wales, who they have beaten twice, have enjoyed winning both their games against Queensland this season.

"The tourists have established their headquarters for their month in Brisbane at the Daniel Hotel and will train at the Queensland Cricket Ground, better known as the Woolloongabba Oval."

On Saturday June 22, the tourists faced Queensland and Arthur Morley reported: "In the most sensational upset of the tour the British team were beaten by Queensland by a single point, 25-24

"Gus Risman again had a bad day and kicked only three goals from eight attempts while the tourists' handling was well below their usual standard until two minutes from time when Albert Johnson gathered a long pass from Ike Owns and sprinted over from half-way. Risman was well off target with the goal attempt.

"Great Britain's tries came from Johnson (2), Joe Egan, Jack Kitching, Willie Horne and Eric Batten. Owens and Egan were outstanding but the full-back Joe Jones splintered a bone in his finger as he attempted to catch the ball with the sun in his eyes. The ball struck the end of his digit and he had to leave the field."

After training the next day the team took the overnight train to Bundaberg for their next game and an incident was reported in 'Sportspots':

Albert Johnson ready to tackle his man in the defeat by Queensland in Brisbane.

Albert Johnson and Bryn Knowleden in action against Queensland.

"The English rugby league team's 'Iron Man' Frank Whitcombe, who played against Queensland yesterday, assisted an elderly lady to board a train at Paddington. 'Thank you very much,' said the lady, 'I can see you are not one of those rough men who play football.'"

From Bundaberg, Alfred Drewry wrote: "The tourists may travel by air during the final stage of their stay in Queensland in order to have as much rest as possible before the second Test match.

"They have 1,450 miles to cover in the next nine days and although a train schedule has been drawn up coal shortages have meant that rail services have had to be curtailed and there is doubt whether satisfactory new arrangements can be made.

"The tourists will travel by rail to Rockhampton for Thursday's game and then to Townsville for a match on Sunday. Townsville is 800 miles from Brisbane. Test men who can be spared will probably be flown straight back to Brisbane and the remainder will go to Mackay. If the Test players returned to Brisbane by train they would arrive only 24 hours before the Test so it is proposed to fly them back to give them two days' extra rest.

"In today's match with Wide Bay, which the tourists won 16-12, Ernest Ward played at full-back for the first time on tour, although he has often filled the position at home. The return of Fred Hughes after injury enabled Frank Whitcombe to rest after playing in nine successive matches. Bundaberg has had no rain for three months and the ground was so hard the top was raked and loosened to minimize bruising."

The next appointment was in Rockhampton and during the journey trainer Tom Langridge worked on the injured players. Jim Mulcahy wrote for the *Courier Mail*: "The English rugby league team made a triumphal entrance into Rockhampton late last night behind a wagon-load of beer, 200 squealing pigs and six prize Herefords on a 500ft goods train which averaged 13mph for the 179-mile journey.

"Because of the restrictions it was the only way to get the team to Rockhampton for the match against Central Queensland, two carriages for the team were hooked on to the back of the train and the tourists voted it a better trip than their trek on the transcontinental troop train from Perth to Sydney.

"The heaviest man in the party, genial 17st forward Frank Whitcombe, did a little training by trotting alongside the train near Gladstone. The team has lost 10 full days in wearisome train travelling and this may presage air travel for future touring teams."

There were problems when the team arrived at their hotel, as Reuter's news agency reported: "The English rugby league team walked out of their hotel, claiming the accommodation was unsatisfactory and without privacy.

"One player said he had been badly bitten by insects while another said the sanitary and washing arrangements were inadequate. After an inspection the tour business manager Wilf Gabbatt agreed with the players and found suitable accommodation elsewhere.

"Better play and superior speed among the backs gave the England team a well-deserved 35-12 success over Central Queensland. Their tries came from Eric Batten (3), Bryn Knowleden, Frank Whitcombe, Doug Phillips and Les White with Ernest Ward (5) and Ted Ward (2) kicking goals."

On July 1, Ernest Cawthorne wrote for the *Telegraph and Argus*: "Playing what, with one exception, will probably be their Test team for Brisbane, the Great Britain tourists beat North Queensland 55-16 at Townville yesterday.

"The tourists put up splendid exhibition of fast, open football; the try-scorers were Eric Batten (4), Arthur Bassett (3), Willie Horne (2), Ike Owens (2), Les White, Gus Risman, Ernest Ward and Doug Phillips with goals coming from Ernest Ward (2), Horne (2) and Owens.

"In preparation for the Test in Brisbane next Saturday: Arthur Bassett, Eric Batten, Gus Risman, Ted Ward, Willie Horne, Dai Jenkins, Les White, Joe Egan and Frank Whitcombe flew back to the Queensland capital today. Batten has a slight thigh strain but will be fit for the Test."

In their final game before the second Test, against Mackay, Harry Sunderland provided this pen-portrait of Frank Whitcombe for the match

Proudly displaying their tour blazers are, from left to right, George Curran, Trevor Foster, Bob Nicholson, and Les White.

programme: "Frank Whitcombe (Bradford Northern) is an amazing man. He was 18st when he arrived in Australia and has been busy cutting his weight down since.

"He will amaze you with the speed with which he carries his bulk about the field. He is a really tough front-rower and a great all-round footballer."

The tourists ran up a record 94-0 score against Mackay with Joe Lewthwaite scoring seven of their tries, the others coming from Albert Johnson (4), Jack Kitching (3), Bryn Knowleden, Willie Davies, Ike Owens and Fred Hughes.

The team were soon back in Brisbane, where there were strikes and power blackouts, on July 4 when Jim Vines wrote in the *Courier Mail*: "England in wartime inured burly rugby league forward Frank Whitcombe to drive through the black-out but never, as in Queensland at strike time, did the black-out cause him to lose his underpants.

"Actually it was a case of indirect cause and effect. Laundry for a touring team is always a problem but with strikes and blackouts is serious indeed. But Frank is nothing if not 17st of resourcefulness so he decided to wash a few things out for himself.

"His washtub was the hotel room bath; his soft washing included four pairs of not-so-dainty underpants. The rubbing part was completed over the half-filled bath, then he pulled out the plug to let them drain.

Three Great Britain tourists before the first Test; Albert Johnson, Arthur Bassett and Frank Whitcombe.

"When he returned to the washtub only three of the four pairs of underpants were there; he glared suspiciously at Arthur Bassett and thought thoughts about Ted Ward but the underpants stayed missing.

"The next man to take a bath discovered them when the water refused to run away, washed down the pipe they had made a most effective plug."

Harry Sunderland wrote on the eve of the second Test match: "Team manager Walter Popplewell will not have any excuses if England are beaten tomorrow; as soon as his team was announced he said 'they are all 100 per cent fit.'

"There is no change in the forwards but Gus Risman moves to the centre with Ernest Ward going to full-back. Jack Kitching is suspended and his place is taken by Ted Ward who has played at centre, full-back and loose-forward on the tour.

"It is expected that Martin Ryan, who has had surgery on his groin, will be in Brisbane to see the game."

The *Daily Advertiser* carried this report on the Test on Monday July 8: "England defeated Australia 14-5 in the second Test in Brisbane and so retained the Ashes.

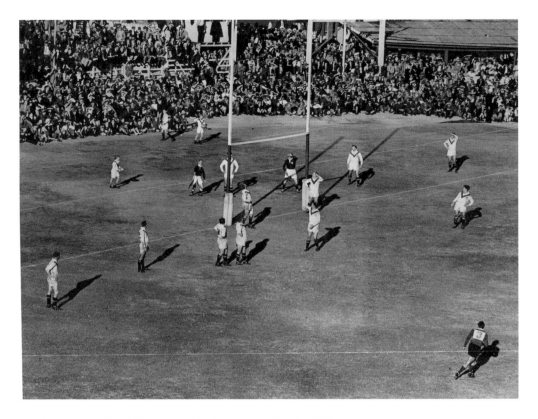

Joe Jorgenson (No 3) kicks a goal in the second Test in Brisbane.

"They led 5-0 at half-time and throughout the game England were superior. At the conclusion of play Tommy McCue, their vice-captain, said he was amazed at the ease with which he was able to run from the scrum base and the weakness of the Australian blind-side defence."

The Test confirmed the amazing interest in the game among the Australian public; the gates being closed at noon with a record 55,000 spectators inside and another 5,000, many of whom had travelled from Sydney, locked out.

The attendance was doubly amazing considering the fact that many trains into Brisbane were cancelled due to the strikes.

Australia passed the captaincy from Joe Jorgenson to Ron Bailey following the alleged biting incident in Sydney, and Newcastle's Jack Hutchinson replaced Noel Mulligan at loose-forward.

The game was a personal triumph for Arthur Bassett who, on his Great Britain debut, scored a hat-trick of tries and in doing so ensured his team

Frank Whitcombe (left) and Les White (No 23) are in support as Willie Horn makes his tackle in Brisbane.

would retain the Ashes, no matter what happened in the third and final Test in Sydney.

Great Britain were superior in all departments with Albert Johnson adding a further try and Ernest Ward kicking one goal.

The forward exchanges were exactly the same as those in the first Test: brutal. The tourists again finished with 12 men after hooker Joe Egan was sent off near the end of the game for punching second-row Arthur Clues. Egan was unlucky, insisted Eddie Waring. Any of the players in either pack could have been sent off, he said.

Australian prop Frank 'Bumper' Farrell left the field at the final whistle with his jersey covered in blood, some of it his, the rest from his opponents. One journalist described his face in graphic terms: "He had two beautiful black eyes, he had crimson lips which could have provided all the make-up for a Hollywood studio and his jaw looked as if it had been drawn slowly through a blackberry bush."

Farrell's immediate opponent Frank Whitcombe had enjoyed another towering game and was by now attracting interest from Australian clubs. The St George club offered the best deal: a two-year player-coach contract

Arthur Bassett tackles Lionel Cooper in the second Test.

at £600 per season, plus travelling expenses and a lucrative job away from rugby league. As Alfred Drewry reported in the *Yorkshire Evening Post*:

"Frank Whitcombe, the Bradford Northern front-row forward, is almost certain to return to Australia for the start of the next season over here.

"Whitcombe told me today he had come to an agreement on terms with the St George club in Sydney and is only awaiting a letter from his wife before signing the contract. His contract is for two years as captain and coach and he will receive £600-a-year and be guaranteed a job.

"He told me: 'In view of the fact that my football career is nearing its end the terms are generous but more important than the football angle to me is that I have been guaranteed a job better than I could command in England.'

"If Whitcombe carries out his present plan he will be the first player from an English club to sign for an Australian club but the signs are he will not be the last provided the no-poaching agreement is not revived."

At 32, Frank knew he was getting towards the end of his career and, after much deliberation he decided to sign the contract. However, after the end of the tour and the journey home, he discussed the contract with his

Frank Whitcombe (left) waits his turn to meet the Mayor of Brisbane.

family back in Bradford and they eventually agreed that they would stay in Yorkshire.

He was not the only player to be approached by wealthy Sydney clubs but none of the Great Britain party decided to take up the offers and, remarkably, the flow went in the other direction with Pat Devery and Lionel Cooper signing for Huddersfield, George Watt for Hull and Arthur Clues for Leeds. They happily left the sunshine of Sydney for the austerity, smog and rationing of England.

Three days after the second Test Frank Whitcombe played against Brisbane at the Gabba and Ernest Cawthorne report for the *Telegraph and Argus*: "The English touring team beat Brisbane 21-15 after leading 12-10 at the interval. Their try-scorers were Willie Davies (2), Jack Kitching (2) and Ted Ward with the latter adding one goal.

"There was as scene at the end of the match when Jack Kitching crossed the line but appeared to lose the ball as he touched it down. The referee allowed the try amid a loud demonstration which was renewed as the teams left the field."

Whitcombe played again on July 11, and Alfred Drewry reported on the game against Ipswich when another record was set: "The rugby league tourists set up a new scoring record for any England team to tour Australia when they beat Ipswich 29-12. Gus Risman's team have now scored 495 points in 17 games, compared to the previous best aggregate of 483 points from 18 games set by Jim Sullivan's team of 1932.

"It was fitting that Jim Lewthwaite should be the man who broke the record; it was he who scored seven tries at Mackay last week which is believed to be an individual record for a man on tour.

"Willie Horne, the Test stand-off, played at centre for the first time in his career and had a particularly good game, Arthur Bassett ran with great speed and determination on the left wing and Ike Owens's speed was another telling factor in a hard game."

On July 13 the tourists played Toowoomba, a game which marked Trevor Foster's return to fitness after injury and the return to his home-town of a famous Australian, as the match programme delighted in telling the crowd: "Accompanying the English visitors to Toowoomba is Toowoomba-born Harry Sunderland.

"Toowoomba has produced many famous sons and daughters but none more illustrious in the world of administration than the mercurial Harry Sunderland. It is good to see you looking so well Harry, after your lengthy *sojourn* in England during the grim war days and nights. We wish you well in any sporting or commercial venture you may have in mind, in this country or overseas."

Ernest Cawthorne wrote for the *Telegraph and Argus*: "Nine of the prospective Test team to play at Sydney on July 20 will travel direct from Toowoomba to Sydney on Monday instead of accompanying the team to Grafton where there is a match on Tuesday.

"Arrangements for the New Zealand flights have been modified and the first consignment will leave Sydney on Sunday week, thus enabling all the players to see the final Test.

The following report appeared in an Australian newspaper: "Superior in all phases of the game, the English tourists had their eighth successive win when they overwhelmed Toowoomba 34-5."

On Tuesday July 16, Frank Whitcombe played in the last match before the third Test, against North Coast at Grafton which the visitors won 53-8 but three days later Alfred Drewry reported in the Yorkshire Evening Post:

"Manager Walter Popplewell has sprung a surprise by dropping Whitcombe from the team for the third Test here tomorrow."

Popplewell knew Whitcombe had run himself into the ground, figuring in 15 of the tourists' 20 games so far on tour.

The *Sydney Morning Herald* told its readers: "England's team to play Australia in the third Test at Sydney Cricket Ground does not include the 17st top forward Frank Whitcombe.

"He has had a surfeit of football, particularly in the early stages of the tour when injuries to other players meant he was in constant demand, and his form in the last two matches has shown signs of deteriorating. His place in the team will be taken by either George Curran or Fred Hughes."

It had been decided that the players not required for the Test would be among the first group of tourists to leave for New Zealand. Taking off from Rose Bay at 5am on the day after the Test would be Willie Davies, Bob Nicholson, Jim Lewthwaite, Dai Jenkins, Joe Jones and Bryn Knowleden. They would be joined by Harry Turner, the baggage man, and the four journalists, Alfred Drewry, Harry Sunderland, Eddie Waring and Ernest Cawthorne.

They would leave secure in the knowledge that the tourists had proved their superiority over their hosts, winning 20-7 with tries from Arthur Bassett (2), George Curran and Ike Owens plus four goals for Gus Risman; Australia's points came from a try by Clem Kennedy and two goals from Joe Jorgenson.

Walter Popplewell (in spectacles) receives The Ashes trophy from the President of Tattersall's Club in Sydney, with his players gathered in triumph.

Being interviewed by an Australian journalist (in trilby) are Tommy McCue, Ken Gee, Ernest Ward, Les White and Fred Hughes.

Pat Devery one of the Australians who moved to England

In his book, *The Life and Times of Frank 'Bumper' Farrell*, Larry Writer recalled the camaraderie between the two teams: "That night, as they had in Sydney after the first Test, Bumper, Arthur Clues, Ken Gee, Frank Whitcombe, Ike Owens and others forgot all about the damage they had inflicted on each other during the tour and drank heartily together at the Dolphin Hotel in Surry Hills.

"There was an old fellow singing Irish songs that night and 'Bumper', with tears coursing down his cheeks, had him sing until 3am. Later that morning, when he tried to hold his baby daughter Susan, his arms were too sore from the game to lift her."

When the tourists had left Australia for New Zealand an article was published in the *Newcastle Sun*: "In a summing up of Australia's rugby league players, members of the England team nominated only seven as 'class' performers and three of the seven – Oriel Kennerson (Orange), Bob Bartlett (South Coast) and Alf Gibbs (Newcastle) did not get a chance in the Tests.

The other Australians to make an impression on the tourists were Lionel Cooper (Eastern Suburbs), Clem Kennedy (South Sydney), Pat Devery (Balmain) and Arthur Clues (Western Suburbs).

"Another impression gained by the Englishmen was that Australians have temporarily forgotten that unity and understanding are strengths."

Frank Whitcombe (second right) looking at the camera, singing in the Welsh choir at Melbourne railway station.

16

MUD-BATHS IN NEW ZEALAND

The touring party arrived in New Zealand in three groups, crossing the Tasman Sea to Auckland in Sandringham flying-boats, converted from the Sunderlands flown during the war and owned by Tasman Empire Airways Limited, the forerunner of Air New Zealand.

The players then travelled by train to Christchurch where their first game would be played on July 27. Frank Whitcombe was originally selected to

Mechanics Bay, Auckland, the centre of New Zealand aviation when flying boats were the popular means of transport across the Tasman Sea

play against South Island but withdrew with a pulled muscle in his leg, and was replaced by Ken Gee in a 24-12 victory.

Alfred Drewry filed his report on the match to the *Yorkshire Post* from Greymouth where the second fixture of the tour was to be played. He wrote: "Having beaten South Island yesterday the tourists play their next game here tomorrow.

"Their opponents will be West Coast who will include nine members of the side they met yesterday, among them Ken and Bill Mountford whose brother Cecil will be seen in Wigan's colours when the English season opens.

"Though the tourists played sparkling football at times against South Island the match showed that the forwards will have to adopt different tactics in the New Zealand mud from those which carried them triumphantly through Australia.

"The Barrow contingent had a successful day. Joe Jones did not figure among the scorers but the Welsh full-back, who disappointed in Australia, came back to what the other Welshmen in the squad call his Swansea form. He ran brilliantly to help make three tries for the resolute Barrow winger Jim Lewthwaite and the third Barrow man Bryn Knowleden scored two tries. The first try in New Zealand was scored by Ernest Ward, who also kicked three goals."

Alfred Drewry's report on the game against West Coast – in which Frank Whitcombe made his bow in New Zealand – was filed from Greymouth on Monday July 29. "The tourists met an unexpected setback here today, the West Coast Division of South Island beating them 17-8. It was the fourth defeat of their tour, their first in New Zealand and heaviest margin against them.

"The tourists' side included 10 Test players but West Coast won on their merits in atrocious conditions.

Frank Whitcombe poised to tackle South Auckland's Maori forward Hilton at Huntley.

Heavy rain for 36 hours before the match had waterlogged the ground in several places and good, honest booting and backing up won the day.

"There was little or no opportunity for displaying any other kind of football skill; the tourists failed because they persisted in their efforts to play the open game when tactics calling for less skill would have paid them better.

"The sodden, slippery ball was difficult to handle and every dropped pass was quickly seized upon by the enthusiastic West Coast forwards who, though lightly built, swarmed everywhere and lasted the pace of a gruelling game amazingly well.

"They were assisted to a certain extent by liberties which the referee allowed them to take with the off-side rule but apart from that there was no denying their enthusiasm and team work.

"Great Britain opened the second half as if they were going to sweep all before them but their finishing was lacking and with 20 minutes to go West Coast led by 10 points. After that they sat tight and whenever the tourists got within their 25 one of their backs deliberately ran offside at the scrum."

Eddie Waring added in his *Sunday Pictorial* column: "Many expatriate Yorkshiremen and Lancastrians made the journey to the mining town of Greymouth for the game and Ken Gee, Joe Egan, Martin Ryan and Ted Ward – all from Wigan – were loaded with food parcels from former Wigan residents.

Taken at the buried Maori village near Rotorua, the tourists are accompanied by the Yorkshire Post's Alfred Drewry on the far right, cigarette in hand.

"An all-night train journey was lightened by some young Maoris teaching the players their war cry and other songs. To see Trevor Foster, Ted Ward, Fred Hughes and Bob Nicholson singing the war cry was really funny and in return we taught the Maoris how to sing 'Ilkla Moor baht 'at.'"

The touring party arrived in Wellington where they were to play the New Zealand Maoris in a ground-breaking game on Wednesday July 31. This report appeared in a Wellington newspaper: "In the first game ever played between an English rugby league touring team and one representing the New Zealand Maoris the visitors gained an easy win by 32-8. The Maoris could not cope with the speed, crisp handling and combinations of the Englishmen who were quick to take advantage of weak tackling.

"Bryn Knowleden was outstanding for the tourists and his try after a 60-yard run in the second half, selling the dummy beautifully, was the feature of the game. Ernest Ward captained the side and was another English star,

Being entertained by Princess De Peau at the Maori Guest House, Huntley. Seated left of front row is a smiling Frank Whitcombe

scoring two tries and kicking four goals. The tourists' try-scorers were Ken Gee, Jim Lewthwaite, Albert Johnson (2) and Knowleden (2)."

The next game was against Auckland at Carlaw Park and Harry Sunderland reported on the match for the *Sunday Despatch* on August 4: "The heaviest rain and the most mud-spattered players I have ever seen were the features of a remarkably well-sustained struggle yesterday between the rugby league tourists and Auckland.

"It gripped the interest of a crowd of almost 18,000 who saw a 9-7 result in England's favour. The game had to be stopped frequently for players' eyes to be cleared of mud and long before half-time the forwards of the two teams could hardly be distinguished, because they were plastered with it.

"Under the circumstances the handling of the ball by both full-backs, Gus Risman and Warwick Clarke, was the highlight of the game. England had

One that got away, Auckland winger Read gets away from Frank Whitcombe in the mud of Carlow Park.

started by trying to exploit their passing with Eric Batten thrusting infield to join Willie Horne, thus making an extra man, but Auckland's tacklers were too grim.

"So the tourists altered and adopted wet-weather tactics, kicking through and following in close formation. Occasionally brighter-minded players detected chances to kick the ball out into the open, behind the wingers and away from the full-back, this presenting try-scoring chances.

"It was Arthur Bassett's opportunism in dashing to the corner after Frank Whitcombe had kicked across that gave England their 3-2 lead at half-time, Clarke having kicked a penalty for Auckland after 14 minutes.

"It had been a grim battle all through the first half with Whitcombe and George Curran grand warriors in the close play that the rugged Aucklanders revelled in. The same players were instrumental in creating the tries by Bassett and Bob Nicholson which appeared to have set up England for a comfortable win.

"Then, in scenes reminiscent of the best Yorkshire and Lancashire Cup fervour, the frantic crowd saw Rex Cunningham's try and Clarke's goal give England the stoutest battle to hold on to their slender lead in the last 10 minutes. For the big game next Saturday the tourists will have to be at their best to retain their unbeaten record in Tests."

In the *Auckland Sporting Times*, 'The Winger' assessed

Frank Whitcombe is tackled by Johnson (high) and Cunningham (low) in the game against Auckland. It always took at least two tacklers to down the mighty Welshman.

the performances at Carlaw Park of two of the tourists' star players: "The big crowd got a thrill out of seeing Frank Whitcombe, the burly English forward, trying to push his 17st 10lb past the Auckland forwards. Whitcombe is perhaps the biggest front-row forward seen here with an English team.

"He is 31 years of age and a truck driver at home. On several occasions it took four Auckland forwards to pull him to earth but at the end of the game he was still looking for more football. He is perhaps the fastest man for his size the writer has seen.

"Willie Horne, the fly-half who built up a fine reputation in Australia, proved a clever side-stepper with a tricky swerve. He is the fastest half-back to be seen at Carlaw Park since Les Fairclough or Billo Rees."

With the end of the summer-long tour in sight, the weary tourists next faced South Auckland at Huntly on August 7, and Alfred Drewry wrote for the *Yorkshire Post*: "The rugby league tourists ran up their highest score in New Zealand today when they beat South Auckland 42-12, scoring six tries in the process.

"They were without Joe Egan for three parts of the game after the hooker suffered concussion in a heavy tackle but he is expected to be fit for the Test match on Saturday.

"Winger Albert Johnson scored three tries but the happiest feature of the match, on which the tourists had a firm grip, was the half-back combination of Dai Jenkins and Willie Davies. Scrum-half Jenkins has found the soft New Zealand grounds much more to his liking than the bone-hard pitches of Australia and he celebrated the last match but one before the tourists set sail for home on the RMS Rangitiki next Wednesday by scoring his first try of the tour.

The Great Britain and South Auckland teams before their match at Huntley.

"Bob Nicholson not only took over Egan's hooking duties with complete success, he also found time to use his pace to score two tries. Les White also crossed twice and others to touch down were Jim Lewthwaite and Jack Kitching, with Ted Ward adding six goals."

As the Test match approached, all the talk among rugby league followers was of how many of the tourists would be returning to Australia to play for Sydney clubs when the new season started Down Under in 1947.

Alfred Drewry wrote: "According to Australian advices, Eric Batten has agreed to return to Australia after the completion of the tour. Frank Whitcombe, Ike Owens, Ted Ward and Harry Murphy are others said to be considering offers.

"Rather strangely, club officials here are not unduly worried by these statements. Harry Hornby, Bradford Northern's managing director, is obviously not upset. He told me to wait until Batten gets home before taking too much notice about what Australia was saying. John Wood, the secretary of Wakefield Trinity, has told me he was looking for a forward, but not one to replace Murphy.

"The general opinion here would appear to be that when the tourists come home there will be a different side to tell concerning the offers, even if they are used as a plank when discussing terms for the new season with their clubs."

The air of uncertainty surrounding the teams deepened when the players intimated they wanted more money for their efforts in such a successful tour and Ernest Cawthorne wrote in the *Telegraph and Argus* on August 8: "The players have asked managers Popplewell and Gabbatt to notify the Rugby League Council of the players' application for extra bonus payments, irrespective of the one third share of the tour profits arrangement.

"Reasons for the application are the considerable inconvenience in travel and accommodation involving all in expense and ruined and lost clothing. The success of the tour, the players argued, was in no small measure due to the way the players had stood up to the gruelling schedule without any complaint.

"We feel we are entitled to some measure of compensation, say the players. The prestige of the Rugby Football League has been upheld when it might easily have been otherwise.

"Bill Fallowfield, the secretary of the RFL, said in response, 'As it happens the tour has been a success but I don't suppose they would have taken less money had we made a loss. The fact is the players have signed a contract and are expected to abide by it. We don't yet know what the surplus will be but expenses have been higher than expected.

"They have been travelling by air between North Island and South Island at £8-a-head and that amounts to £240 a trip for 30 men; we cannot make much. In other years players have received a bonus of £100 each or a little more, averaging at about £3,000 for the players from a profit of £9,000; it may be a little more this time."

Concentration had re-focussed on rugby when the tourists trained at Carlaw Park, in poor weather, on Friday August 9. Frank Whitcombe was not selected for the Test – his body was still recovering from his efforts in Australia – but there was joy for his Bradford Northern team-mates Trevor Foster and Willie Davies who were both chosen to make their Test debuts against New Zealand.

Other newcomers to Test rugby were Joe Jones, Bryn Knowleden and Bob Nicholson with Tommy McCue captaining the side in the absence through injury of Gus Risman.

Trevor Foster (back) makes his Test debut in Auckland.

The *Sunday Despatch* reported on the Test: "New Zealand won the sole Test at Carlaw Park 13-8. Although England scored two tries to New Zealand's one they could not make up the leeway created by Warwick Clarke's four penalty goals for the home side.

"England made the mistake of trying to keep the game open and New Zealand's tackling broke up their movements time after time. The weather broke on Friday and made the ground almost a quagmire. This was unfortunate for England as, given a firm field, the result would probably have been reversed.

"Ernest Ward just prevented a New Zealand try in the opening minutes but rough play by the English forwards resulted in a penalty with which Clarke made no mistake. He added two more goals from penalties before half-time when New Zealand led 6-0.

"Shortly after the break Tommy McCue sent up a short punt which Ernest Ward collected to dive in the corner for a try which he improved. Another penalty put the home side further ahead but with a beautiful back pass Ward sent Eric Batten over for a try to which Ward could not add the goal.

"A penalty by Clarke hit a post but forward Robert Graham snapped up the rebound to dive over between the posts, Clarke adding the goal. New Zealand had the luck but their ability to cope with the conditions justified their win. Ward was undoubtedly the best player on the pitch, his kicking and handling being perfect."

Frank Whitcombe was selected for the final game of the tour – against Auckland again at Carlaw Park on Monday August 12 – when 12,000 would see Ernest Ward top 100 points for the tour.

The 1946 British touring team
Back row L-R: Ken Gee, George Curran, Les White, Bob Nicholson, Arthur Bassett, Joe Jones, Eric Batten;
3rd row L-R: Trevor Foster, Ted Ward, Ike Owens, Doug Phillips, Jack Kitching, Ernest Ward, Harry Murphy, Joe Lewthwaite;
2nd row L-R: Martin Ryan, Albert Johnson, Tommy McCue, Walter Popplewell, Gus Risman, Walter Gabbatt, Frank Whitcombe, Joe Egan, Fred Hughes;
Front row L-R: Willie Davies, Bryn Knowelden, Dai Jenkins, Willie Horne.

An Auckland newspaper reported: "England finished their tour of Australia and New Zealand in fine style, beating Auckland 22-9.

"The Englishmen were not at their best before the interval and crossed over four points in arrears but they gave a brilliant second-half display when the quick bursts of Jim Lewthwaite, Gus Risman and Willie Horne cut holes in the Auckland defence.

"Auckland fought hard but did not possess the speed or the cleverness necessary to break down the solid English defence. After losing most of the early scrums, the English forwards settled down and eventually got the measure of their opponents through strong, bustling tactics.

"The tourists' only score of the first half was a penalty goal by Ward, who kicked four more goals in the second period when their tries came from Albert Johnson, Ike Owens, Jack Kitching and Lewthwaite."

Frank Whitcombe had played 19 games in Australia and New Zealand – more than any other member of the Great Britain party – and as they prepared to leave for the long journey home, Trevor Foster said of his great friend and team mate: "Frank was an outstanding player on the tour, scoring tries and being the best forward in the scrums. He took on the Aussie pack on his own and was genuinely feared by the Australians.

"It took sometimes three and four defenders to pull him down in the tackle; he was so strong and fearless."

17

BACK TO BRADFORD

Before the touring party boarded RMS Rangitiki for the long journey across the Pacific Ocean, through the Panama Canal, up the Eastern seaboard of North America then across the Atlantic to London, Alfred Drewry compiled an end-of-term report on the five-month tour.

"The rugby league tourists who leave Wellington for home tomorrow cannot look back on their visit to New Zealand with the same pride that was justified by their achievements in Australia but there is no doubt the tour as a whole has been a great success.

Tommy McCue, one of the tour's outstanding players, in action against New South Wales.

Captain 'Dutch' Holland of RMS Rangitiki.

"Outstanding individual successes in big matches have been Ike Owens, Les White, Ernest Ward and Tommy McCue. The combination of McCue's cunning and Owens' devastating burst of speed from the base of the scrum was a masterstroke to which the Australians never found an effective reply.

"The Leeds man has proved himself as a great loose-forward, as we already knew McCue was a scrum-half.

"It is not difficult to see in Ernest Ward, whether as a centre or full-back, a ready-made successor to the great Gus Risman. Ward, cool and stylish, has proved a complete footballer and one young enough to develop into a first-class leader.

"Jack Kitching was just about the fastest man in the side and his ability to run straight brought him more tries than any other centre. If he can correct tendencies to wander out of position and mistime the occasional pass England need look no further for a centre."

On Wednesday August 14 at 3.15pm, under the command of Captain 'Dutch' Holland, RMS Rangitiki of the New Zealand Shipping Company

RMS Rangitiki in Auckland.

The meeting of two oceans: 'The Kiss'.

sailed from Wellington for England, her forward-facing 4.7in gun having been removed along with the rest of her war-time equipment

In his report to the Rugby League Council, Wilf Gabbatt, the business manager of the tour, wrote: "During the voyage to Panama it was learned that the Rangitiki would call at New York and probably stay for three days. Later, owing to a strike of dock workers on the wharves of New York, the ship was diverted to Halifax, Nova Scotia.

"The ship arrived on the Pacific side of the Panama Canal on September 2 and made the crossing the following day, arriving at Cristobal on the evening of that day. A few hours shore leave were given, the first for three weeks.

"RMS Rangitiki reached Caracas, the capital of Venezuela, on September 7 and again shore leave was granted for a few hours before we sailed for North America.

"On Thursday September 12 the Rangitiki berthed at Halifax and a full day was spent ashore before we departed on September 14, arriving at Tilbury on Sunday September 22 at 10pm.

"I desire to put on record appreciation of the arrangements made for our comfort and convenience on arrival at Tilbury. We appreciated the Council's desire to mark our arrival with a dinner but this, by mutual consent, was deferred".

The *Yorkshire Observer* carried this article under the headline "Rugby league tourists arrive home": "Members of Great Britain's successful rugby league touring team arrived back in their home towns last night after leaving their ship earlier in the day.

"Bradford Northern's six players, all looking very fit, were met in London by Mr Harry Hornby, managing director of the club, who had travelled down by road. He returned with three of the players, Ernest Ward, Willie Davies and Frank Whitcombe. The others travelled by train, Trevor Foster to his home in Wales, Eric Batten to Barnsley and Jack Kitching offered to take all the luggage back to Bradford by rail.

"Relatives and friends waiting at Bradford Exchange Station were surprised when Mr Hornby and his passengers drove up. Frank Whitcombe was greeted by his wife Doris and sons Brian and Frank and Ernest Ward by his wife and son Trevor, who was heard to ask his father if he had brought a kangaroo home for him.

Frank Whitcombe, looking very fit and well, was in his usual good humour and mentioned that he had brought "thousands of pairs of nylons" back with him. Speaking of his weight he said he now tipped the scales at 17st 12lb which was 'just right'.

Happy to be home, the Great Britain touring party come ashore at Tilbury.

"The man who had put on the most weight, he said, was Ernest Cawthorne, the *Yorkshire Observer*'s representative. Whitcombe added that one of the reasons for the team's failure in New Zealand was the softness of the grounds.

"In Australia, he said, the grounds were baked hard while in New Zealand they were water-logged and like glue. On several occasions we were all at sea, playing an open game against the Kiwis' rugged rugby.

Back at Bradford Exchange station, are three tourists who would all win the Lance Todd trophy; Willie Davies, Frank Whitcombe and Ernest Ward.

Welcome home! Frank Whitcombe is greeted by Harry Hornby whilst Dai Rees, Willie Davies (left) and Ernest Ward (right) look on

"The prized possessions of the players were boomerangs. Frank Whitcombe received his in Sydney; the others were presented with similar souvenirs at Ipswich in Queensland.

"The Northern players looked fit enough to start playing immediately but Mr Hornby was doubtful if they would, saying it would be better to let them settle down and spend time with their families before getting back into action.

"It has been announced that the Rugby Football League's share of the profits from the tour would be about £27,700 and the bonus for each player would be £140."

Just three days after five of the Northern players had arrived back in Bradford the *Yorkshire Post* told its readers: "Ernest Ward, Willie Davies, Eric Batten, Jack Kitching and Frank Whitcombe have all signed new contracts with the club and Trevor Foster, who is still in South Wales, is also expected to do so.

"Asked if this meant that none of Northern's returned tourists would be accepting Australian offers, team manager Dai Rees said: ' You can take it for granted that all the Australian stuff is cut out.'"

On September 28, just five days after docking at Tilbury, Frank Whitcombe played alongside Eric Batten, Ernest Ward, Willie Davies and Jack Kitching for Northern in a 5-5 draw against Halifax at Thrum Hall, Arthur Bassett appearing on the wing for the home side.

On the same day Frank Townsend, a 20 year-old Wakefield Trinity winger, was fatally injured by a neck tackle in an otherwise clean game with Featherstone Rovers at Post Office Road. He was buried on Wednesday October 2.

Trinity had been due to face Castleford in a Cup-tie that day; the game was postponed and played the following day to allow the Trinity squad to attend the funeral, some of them acting as bearers. The rugby league community rallied round and all six of Bradford Northern's tourists appeared in a fund-raising game for the family on October 9.

The *Yorkshire Evening Post* reported: "The biggest array of rugby league football talent ever to be seen at Featherstone, including 10 of the returned touring team, will figure in the match to be played for the benefit of the family of Frank Townsend, who died in Pontefract Infirmary after injuries received in a match against Wakefield Trinity.

"The teams for the match, selected by Vic Darlison (Bradford Northern) and Alex Fiddes (Huddersfield) are:

Darlison's XIII (from): W McWatt (Hull KR), E Batten, J Kitching, E Ward (all Bradford Northern), A Longley (Featherstone), G Langfield (Castleford) Willie Davies (Bradford Northern), D Jenkins (Leeds), F Whitcombe, V Darlison (both Bradford Northern), M Exley, H Murphy (both Wakefield Trinity), T Foster (Bradford Northern), I Owens (Leeds).

Fiddes XIII: B Leake, J Bawden, A Fiddes, W Davies (all Huddersfield), R Copley (Castleford), G Morgan (Huddersfield), R Rylance (Wakefield Trinity), J Taylor (Huddersfield), J Ramsden (Hull KR), H Wilkinson (Wakefield Trinity), R Robson, R Nicholson (both Huddersfield), A Dockar (Hull KR)."

The match drew a crowd of 6,000 and raised £200 for the Townsend family.

Northern had started the season by signing winger Alan Edwards just 24 hours after he had asked Salford for a transfer. Moving to Odsal was not a surprise; the former Aberavon player and Welsh international had played for Bradford during the war.

Changes were afoot both on the field and off it. To accommodate Edwards, Walter Best was sold to Leeds for a record fee. He made his debut against Batley and went on to make 37 appearances for the Headingley club, scoring 17 tries.

In addition, the end of the war had allowed prop Herbert Smith to resume his rugby career while second-row Sandy Orford had become a

Herbert Smith resumed his career after the war.

Vincent Dilerenzo moved to St Helens.

Laurie Roberts left Northern to join Featherstone.

professional wrestler whose new trade would take him all over the world.

In the board room, Sir James Hill, a prominent figure in the wool trade, took over as chairman while managing director Harry Hornby was installed as vice-chairman of the Rugby Football League. After the home game with Barrow on October 5, a 'welcome home' dinner for Bradford's tourists was given at the Great Northern Hotel by the clubs' players and directors, at which the new chairman was introduced to the team.

In October, hooker Vincent Dilorenzo was sold to St Helens, second-row Laurie Roberts joined Featherstone Rovers and Alf Marklew moved to Keighley, while on the Saturday October 12, Frank Whitcombe earned his 10th cap for Wales in a 19-5 defeat against England at Swinton.

Frank was now employed as a wagon driver by Ryburn United Transport Ltd who were based just off Wakefield Road in Bradford, but he was looking to a future beyond rugby and, like many professional rugby players, was turning his attention to running his own public house.

In Bradford, Frank Mugglestone's family ran the Unicorn on Ivegate, Bill Hutchinson's family had the Wagon and Horses on Manchester Road, George Carmichael was mine host at the Flappit in Cullingworth and Leeds forward Ken Jubb was landlord at the Red Lion.

Former Wigan and Wales forward Harold Edwards had joined Bradford Northern towards the end of his career and had played with the young Frank Whitcombe, who had recently arrived from Broughton Rangers. Together with his wife Edna, Edwards – nicknamed the 'Welsh Bull' – ran the Truncliffe Gate public house at Odsal top, and the pair were happy to show Frank Whitcombe and his wife Doris how to run a business in the licensed trade.

The Whitcombes became partners with Harold and Edna Edwards and helped provide outside catering for major companies like department stores Busbys and Brown Muffs at the Connaught Rooms on Manningham Lane in Bradford.

Roll out the barrel, Frank Whitcombe at the Hallfield Hotel in Bradford.

It was not long before Frank and Doris Whitcombe took on the Hallfield Hotel at the top of

New signing Gwylfa Jones (left) and Barry Tyler (centre) with Mr & Mrs Hornby and Trevor Foster.

157

Trafalgar Street in Bradford and nearby was the Police Boys' Club where their sons Brian and Frank junior attended the youth club. They later moved to Sedbergh Boys' Club where they had their first experience of playing rugby.

Later, in the same spirit he had been shown by Harold Edwards, Frank educated Alan Edwards in the licensed trade and Edwards would later take over the Albion in Skipton.

While Frank Whitcombe was gaining experience in his new trade, Bradford Northern were looking for new talent and three new signings, all from rugby union in Wales, were made.

Gwylfa Jones, a former Llanelli and Swansea scrum-half who had been educated at Gowerton Grammar School, made his debut in a 16-8 win over Keighley on Boxing Day; on January 6 1947 they landed Ron Greaves, who had played at prop for Abertillery and had a trial with Monmouthshire: and finally, they signed Hagan Evans, a forward from Llanelli who had once scored five tries in a game against London Welsh. After only five games for Northern, Evans would play in the Challenge Cup final against Leeds.

18

HARD MEN

Frank Whitcombe was a hard man in an era when the game of rugby league football was at its toughest. This was the time of the contested scrum, when there was no six-tackle rule and possession from the scrum was the difference between winning and losing.

The dark side of the game was the front row, where every team had at least one, usually two, enforcers; the practitioners of the dark arts which were never taught at school. Frank was the enforcer in the Bradford team at a time when the head-butt was not uncommon and stiff-arm tackles almost the norm.

Intimidation of opposition players was part of the game and it was one of Frank's jobs to ensure that none of his team-mates were knocked about or put off their game by threats. Each week he would particularly watch over Willie Davies, Northern's slightly-built, mercurial stand-off, who would be targeted in every match.

Former Northern forward of the 1940s, Frank Mugglestone, was a keen observer of Frank's devotion to his team: "Whenever you made a mistake on the field Frank would always be the first to come up to you to reassure you; he knew what to say at the right time.

"If a player was injured Frank would joke 'It's OK, there are no broken bones' then he would be serious and ask 'who did this'? After a match, if it had not gone the way we wanted, Frank knew what to say and how to break the ice. It was a unique gift he had."

Frank's rival enforcers included Jim 'Ginger' Crossley from Castleford. Frank had a photograph of Crossley and had written on the back 'A formidable opponent'. Wigan had two, Ken Gee and Joe Egan, with whom Frank packed down during the 'Indomitables' tour. Warrington had Dave Cotton, their hooker, who played against Frank from his early days at Broughton Rangers until the end of his career with Bradford Northern.

Willie Davies who had Frank Whitcombe as his protector.

Cotton's son, Fran, would later captain the England RU XV and play for the British Lions. Another son, Dave, would include Keighley among his clubs in a long rugby league career.

Rivals are one thing, adversaries another and Frank's chief protagonist was Arthur Clues, the Australia and New South Wales second-row who signed a lucrative contract with Leeds, becoming the first Aussie to join an English club after the war.

Former Bradford Northern player Charlie Ebbage knew Frank Whitcombe well. "For a big man you have never seen anyone as light on their feet as Frank," he remembered. "He always had a smile on his face. He had very small feet for a man of his size. He used to sneak out wearing Willie Davies' boots. I don't know if Willie wore Frank's!

"Some people might think he was a dirty player but he wasn't. He did, however, know how to look after his team-mates. He was very deceptive for a big man; he could run like the wind and had tremendous ball skills.

"Frank had very few rivals in the game as far as scrummaging goes. I think the nearest to him at open-side prop would be Ken Gee at Wigan. But his great adversary was Clues. Their confrontations started in the first Test in Sydney; Clues said something as the first scrum went down and

Harry Royal the Dewsbury scrum half receives the Yorkshire League Trophy from Bill Fallowfield. Royal would later feel the boot of Frank Whitcombe.

the result was that Clues flew out of the top of the scrum. First round to Whitcombe. Their battles continued to the end of Frank's career.

"Frank was great fun off the field; he was a great humourist and always said something to make you laugh. But on the pitch he was a different person; no-one took liberties when Frank was on the field. Opposing forwards always used to look round to see where he was."

Another bout in the Whitcombe v Clues series came when the clubs met in the second leg of their Yorkshire Cup tie at Odsal on September 24 1947. Trevor Foster recalled the match, which Northern won 11-9 despite having 12 players unavailable through injury.

"Arthur Clues kicked out violently at our scrum-half Gwylfa Jones at a scrum, missing his head by inches. Immediately Frankie stood up from the scrum and confronted Clues, running towards him with both fists clenched. He drove the full force of his 18st frame into Clues and pole-axed him. Then, as Arthur hit the ground, Frankie dropped to his knees, crushing Arthur's ribs.

"The Leeds supporters in the Main Stand erupted, calling out 'off, off, off'. The Leeds trainer was on the field quickly to treat Arthur who was in a real state of distress and could not get his breath. He made some horrible noises; I feared he was in dire straits and gasping for life.

"This went on for several minutes and eventually the referee (Walter Hemmings from Halifax) turned to Frankie and ordered him to the dressing room. I think by then Frank was walking that way anyway. The crowd erupted again as he made his way off the field. Arthur was carried off on a stretcher and was also sent off.

"Arthur later admitted it was the hardest he had been hit in his rugby career and he would never tangle with Frank again, which, of course, he did.

"After the match we were all in the bath when Arthur came into the dressing room and in time-honoured fashion shook hands with Frank to show their mutual respect."

To confirm there were no hard feelings, victim and assailant went to the Hall Field Hotel and drank together until the early hours.

The Rugby League's Disciplinary Committee met on October 2 and suspended Arthur Clues for two matches and Frank Whitcombe for four, which mean he had to miss the Wales v New Zealand international on October 18. The tourists no doubt appreciated the action taken by the committee – they had been in the stand at Odsal when the incident occurred.

Trevor Foster continued: "That was Frank; always in the thick of things and always the first to help a team-mate in trouble. When the battle was on in those really big games Frank was always in the front line.

"Scrums in those days were immensely hard and uncompromising. The weakest fell and Frank never fell. The most important thing was to get a fair share of the ball from the scrum; Frank was instrumental in ensuring we always got our share."

Frank was only playing his second game after his suspension when he was sent off again under very different circumstances as Northern won 3-0 at Dewsbury on November 15. Harry Waring remembered the match: "Frank was sent off at Crown Flatt when Dewsbury's Welsh international scrum-half Harry Royal conned Frank into kicking him from the open-side prop position, where in those days both props would try to scoop the ball towards their hooker.

"Harry stood nearer the scrum than he normally would and Frank's effort resulted in Harry being kicked in the 'Crown Jewels'. Harry made a song-and-dance about it and Frank had to make the long walk from the Sugar Lane bottom corner to the dressing room to the accompaniment of vitriolic abuse from the partisan crowd."

Need we say more, except that our confidence in our boys is intensified by the heroic efforts that our forwards made to save the game and the knowledge of what our regular backs can do.

Wigan, our visitors to-day, deserve every encouragement. They have worked hard to build up a team of young players of their own—no weekly variety show for them—no fear of that—and to what extent they have succeeded can be judged by their achievements this season. Last Saturday they scored over 40 points against Oldham. So with the knowledge of our team difficulties due to the Northern Command Match at Hull, they will be all out to liquidate the heavy defeat they sustained when last at Odsal.

The policy adopted by the Wigan Club during the war period so far bears the hallmark of sound legislation, and the benefits to be derived therefrom in the post-war era of Rugby League Football will undoubtedly be great.

Since our elevation to a "place in the sun" of Rugby League football, our Club's association with the Wigan club has been a very happy one. Long may the names of Wigan and Bradford be associated with each other as they are to-day—keenly competitive, yet as keenly appreciative.

Good News.

It is expected that our Managing Director, Mr. Harry Hornby, who three weeks ago had an operation on his knee, will be discharged from hospital next week.

BRADFORD NORTHERN v. WIGAN

Bradford Northern	Wigan
Colours— White Jerseys, Red, Amber and Black Stripes.	★
Full-Back 1 ANOTHER	**Full-Back** 1 JONES
Three-Quarters 2 BEST 3 BILLINGTON 4 RULE 5 WALTERS	**Three-Quarters** 2 KERWICK 3 LAWRENSON 4 MALONEY 5 ASPINALL
Half-Backs 6 DAVIES or BENNETT 7 WARD, D.	**Half-Backs** 6 HUGHES 7 RYAN
Forwards 8 ANOTHER 9 HALEY 10 HIGSON 11 SMITH 12 MUGGLESTONE 14 HUTCHINSON	**Forwards** 8 GEE, K. 9 EGAN 10 BLAN 11 CAYZER 12 SIMPSON 13 BOWEN

Referee — Mr. L. THORPE.
Touch Judges—
Messrs. R. Rawlinson and R. Stead.

Hard evidence, Frank Whitcombe is named as 'Another' in Northern's programme for the game against Wigan

Frank was suspended for six matches but appealed against the length of the suspension and called upon Harry Royal to give evidence on his behalf. The appeal was heard on December 4, and after hearing from both parties the committee reduced the ban to four matches in all and added that as Whitcombe had already missed two games he would be available for selection from December 13.

Frank Whitcombe's first brush with authority had come five years earlier. He had been selected for a Rugby League XIII to play in a charity game against Northern Command at Hull's Boulevard ground. Unfortunately that game was to be played on October 10, the same day as Bradford Northern were due to play Wigan at Odsal.

Dai Rees withdrew Whitcombe from the select team, claiming he was injured, and then picked him under the name of 'A N Other' to face Wigan in a game Northern won 12-6. The ruse did not work and a disciplinary meeting was inevitable.

The *Hull Daily Mail* reported: "For breach of rules in playing Frank Whitcombe, who had been chosen to play for a League XIII against Northern Command in Hull, Bradford Northern were fined £20, the team manager Dai Rees was severely censured and Frank Whitcombe was suspended for two matches."

Another ban came when he was suspended for fighting in November 1943. The four-match ban meant he had to miss the two-legged Yorkshire Cup final against Keighley, the only final for which he was unavailable during his Odsal career.

19

THE ROAD TO WEMBLEY

The dawning of 1947 saw rugby league settling into what would become a hugely successful period with matches attracting massive crowds, the people being determined to enjoy themselves to the limit after the restrictions imposed by war.

Travel was almost back to normal and Frank Whitcombe was selected for the Welsh team to face France in Marseilles on January 18. As ever, though, the mandarins at RL Headquarters kept a careful eye on the costs of such trips and the *Hull Daily Mail* heard from the secretary Bill Fallowfield.

"Costs to the RFL of the match in Marseilles will be in the neighbourhood of £1,250," said Fallowfield. "The party, consisting of 13 players, two reserves, a coach, six members of the Council and the secretary, will be away for a week and the expected cost of hotel accommodation and travelling costs is £45 per head.

"The players will receive £10 each if they win and they have to be reimbursed for loss of time at work." The players did not get their £10, as France won 14-5.

George Carmichael an outstanding servant to Bradford Northern.

Three of Bradford Northern's stalwarts who had served the club at Birch Lane and Odsal were given a benefit match against Huddersfield on Easter Monday, April 7.

George Carmichael, who was signed from Hull KR in 1934, would play 16 consecutive seasons for Northern at full-back, scoring 18 tries and kicking 409 goals. He played 473 games for Northern and totalled 872 points.

Prop forward Len Higson started his career at Wakefield Trinity at the age of 19, ironically making his debut against Bradford Northern in 1927 and moved to Leeds for £600 in August 1934. He signed for Northern in the same year and played 380 games for the club, scoring 25 tries, and scrummaged with Frank Whitcombe in four

Championship finals and two Challenge Cup finals. He also played for England at hooker in their 14-13 win over Wales at Headingley in 1932.

Higson continued to serve Northern after his retirement as a player, taking up the role of coach with the 'A' team and also acting as sponge man for the first team.

The third player to enjoy the benefit was loose-forward Billy Hutchinson who played 213 matches and scored 40 tries in a career that started in 1933. He appeared in two war-time Cup finals, against Wigan and Huddersfield, and was capped by England in the 9-9 draw with Wales in 1944.

The recruitment programme went on for Bradford Northern with Ken Traill, recently released by the RAF, signed from Hunslet for £500 on May 25. He made his debut in a 19-10 defeat to Wakefield Trinity at Odsal the following day – Whitsuntide Monday – but he collapsed and was taken to hospital suffering from sun-stroke and concussion.

Len Higson another player who was revered at Odsal.

One of Bradford Northern's foibles in the war years had been an insistence that, because the number 13 was thought to guarantee back luck, their loose-forward always wore No 14 on his jersey.

When Frank Mugglestone was released from the RAF he became a regular at loose-forward and when the board reconsidered their numbering policy he was quite happy to fall in with their plan to restore the No 13 jersey.

"I'd survived the war and was doing what I loved – playing rugby league football for Bradford Northern," he said. "Wearing the No 13 jersey was no problem for me."

Mugglestone also remembered walking down the steps from the dressing room to the pitch at Odsal and hearing Eric Batten whisper: "Now then 'Kid' don't go giving all the ball to those bloody Welshmen; remember me on the blind side."

The season had not gone well for Bradford Northern despite their investment in new players and they could only finish fourth in the league table but they had enjoyed better fortune in the Challenge Cup, earning a meeting with Warrington in the semi-final.

The week before the semi-final, Dai Rees asked Frank Whitcombe and Donald Ward to watch Warrington in action at Batley and Alfred Drewry reported in the *Yorkshire Post*: "There was a broad smile on Frank Whitcombe's face as he left Mount Pleasant but he knows too much about rugby league to believe the side Northern face in next Saturday's Cup semi-final will be as slipshod as the one soundly beaten by Batley".

Warrington did play much better when they faced Northern at Swinton but the Yorkshire side took the honours with an 11-7 victory thanks to tries from Jack Kitching, Donald Ward and Eric Batten, with Ernest Ward adding one goal.

In 1943 the Rugby Football League's Emergency Committee had decided that the first five Challenge Cup finals after the war would all be played at the Empire Stadium, Wembley; the stadium authorities would provide all the facilities for the game for which they would be paid 20 per cent of the net takings.

The first final back at Wembley had been the previous season when Wakefield Trinity had beaten Wigan 13-12 before a crowd of 54,730. Now the players of Bradford Northern and Leeds would have the chance to savour the unique atmosphere of Wembley on a Cup final day.

Leeds were warm favourites to win the final and Alfred Drewry interviewed their captain Ike Owens who said: "We have been through this Cup competition without a try being scored against us and I don't see why Bradford Northern should succeed where the others have failed. All we can ask is for an even share of the breaks on the field."

When Drewry questioned Northern's captain Ernest Ward he found him in equally optimistic mood. "I think we have a faster back division than Leeds and we intend to make every use of our speed," he said. "This is Northern's first Wembley final and we intend to make it a winning one."

Drewry then reported on what would become a pre-Cup final tradition. "Both teams visited Wembley today but did not meet," he wrote in the *Yorkshire Post*. "All the Northern players changed into their football gear and had a business-like half-hour this morning under the watchful eye of their coach Dai Rees.

"There was a strong, cold wind when Leeds arrived in the afternoon and the only player to change was Bert Cook, the New Zealand full-back and goal-kicker. Because of the peculiar eddies which swirl around the Wembley bowl practice for him was essential.

"The goal posts were not in position but Ike Owens and Ken Jubb stood on the marks and Cook gave himself a thorough trial. His accuracy both with and against the wind surprised everyone and if he can find the same game tomorrow Northern will pay dearly for any penalties they concede.

"Leeds are favourites because they have never been beaten in a peace-time Cup final and because they have what is considered to be the best pack of forwards in the club's history."

Northern had based themselves out of London at Westcliffe-on-sea, and the players were greeted with brilliant sunshine when they took their final exercise along the promenade. They had been instructed to have a lie-in that morning, before a light lunch at 10.45, but hooker Vic Darlison was up and about at 8am. He explained: "I'm a miner and my work does not allow me to stay in bed in the morning."

Problems began after Northern left their hotel for the two-hour drive to Wembley. Trevor Foster takes up the story: "On our bus journey we were caught up in a traffic jam and running late. The bus driver was panicking, which could have had something to do with him not being sure of the route through London.

"Much to our amusement, Frank Whitcombe took over the driver's seat and proceeded to put his foot hard on the accelerator. We sailed through the centre of the city, past the Palace of Westminster, with motorists bellowing and waving their fists at our bus.

"With a huge smile, Frank drove on and we arrived at Wembley bang on time. There was no nervous tension for Frank before turning out at Wembley."

In Bradford Northern's match brochure Frank's pen-portrait read: "Genial giant Frank Whitcombe is the wit as well as the heavyweight of the team. He turns the scales at over 18st and opposing forwards really know they have been in a game after 80 minutes with him.

"But as a boy in Cardiff, where he was born, Frank was a full-back, turning to the pack after joining the Army. He played 27 times for the Army and appeared in a Welsh trial. In 1935 Broughton Rangers signed him and he won his first Welsh international cap the following season. He has been Wales's first-choice at prop ever since.

"In 1946 he toured Australia with Gus Risman's team and played in the first two Tests. Northern made one of their best moves when they signed him from Broughton Rangers in 1935; he takes a well-earned benefit this season."

Eddie Waring commented prior to the kick-off at Wembley: "The Rugby League Challenge Cup final brought new ideas to Wembley, adopting the French system of individual introduction to the record crowd of 77,605 as the players ran to their respective positions on the field."

Bradford Northern's Willie Davies should have struck the first blow when he intercepted a pass and ran 50 yards before kicking over full-back Bert Cook's head but the race for the ball was won by Ike Owens. Davies then put centre Jack Kitching through but Cook used the touchline to good effect to make the tackle.

The Bradford Northern and Leeds teams take the pitch at a sun drenched Wembley for the 1947 Rugby League Challenge Cup final.

Leeds took the lead with a penalty from Cook and held their advantage until the interval, then Bradford went ahead with a spectacular try from Emlyn Walters, before Cook struck again to give Leeds a 4-3 advantage.

Ernest Ward restored Northern's lead with a 30-yard drop-goal 15 minutes after the restart then, five minutes from the end, Cook and George Carmichael began a kicking duel which ended when the New Zealander fumbled the ball and slipped at the same time which gave Trevor Foster the chance to gather the ball and score the try which finished the Leeds challenge.

The Leeds forwards – known by their supporters as 'the super six' – had been outplayed by the Bradford pack on the day so justifiably the Northern forwards considered themselves 'the superior six' and the icing on their cake was the award of the Lance Todd trophy, for the final's outstanding player to Willie Davies.

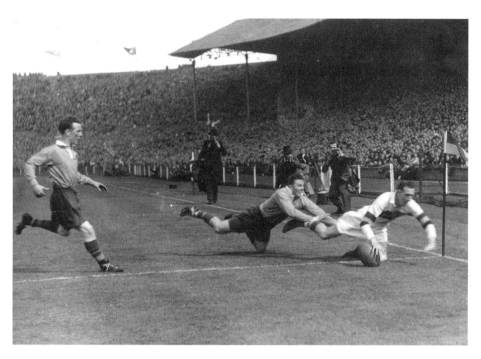

Emlyn Walters opens the scoring with a spectacular try as he evades Bert Cook and Dickie Williams.

Northern's Vic Darlison (No 9) and Frank Whitcombe (No 8) watch as Bert Cook kicks at goal.

Herbert Smith makes a tackle, with Eric Batten (left) and Frank Whitcombe (right) in attendance.

Ike Owens said afterwards: "The better team won. We cannot understand why we played below what is our usual form."

Bert Cook had one great regret – that he missed a penalty chance in the first minute. He said that had he had that opportunity later in the game, when there had been time to judge the breeze, there might have been a different tale to tell.

Of the 26 players who took part in the final, half of them were from Wales, namely Bradford's Frank Whitcombe, Emlyn Walters (try), Willie Davies (Lance Todd trophy), Trevor Foster (try) and Hagan Evans. Whilst from Leeds, Wales was represented by: Ike Owens (captain), Tommy Cornelius, Gareth Price, Thomas Williams, Dickie Williams, Dai Jenkins, Dai Prosser and Con Murphy.

In addition to the 13 Northern players who were awarded winners' medals others went to Len Higson, for his services to the club, and Alan Edwards, who had broken a collar-bone in the 5-3 defeat at Hunslet on April 3.

The day after the Wembley triumph a Civic Reception was arranged for the players at Bradford Town Hall where they were greeted by the Lord

Bradford Northern bring the cup home greeted by 100,000 delirious supporters.

Mayor, Alderman Clough, who had been at the match the previous day and had played for Bradford Northern 30 years earlier. He told the players: "Everyone from Bradford is proud of you."

Along the route from Odsal to the Town Hall Square in the centre of the city, it was estimated that over 100,000 people had lined the streets of Bradford to welcome the Cup-winners home. It was a special day for the Ward family.

Brothers Ernest and Donald who had been on the pitch at Wembley the previous day, were greeted by another brother Stanley, a former Dewsbury player, and their father Ernest senior, who had won a Challenge Cup-winner's medal with Dewsbury in 1912. Ernest Ward introduced the players to the crowd and Lance Todd trophy winner Willie Davies addressed the gathering.

Northern's managing director Harry Hornby, also the vice-president of the Rugby Football League, said: "I am a very proud man; the team won the Cup playing good, clean football." Sir James Hill, the beaming President

Ernest Ward displays the Rugby League Challenge cup, with his son Trevor seated and Frank and Brian Whitcombe looking on

of Bradford Northern added how fitting it was that Northern had won the Cup in Alderman Clough's year of office.

On May 21, Northern played Leeds at Headingley where the honours where shared in a 2-2 draw. During the game a collection was organised with the takings to be shared between the families of two prominent rugby players who had died in tragic circumstances.

Former Leeds forward Harry Dyer was only 37 when he passed away suddenly and Halifax forward Hudson Irving – who had played for Northern as a loan player in the 1942-3 season – had died of a heart attack while playing for Halifax against Dewsbury at Thrum Hall on April 11.

Because of the severity of the winter, the 1946-7 season became the longest on record, Northern playing their final match of the campaign, a 24-16 home win over Batley, on June 11 1947.

Frank Whitcombe's elder son Brian recalls growing up in the Wibsey area of Bradford in the years immediately after the war. "We couldn't wait to wake up on a Sunday morning during the rugby season to see who had stayed over on the Saturday night at the family home in Wibsey Park Avenue," he remembered.

"Trevor Foster always had the spare room; that was his. During the war years, whenever he came back to Bradford on leave he lived with us. Emlyn Walters and Des Case were also regular guests at our home.

"The first job for my brother Frank junior and I on a Sunday was to take the empty beer bottles back to the pub. There was always three tea-chests full and we got a penny for every bottle we returned.

"When we got back home we would all sit down and eat the breakfast Mum had cooked for everyone. Then, after breakfast, we played touch-and-pass in Wibsey Park with our house guests. Can you imagine being taught to pass and tackle by my Dad, Trevor Foster, Des Case and Emlyn Walters?

"During the summer, the Welsh players at Northern would come and play cricket with us. The game always ended in a draw at 8pm; Frank and I would go home and Dad and his friends would all go for a pint at The Park Hotel.

"It was a different era in those days; there was a real community spirit among the people and the Bradford Northern players were at the heart of the community. When Emlyn Walters got married he and his wife came and lived with us for six months until they could arrange their own house.

"Later, when Dad had retired from playing rugby and had become a director at Odsal, Joe Phillips, Norman Hastings and Jack McLean joined Bradford Northern from New Zealand. By then we were at the King's Head public house in Bradford and they would come and eat Sunday lunch with us. When Norman later became tour manager for New Zealand he came to Bradford to see my Mum and Dad. The spirit in the club was second to none at that time."

20

THE LANCE TODD HERO

The 1947-8 season was quickly upon the players, who had barely had time to recover from the exertions of the previous, marathon campaign, and, as usual, Harry Hornby had been trying to further strengthen his squad.

For the game against Wigan at Odsal on September 16, the *Yorkshire Evening Post* informed the rugby league public: "Bradford Northern will have Bill Leake, who learned his football at Featherstone, in the full-back position tomorrow evening when Sandy Orford will return to the home pack.

"Leake was transferred from Huddersfield to Northern today at a fee of £600. He went on the transfer list at Huddersfield at his own request a month ago when the fee was fixed at £900 but Leake, on appeal to the RL Management Committee, had the fee reduced.

"Leake went to Fartown in 1943, was a member of the team which won the Challenge Cup final in 1945 and held his place until the arrival of Johnny Hunter from Australia. He will not be eligible to play for Northern in Yorkshire Cup football but George Carmichael, who intimated at the beginning of the season that he was ready for retirement but would play on until they signed another full-back, will fill in.

"Sandy Orford, who played for Northern before the war, returns to Odsal from Trinity on a free transfer and will take the place of Frank Whitcombe, who is ill."

Early season form had not been good for Northern with five defeats, but they turned the corner in typical style and their form picked up so markedly that they won the Yorkshire League title. They also made progress in the Challenge Cup; victories over Huddersfield, Wakefield Trinity, Oldham and Hunslet setting up a final against Wigan.

Before the trip to Wembley there was the matter of a benefit game for Frank Whitcombe, Des Case and Donald Ward. The match in question was against Wakefield Trinity at Odsal on April 10 1948 and Trevor Foster celebrated the occasion in remarkable fashion, scoring six tries in a 28-16 home victory.

Harry Hornby (left) presents benefit cheques to Donald Ward, Des Case and Frank Whitcombe.

His feat equalled that of Eric Batten, who had scored six tries in a 54-3 win over Leeds at Headingley, a match in which scrum-half Donald Ward crossed for five tries himself.

Northern secured a top-four place in the league table, thus ensuring another hectic finale to the season for their players, who knew they had much hard work before they could look forward to a return to Wembley.

Between March 19 and April 24, Frank Whitcombe and several of his Welsh team-mates played nine matches for Northern and one for Wales, in a 20-12 defeat against France at the St. Helen's ground in Swansea. No wonder the supporters were wondering if their heroes would run out of energy and enthusiasm before the big day at the Empire Stadium.

Northern's string of matches over that period read: March 19 won 11-6 at Keighley; March 27 lost 21-5 at Warrington; March 30 won 7-2 at Huddersfield; April 3 Challenge Cup semi-final beat Hunslet 14-7 at Headingley; April 10 beat Wakefield Trinity 28-16 at home; April 14 beat Workington Town 22-16 at home; April 17 beat Leeds 9-3 at home; April 19 won 13-6 at Workington; April 21 won 23-12 at York; April 24 won play-off semi-final 15-3 at Wigan, Northern's last game before Wembley.

But, when the flood of matches was over, there was time for a group of the players to attend a social function at Buttershaw Lane Working Men's Club in Bradford on April 29, in support of the benefit funds of Frank Whitcombe, Des Case and Donald Ward.

They took the Yorkshire League trophy with them and Ernest Ward was pictured with a bouquet of carnations which he hoped to attach to the Challenge Cup after the following Saturday's final against Wigan at Wembley.

This was to be a special final on several fronts. It would be the first time the Rugby Football League Challenge Cup final had been honoured by the presence of the reigning monarch, His Majesty King George VI; for the first time the game would be televised live with 17 cameras spread round the stadium; it was the first all-ticket final and attracted a record crowd of 91,465; and it was the first time 'special excursion' trains had been run since the outbreak of the war, 17 such trains being laid on for supporters from Yorkshire alone.

Getting their hands on a ticket was the major problem for the majority of supporters. 'Little John' wrote the following in the *Yorkshire Evening Post* on April 12: "Mr Harry Hornby, the managing director of Bradford Northern, is in the market for tickets for the Challenge Cup final on May 1. He is eager to buy them at any price from 2s 6d (12.5p today) to one guinea (£1.05) to respond to some of the thousands of applications stacked in boxes at Odsal.

"Mr Hornby says his club has no more than 1,350 tickets for their followers and of those there are only 92 tickets priced at one guinea; Bradford have 200 Patrons. That gives us some idea of the headache facing the club.

"Mr Hornby told me: 'Over the weekend we have had two men working full-time on the applications and there are still two boxes full of letters for us to tackle. If we had 10,000 tickets we could find a home for every one. As it is, we are searching everywhere in an effort to buy tickets to sell to our followers. The only bit of luck I have had so far was for the purchase of a batch of 12 at 4s 6d (22.5p) each.'

"Wigan sold 2,000 2s 6d tickets last week which they had bought from Wembley when they were drawn with Rochdale Hornets in the semi-final. Today they began to sell stand seats from their RFL allocation to reserved-seat ticket holders at Central Park.

"We have not got a quarter enough," J P Barnes, the Wigan secretary, told me. "In fact we could have sold seven or eight thousand without difficulty. As it is, I reckon

Wigan secretary JP Barnes (centre) tried to satisfy the demand for Wembley tickets.

there will be 10,000 Wigan folk at Wembley. I know that from the number of applications we have referred to Wembley."

"Bradford Northern's Cup final plans are not complete but Mr Hornby says they are well in hand. Northern will go South on the Thursday before the final. Last year their final preparations for the game with Leeds were completed at Westcliffe-on-sea; this time they may stay nearer London, perhaps in the Thames Valley."

'Little John' – in reality John Bapty, the sports editor of the *Yorkshire Evening Post* – reported on Northern's team for Wembley: "Dai Rees, the Bradford Northern team manager, keeps Bill Leake, the former Huddersfield full-back, in the side for tomorrow's Challenge Cup final at Wembley. Though he delayed his announcement until Northern had had a look at the Empire Stadium today, he had decided last Monday that his Cup final team would be the one which failed to complete a victory at Wigan a week ago in the Championship semi-final.

"Leake went to Northern from Huddersfield last September to be ready to replace George Carmichael when the Hull-born veteran retires. He was unfortunate with early injury but he was tested at Workington and again at Wigan and never put a foot wrong.

"Northern's hopes of lifting the Cup are high after last weekend. Still, Dai Rees, as astute a judge of a football situation as there is in the game, does not pay too much attention to what happened at Central Park.

"Rees knows another brilliant Welshman – Jim Sullivan – will have worked on his men this week to restore the fine edge to Wigan's attack and to revive the team's confidence and he contents himself with saying 'I hope tomorrow's Royal final will have as much football in it as last week's League Championship semi-final had"

"Sullivan thinks Northern will win and so do I."

Supporters from both clubs were desperate to get to Wembley, none more so than 48 year-old Alf Townsend of Leigh Street, Golborne, near Wigan. Wearing the cherry-and-white hoops of Wigan, he was interviewed at Euston Station after he had walked the 200 miles to London.

As he was waiting for the special trains to arrive from Wigan he told a reporter: "My feet are sore but I will just about manage the remaining miles to Wembley." Townsend, who spent the night in hostels as he passed through Warrington, Stafford, Coventry and Daventry, added "I don't think I'll walk back."

As Wigan supporters surged down the platform from the first of the 12 trains due from Lancashire, hundreds of them shook hands with the beaming Townsend.

Rugby League Parade published a Cup final special edition which carried interviews with both captains. Northern's Ernest Ward said: "The team and I are very pleased to be appearing at Wembley for the second year in succession.

"Our performances at the beginning of the season did not merit such a reward but we have improved in spirit and in our play which has taken us once more to Wembley. We have a very hard task to beat the giants of rugby league but the boys are confident of setting a record of winning the Cup twice in succession. Whoever wins, it will certainly be the greatest Cup final to have been played at Wembley."

Wigan's Joe Egan responded: "Our boys are full of confidence and are hoping to improve on our failure to win the Cup two years ago. If we had been asked to select opponents for the final we would have chosen Bradford Northern for in playing against them we are practically assured of having a good game and one worthy of the Royal occasion."

Frank Whitcombe's pen-portrait in *Rugby League Parade* read: "Nick-named 'man mountain' by the Australian spectators during the 1946 tour,

The Bradford Northern team line up, waiting to meet the King, before the rugby league Challenge Cup final.
L-R: Ernest Ward (captain), Bill Leake, Eric Batten, Des Case, Alan Edwards, Willie Davies, Donald Ward, Frank Whitcombe, Vic Darlison, Herbert Smith, Trevor Foster, Barry Tyler, Ken Traill, Dai Rees (Team Manager).

Frank is now a stone heavier than when he played at Wembley last year and will certainly create a record all of his own in this year's game.

"He left Broughton Rangers to join Bradford in 1938 and has been a regular selection for Wales in the last 10 years. He played in the first two Test matches against Australia in 1946. A native of Cardiff, Whitcombe is now mine host of a Bradford hotel and although a heavy player he can still get around and take his share in the loose."

Whitcombe went into the match as the heaviest player to take part in a Challenge Cup final, the previous record-holder being the South African Gert 'Tank' Van Rooyen at just over 16st. The lightest player on the field was Wigan's scrum-half Tommy Bradshaw at 10st 8lb.

Wigan had made arrangements to stay in Weybridge, using the same hotel Manchester United had occupied the night before they had beaten Blackpool 4-2 in the FA Cup final. When they visited Wembley the day before the final, coach Jim Sullivan was keen for Ted Ward, who could not land a goal in the previous week's Championship semi-final, to have some kicking practice to acquaint himself with conditions at the massive ground.

King George VI shakes hands with Herbert Smith, having all ready been introduced to fellow front row forwards Frank Whitcombe and Vic Darlison.

There had been 47 Challenge Cup finals previously and the stage was set for the 24th 'War of the Roses' match, in which Northern would equal Salford's feat of appearing in consecutive Wembley finals.

Prior to kick-off the King met the two teams on the pitch and Trevor Foster remembered: "We were introduced to the King before the game and Frank was bursting with pride as he shook the King's hand with that almighty 'squeeze' of his."

On Sunday May 2, the *Sunday Post* published a report on the final: "In defeating the holders of the Rugby Football League Challenge Cup, Wigan equalled the record of Widnes in succeeding twice in three Wembley finals. The contest, although it did not produce the spectacle anticipated, kept the world-record crowd of 91,465 who paid £21,000 on tenterhooks to the end.

"The most dramatic incident of a stern battle, played on turf moistened by rain and offering insecure foothold, came midway through the second half when Ernest Ward, the Bradford skipper, had the opportunity to equalize with a penalty kick from an easy position but most unusually missed.

"The incident seemed to unnerve both teams and caused the players to make innumerable mistakes. All the scoring resulted from errors and constructive play achieved nothing because of the relentless tackling and quite a few players received temporary injuries.

"There were few outstanding individuals but credit goes to Tommy Bradshaw, Les White, Billy Blan and Bill Hudson of Wigan and Frank Whitcombe, Trevor Foster and Alan Edwards of Bradford, for whom the experiment of playing the inexperienced Billy Leake at full-back proved unwise.

"Wigan scored a try after 20 minutes when Northern winger Eric Batten had a clearance kick charged down by his opposite number Jack Hilton who beat Batten in the race for the line and scored the opening try, to which Ted Ward added the goal for a 5-0 lead.

"Alan Edwards responded with a try for Bradford four minutes later and the score stayed at 5-3 until the 79th minute when prop Frank Barton sealed the game with a try for Wigan making the final score 8-3."

Bradford's only consolation was the awarding of the Lance Todd trophy, given for the outstanding performance on the day, to Frank Whitcombe. He became the oldest player, the first forward and the first man from the losing team to receive the award.

The *Yorkshire Post* reported: "The Lance Todd trophy was awarded to genial Frank Whitcombe, Bradford Northern's 34-year-old front-row forward. He had an emphatic majority over Martin Ryan and Tommy Bradshaw of Wigan and Bradford's captain Ernest Ward in the votes cast by journalists after Saturday's match."

Trevor Foster recalled: "All the players applauded Frank back into the dressing room. Even though we had lost it was really quite emotional."

Some years later, cricket and rugby league broadcaster George Duckworth commented: "No-one who witnessed it will ever forget Frank's performance that day in the pouring rain.

"The game was a low-scoring, hard fought win for Wigan, whose solid defence was just too much for Bradford Northern. So it was all the more remarkable, that Northern's No 8, Frank Whitcombe, could continually tear through this great Wigan defence".

"It took the defence *en masse* to slow and halt the inspired Frank, I doubt that he ever played a better game. The Lance Todd trophy was probably, in Frank's mind, a poor substitute for the Rugby League Challenge Cup, as it was plain to see that his goal was nothing less than going home with the Cup.

"If the Cup had been awarded to the best player, rather than the highest scoring team, Frank would have won it by a huge margin; one could not help but feel sad afterwards for the man, that his superb efforts were not matched by his team mates."

Northern's players had to recover quickly from the disappointment of losing at Wembley as they had a date with Warrington at Manchester City's Maine Road ground in the Championship final the following Saturday.

The *Yorkshire Evening Post* preview of the game on the Friday read: "There seems to be all the makings of another big rugby league crowd for the League Championship final between Bradford Northern and Warrington at Maine Road, Manchester, tomorrow.

"Neither club has yet named their side but of all the stars in both teams only Albert Johnson, Warrington's brilliant left-winger, is likely to be missing with a troublesome knee. His place will be taken by Stanley Powell, the Welsh utility back.

"Northern inevitably lost favour for tomorrow's final after their dull display in the dour Cup final against Wigan but we all know the heights they can reach and they were all well below normal form – as were Wigan – last Saturday.

"Northern did well in the scrums at Wembley, heeling on 32 against Wigan's 37, and they will have to produce a similar count against Warrington's redoubtable steam-roller pack.

"Behind the scrum there is a dire need for Northern to keep a close watch on Brian Bevan, Warrington's fleet and tricky wing who topped the try-scoring list for the season. But he too can give his opposite number Alan Edwards no scope without paying for it. Their duel should be a highlight of the match."

Warrington, who had finished the season in second place in the table against Northern's fourth, fielded seven of the players from the previous season's Challenge Cup semi-final when Northern had prevailed.

A crowd of 69,143 – a record for a match outside Wembley – saw Warrington open the scoring after 10 minutes with a penalty from Harold Palin and shortly afterwards Brian Bevan scored his 62nd try of the season to give them a 5-0 interval lead.

In the second half Warrington took a grip on the game with a try from centre Bryn Knowleden to which Palin added the goal for a 10-0 lead, and although Des Case cut the deficit with a try, to which Ernest Ward added the goal, despite protests from the Warrington players who insisted the ball had not passed between the posts, Warrington were assured of the title when centre Albert Pimblett crossed in the 77th minute and Palin added the final touch with a penalty to make the final score 15-5.

Warrington hooker Dave Cotton won the scrums 36-28, it was first time Warrington had won the Championship and the first time since the 1933-4 season that the team finishing at the top of the table had not gone on to win the title.

Boarding their aeroplane at Ringway airport, Manchester, the Bradford Northern party depart for the south of France with Frank Whitcombe at the top of the stairs

Bradford Northern had won the Yorkshire League but lost the Challenge Cup and the Championship at the final hurdle. In doing so they had enjoyed amazing financial success. In seven Cup-ties and two Championship play-offs they had been watched by more than 411,000 spectators – an average of almost 50,000 per game – which had brought receipts of over £55,000. Northern's share of that figure would be £10,000.

They rewarded their players and staff with an end-of-season treat – an event previously unheard of in rugby league. The week after the Championship final they flew from Manchester's Ringway airport, which had just opened as a civilian facility after being an RAF base during the war, to the South West of France where they were to play matches against Toulouse and Carcassonne on the Saturday and Sunday then spend the rest of their week away sight-seeing and relaxing.

New Zealander Kia Rika joined Halifax, after serving in the 28th Maori Battalion during the Second World War.

They won both matches, overcoming Olympique Toulouse 21-17 and AS Carcassonne 16-10, the latter game being the club's first experience of playing on the Sabbath. There was also sporting entertainment for several Northern players during that summer. George Bennett played baseball, as did the great Jim Sullivan, while professional sprinting had its attractions.

Alan Edwards and Jack Kitching were among the entries for a £100 race at the Shay Stadium in Halifax on July 3 1948 where other rugby league players competing included Stan Brogden, Brian Bevan, Kia Rika, Enoka Macdonald and Charlie Smith.

21

BOWING OUT

Frank Whitcombe's 1948-9 season began with a special moment during a Rugby League Supporters' Rally at Belle Vue – the venue where he had first played as a professional with Broughton Rangers – when he was presented with his Lance Todd trophy, earned by his brilliant display against Wigan in the previous season's Challenge Cup final.

The trophy was named in the memory of Lance Todd, a member of the first rugby league touring team from New Zealand to visit Britain – the famous All Golds – in 1907. He joined Wigan after the tour and would later become a major influence as manager of Salford during their successful period in the Thirties.

Bill Kirkbride holds, in his right hand, the Lance Todd trophy he won playing for Castleford against Wigan in 1970, with, in his left hand, the trophy won by Frank Whitcombe, also playing against Wigan, in the 1948 final.

He was killed in a car accident in 1942 and his many friends wanted to establish a permanent memento to his career in the game. Harry Sunderland, who had managed three Australian teams to tour England and also had charge of Wigan for a spell, was particularly close to Lance Todd and he was instrumental in setting up the trust fund to provide the outstanding player in the annual Challenge Cup final with the Lance Todd trophy.

The 'trophy', was actually a cheque for £10 and the recipient could choose to do whatever he wanted with the money. Frank decided to ask Fattorini, the famous Bradford jeweller and manufacturer of trophies and medals – the FA Cup in use today was among their creations – to produce a statue which he and his family could treasure.

As he made a brief speech after the presentation, Frank Whitcombe announced to the rugby league world that the coming season would be his last. That was the serious part of the afternoon; for the rest, the huge gathering of supporters from all over the North of England were introduced to the 1946 'Indomitables' and the 1948 Kangaroo tourists, who gave a rendition of their war cry. They cheered Wigan and Warrington players who had brought the Challenge Cup and Championship trophy respectively and they heard a medley of songs performed by the Welshmen who had figured on the Ashes-retaining 1946 trip to Australia.

Returning to action, Frank Whitcombe and his Bradford Northern colleagues quickly demonstrated their love of knockout rugby league when they played their way into the Yorkshire Cup final in which they were to meet Castleford at Headingley on October 30. Alfred Drewry reported in the *Yorkshire Post*: "The Bradford Northern players had a moorland walk at Denshaw yesterday to prepare themselves for the Yorkshire Cup final today.

"Only three years have passed since Northern last played in the Yorkshire Cup final but it is possible that only four members of the 1945 team – Eric Batten, Ernest Ward, Vic Darlison and Frank Whitcombe – will play against Castleford.

"In addition to those four George Carmichael and Donald Ward are candidates for places and team manager Dai Rees will not decide on his side until just before the match but unless he is going soft I expect him to have Billy Leake at full-back and the much improved young Gwylfa Jones at scrum-half.

"This will be Castleford's first appearance in the final and they will be all the more anxious to do well on that account. They are a sound, fearless, vigorous team with players of outstanding ability in George Langfield at scrum-half and Len Skidmore at centre. Against them is their comparative lack of big match experience.

"The mounting years are beginning to tell on some of the Northern warriors but anyone who underrates them in a final is making a mistake. They are essentially now a team for the important occasions and for that reason they are bound to start favourites, except in Castleford where enthusiasm is running high."

Alfred Drewry's match report in the following Monday's *Yorkshire Post* read: "'We want Edwards' chanted the crowd in front of the Headingley stand as the Bradford Northern players climbed the steps to receive their Yorkshire Cup winners' medals.

"But Alan Edwards, the man who had done more than anyone else to beat Castleford, was in the dressing room, white and speechless with the pain from a dislocated shoulder, waiting for a car to take him to hospital.

"He had been injured in a tackle just before the final whistle. Frank Whitcombe collected his medal for him and Dai Rees will probably deliver it when he visits Edwards at home in Manchester today. Edwards' shoulder joint was re-set at Leeds General Infirmary but it is feared he will be out of the game for a long spell, having damaged the same shoulder before.

"This was not a great final but it will be remembered for the power of Northern's rally having been 9-2 behind. Castleford took the lead in the third minute when Desmond Foreman kicked a great penalty goal from 50 yards and for more than an hour Northern tried vainly to take it from them.

"Then they scored 10 points in as many minutes. The signal for Castleford's defensive collapse was a try from Edwards, a smooth chain of long passes spanning the width of the field giving him sufficient room to make his pace decisive.

"That gave new impetus to Northern and the rest was anti-climax, Billy Leake and Trevor Foster adding tries from movements which Castleford would have easily stopped half an hour earlier. Edwards had 12 points to his name and Ernest Ward had none but Ward's powerful centre play was almost as potent as Edwards' scoring ability.

"Castleford had no-one to match Ward in the skill of manoeuvre but they had at least one man who deserved a winner's medal in Ronald Lewis, whose tackling and fielding at full-back were beyond criticism and he did not lack enterprise in a game which, until the last quarter, was fought with safety-first tactics.

"Desmond Foreman scored Castleford's try, Charlie Staines placed a goal and George Langfield dropped one with a beautiful, firm shot from the base of a scrum 35 yards out. A crowd of 31,300 returned record receipts of £5,039."

Ten days after the final the Kangaroos, led by Wally O'Connell, beat Bradford Northern 21-7 at Odsal in a match watched by 13,287 people, an amazing crowd for a Wednesday afternoon.

'Little John' reported for the *Yorkshire Evening Post*: "Bradford Northern and the Australians gave a fast and clever exhibition at Odsal this afternoon in a match where a try from Pat McMahon gave the tourists an early lead.

"The Kangaroos, with Johnny Hawke and Jack Horrigan in the centre and Bruce Hopkins at scrum-half, tackled a Northern side that had Billy Leake in the centre and George Carmichael at full-back, and they were quick enough in following up to tackle Ernest Ward in possession.

"From the attacking position gained they raided first on the right wing then on the left. Their passing was of genuine Australian standard with men dropping quickly and surely into supporting positions and McMahon gave them a deserved lead.

"It was not long before Northern showed themselves ready to accept the challenge to play open football and they moved the ball well enough to bring their wings into flying action. With Willie Davies and Ernest Ward giving a lead, well supported by Leake, they attacked furiously but were held by the Australians.

"Ernest Ward missed with a penalty shot at goal but again the Australians, with big forwards Jack Rayner and Jack Holland working well, swept the ball back to the Northern line where burly Frank Whitcombe was in the right spot at the right time to deal with a smashing run by Holland. Whitcombe rolled the Australian over to save a try in the corner.

"At the other end, Hawke, who tackled so well in the first Test, was on the job quickly when Northern broke away following an interception by Emlyn Walters. Willie Davies and Bill Leake supported sharply but Hawke wrapped it all up before anything could develop.

"Noel Mulligan and Les Cowie were getting about the field strongly and a magnificent burst from Cowie ended with him giving a scoring pass to Horrigan for the tourists' second try, Johnny Graves again failing with the kick.

"Carmichael scored Northern's first points with a penalty goal after Eric Batten had been obstructed then Batten took the ball after good passing following a scrum and dived over in the corner. Carmichael's kick was wide and the first-half scoring was completed when Vic Bulgin dropped a fine goal for the Australians."

Ernest Ward spent most of the second half limping badly and the Australians took command of the game, eventually winning 21-7 with Horrigan completing a hat-trick of tries and McMahon crossing again.

Rugby history, the Kangaroo tourists performed their war cry from 1908 to 1967.

Disappointed at losing against the Australians at Odsal, Frank Whitcombe suffered another setback when, on his final appearance for Wales, he again finished on the losing side; Australia recording a 12-5 victory before a crowd of 9,224 at the St. Helen's ground in Swansea.

Bradford Northern were again looking to recruit and on December 6 Alfred Drewry wrote in the *Yorkshire Post*: "Something out of the ordinary has to happen to prevent Dai Rees watching a Bradford Northern match. His absences since the war can be counted on the fingers of one hand but he was not at Odsal on Saturday to watch his team's emphatic victory over Leeds.

"Business in Wales kept him away and he has returned with the signature of Brian Radford, a 22-year-old second-rower. Radford, 6ft and 13st 10lb, was born in Kenfig Hill, the same village as Alan Edwards. Like Edwards he moved down the valley to Aberavon and this is his first season in big football. Leeds were also on the track of the big forward."

Frank Whitcombe played in every game Northern played between August 31 to January 22 apart from one, when he was on duty with Wales against the Kangaroos, but then he was sent off for fighting and suspended for four matches. His last game before the ban saw Brian Radford make his debut in a 17-3 defeat at York.

On Saturday April 30 1949, Frank played his penultimate game for Northern at Odsal against Warrington when the programme notes said: "The Dewsbury game on Wednesday May 11 (kick-off 6.15) gives Northern supporters the chance to bid farewell to that jovial personality Frank Whitcombe, our Test and Wales international front-row forward, who hangs up his boots after a notable and distinguished career.

"Mr Harry Hornby, the club's managing director, has had a bronze medal made in Paris and it will be presented to Frank to commemorate him winning the Lance Todd trophy in last year's Challenge Cup final."

Fittingly in Frank's last season, Northern had again battled their way to the Challenge Cup final and in doing so had become the first team to play in three consecutive Wembley deciders. They were to face Halifax at the Empire Stadium and their supporters knew that Dai Rees faced a difficult task in picking his side for the final.

George Carmichael had played at full-back in the three games leading up to the final while Ken Traill and Trevor Foster had not played for three weeks through injury. Frank Whitcombe had played in the 10 games before the final but had not played a game in the team's Challenge Cup run. The biggest issue for Rees was in finding a way to match the weight of the Halifax pack and Whitcombe's 18st 7lb was a major factor in his deliberations.

Alfred Drewry described how the arguments were resolved in the *Yorkshire Post* the day after Northern had trained at Wembley: "Brian Radford, the second-row forward who joined Bradford Northern from Welsh rugby union midway through the season and has played in every round of the Challenge Cup, has been left out of Northern's team for today's final.

"Team manager Dai Rees called his 19 players into the dressing room when they arrived at Wembley yesterday afternoon for training. First news of team selection came when full-back George Carmichael, three-quarters Emlyn Walters and Bill Jenkins, scrum-half Gwylfa Jones and forwards Herbert Smith and Brian Radford emerged still wearing their street clothes. They were out.

"Young Radford was bitterly disappointed at his omission but he was consoled by Carmichael, the victim of a parallel case last year. Carmichael had played through to the final then lost his place to Billy Leake.

"The most important move is the recall of Frank Whitcombe, a clear indication that Rees is determined to have scrummaging strength, even at the expense of speed in the loose. To make room for Whitcombe, the burly Barry Tyler moves back to second row for Radford."

In his preview of the final in the *Yorkshire Post* of Saturday May 7, Alfred Drewry admitted he was unsure of the outcome. "Last night's news from Bradford Northern at their base in Guildford and from Halifax in Weybridge

Winners and losers before the final, those who were selected are in playing kit, those who were omitted are in their 'civvies'.

was that there was no news, which is just how the people most intimately concerned wanted it to be.

"All the plans, secret and otherwise, have been made. Now it is only a question of how they work out on Wembley's green carpet.

"Earlier in the day Halifax had decided to make one change to the team which had represented them in all the previous rounds, Enoka Macdonald, the New Zealander, replacing his compatriot Kia Rika on the left wing to oppose Eric Batten.

"A study of the season's happenings makes Bradford the clearest favourites since Salford beat Barrow in 1938. But Halifax know full well that the form which was good enough to beat the favourites Huddersfield in the semi-final will be good enough to account for Northern.

"No-one expects a classic match. Halifax, fifth from the bottom of the Championship table, have no pretensions to spectacular skill while Northern are slower in the backs than they were when beating Leeds two years ago. The most significant pre-match move has been the selection of Frank Whitcombe, a declaration of strength in the scrums and close-quarter work at the cost of skirmishing speed in the open.

"In the semi-final Huddersfield outpaced Halifax but they never tired them. Dai Rees clearly makes the mastering of the Halifax forwards his first concern. The outstanding figure in the backs on either side is Ernest Ward, the greatest player of his generation.

"Halifax certainly have no-one to match him as a tactician or maker of openings but they say in centre Gareth Price they have a centre better equipped than any other man to stop Ward. There is no better tackler in the game than Price; the individual battle between the two captains should be a connoisseur's piece.

"But Halifax will have to ensure that in watching Ward they do not neglect to keep an eye on Willie Davies who was outstanding in the final two years ago, partly because Leeds were paying too much attention to Ward when Davies had the ball. You cannot afford to do that against a stand-off with the darting skill of Willie Davies.

"Alan Edwards will set a record with his fourth appearance at Wembley, twice with Salford before the war and twice with Northern. Opposite him will be Arthur Daniels, a fellow-Welshman from Pontyberem, a much-improved wing.

"Northern cannot expect much advantage on the flanks but on the counts of experience and resource in attack they seem to have the pull. I say that with some diffidence; the memory of what Halifax did to Huddersfield when the odds against them were much heavier is still fresh. Anything could happen."

A world-record crowd of 95,050 saw both teams being introduced to the Duke of Edinburgh before the kick-off then those from Bradford enjoyed the sight of their heroes taking the Challenge Cup for the second time in three years with a 12-0 victory.

Alfred Drewry's report in Monday's *Yorkshire Post* read: "Ernest Ward, leader of Bradford Northern in three successive Wembley years, captain of the Great Britain Test team and by general acknowledgement the most accomplished centre of his time, is the latest winner of the Lance Todd trophy.

"A panel of rugby league writers voted him the outstanding player in Saturday's Cup final against Halifax at Wembley, giving him twice as many votes as any other player nominated.

"Son of a former Dewsbury player, Ward, who will be 29 in July, has basked in the sunshine of greatness for several years. He has won every honour that a player can, except a League Championship medal.

Almost there. Frank Whitcombe just fails to make the touchdown, surrounded by Halifax players Dennis Chalkley (left), Des Healy (in the scrum cap) and Michael Condon (right).

"Next year he is almost certain to captain the team which visits Australia. He is one of the great ones of rugby to be remembered alongside Harold Wagstaff, Billy Batten and Gus Risman.

"Having paid that tribute to Ernest Ward I hope I will not be misunderstood in saying that had the terms of nomination been wider he might have lost the award to a man who did not even take part in the match. The biggest factor in Northern's victory was a 39-18 advantage in the scrums and that was due to the bold team construction of manager Dai Rees.

"Many people questioned his judgment in recalling Frank Whitcombe, who had played in none of the previous Cup rounds, solely with the idea of getting the ball. Never has a plan worked more perfectly. Whitcombe's 18st 7lb and Barry Tyler's 15st 7lb in the second row was too much for the Halifax front row. There you have the key to the match.

"Experience has taught us not to expect too much from Wembley finals; this was no worse than the average and considerably better in the first half with both sides throwing the ball about freely and Northern keeping the initiative only because they had more of the ball.

"The Northern of two years ago would have won with more comfort. That neither try was scored from long passing moves is a tribute to the

Ernest Ward collects the Challenge cup from the Duke of Edinburgh with Bill Leake and Eric Batten next in line.

elasticity of the Halifax cover and the accuracy of their tackling. But there was evidence in the first half that Northern have slowed down a good deal.

"When Willie Davies was running brilliantly and making openings, some of the moves which ended a few yards short of the line would have been easy tries two years ago, against even the best defences.

"Ernest Ward stamped his personality on the game with a perfectly judged kick to Eric Batten's wing, from which Batten's coolness brought the first try, Ernest Ward landing the finely-judged goal kick from the touchline. Otherwise he and Jack Kitching had scant success against Paddy Reid and Gareth Price, who tackled unerringly.

"Besides ruling the scrums, Bradford's forwards were faster in the loose. Ken Traill, who had a splendid game, was the most consistent while Trevor Foster was brilliant one moment and strangely inept the next. His try near the end was scored as if it was the easiest thing in the world to do.

Ernest Ward leaving the royal box after the presentation of the cup and medals, this was Northern's third successive appearance at Wembley.

Men of the moment: Vic Darlison and Frank Whitcombe hold aloft Ernest Ward and the Challenge cup, all three had just played in their fifth Challenge cup final.

"There was never any question about Halifax's courage and there were touches in their first-half play which suggested that with more opportunities they might have been able to spring a surprise. Stan Kielty made good of the limited supply of ball and Arthur Daniels and Enoka Macdonald several times threatened danger on the wing. But the hard work of chasing and tackling took a lot out of them all and they were flat-footed in the second half.

Bradford's points came from tries by Batten and Foster with three goals from Ernest Ward. Trevor Foster recalled: "Ernest went over especially to shake hands with Frank at the end of the game, one proud Lance Todd trophy winner to another." Frank Whitcombe would play his last game for Bradford Northern four days later.

That night the Bradford players celebrated with a dinner at the Kingsley Hotel in London, among them Eric Batten who had an injured shoulder strapped after an X-ray examination in hospital. He had played for most of the match with a cracked bone in his shoulder, the injury coming in the first few minutes of the game – just after he had scored the opening try – when he tackled Enoka Macdonald. He did not leave the field for attention.

Northern's supporters also enjoyed their night in the capital, as the *Yorkshire Post* reported on May 9: "Jubilant Bradford supporters crowded round Eros in Piccadilly Circus on Saturday night chanting 'On Ilkla Moor bah't 'at' until midnight. They almost stopped the traffic. Everywhere in the West End

Eric Batten with his arm in a sling takes the Challenge Cup to Doncaster fire station.

their colours of red, black and amber could be seen and the harsh notes of their football rattles heard.

"Halifax supporters had perforce to sing in a minor key but their blue-and-white favours were sported and there were many good-humoured encounters as rival parties met, brief witty passages which left Londoners rather bewildered and faintly amused either by this unusual ebullience or the accent of these Northerners who at home live on the opposite sides of the same hill top."

The following day the players and the Challenge Cup travelled back to Bradford, where they were welcomed by huge crowds. From the city boundary to the Town Hall the road was lined with men, women and children cheering and waving and when the team arrived in the city centre they saw 10,000 people, all waving jubilantly, in Town Hall Square.

"Amid deafening cheers, Ernest Ward, carrying the Cup, climbed up to the platform where the Lord Mayor, Councillors, County Councillors and municipal officials waited to greet the team. Close behind Ward were Frank Whitcombe and Barry Tyler, who was carrying the base of the Challenge Cup.

"The Mayor of Bradford, Alderman Cowie, told the team they had achieved something which might never happen again in the history of the game by appearing in the Cup final three years in a row and winning the trophy twice."

The Bradford Northern and Halifax teams walk out at Wembley for the 1949 Challenge Cup final

Bradford Northern's Welsh players at the 1949 Rugby League Challenge Cup victory dinner at the Kingsley Hotel, London Left to right: Frank Whitcombe, Emlyn Walters, Gwylfa Jones, Mr Gablon, Willie Davies, Des Case, Alan Edwards.

Ernest Ward spoke briefly: "We tried to play the same men in all three finals. Twice we won and once we lost but in all three this team proved themselves a great crowd of lads. We won because of our will-to-win, our determination and a great team spirit."

The official party then went into the Mayor's Parlour where the Challenge Cup was filled with Champagne several times so everyone could take a sip. The team then re-boarded the coach and drove up to Odsal, where still more crowds awaited, and the Challenge Cup and Yorkshire Cup were displayed before, looking more than a little tired, the players went home, under orders to rest before the match against Dewsbury on the Wednesday night, the 331st and last game Frank Whitcombe would play.

22

GOODBYE TO A RUGBY GIANT

The programme notes for the Bradford Northern v Dewsbury match gave an indication of the camaraderie between rugby league players at the time. "Tonight's game is for the benefit of Willie Davies and Emlyn Walters. Both are well-known to all supporters and it is hoped that the sporting public of Bradford will show their appreciation by giving generously.

"Dewsbury are the visitors and two of their players – prop forward Harry Hammond and scrum-half Harry Royal – have also been granted a benefit this season. A sporting gesture has been made by Herbert Smith, the Bradford Northern forward, who bought a rugby ball and had it autographed by the two Wembley finalists last week. He is presenting it to Harry Hammond and Harry Royal's benefit fund and it will be auctioned."

Farewell to a great player, Ernest Ward shakes hands with Frank Whitcombe before his final game for Bradford Northern.

More than 19,000 turned up at Odsal to say their goodbyes to Frank Whitcombe, who bowed out on a winning note as Northern beat Dewsbury 10-9 with tries from Trevor Foster and Alan Edwards plus two goals from Edwards.

After the game the supporters lined the steps up to the dressing room, cheering Whitcombe all the way and the mighty prop confessed as he reached the quiet of the inner sanctum: "I have a sinking feeling. I am leaving a great set of players but it is time to retire. I am 35 and could not retire at a better time than when Northern hold the Rugby League Challenge Cup."

Northern's captain Ernest Ward said of his key forward: "He has made a big contribution to team spirit" while Brian Radford, who had been displaced by Whitcombe for the Cup final after playing in all the previous rounds, added: "I am glad Frank was chosen."

He might have finished his playing career at the end of the 1948-9 season but Frank Whitcombe could not bring himself to leave the game he had played and loved for most of his adult life. His first role in his new career at Bradford Northern was as assistant to Len Higson who was in charge of Northern's A team.

One of their charges, Len Hayley – who would go on to captain Northern's first team – remembers an early meeting with the new coach. "I took the mickey out of Frank, saying he had lost his strength since retiring," said Hayley. "My next recollection is of being held upside down by my left leg.

That's that! After his final game Frank Whitcombe had one more job to do, signing the autographs for the youngsters at Odsal.

Frank held me with one hand and suspended me like a flag. He had not lost any of his strength."

Such was the impact Frank Whitcombe had on the club once his playing days were over that in early 1955 he was invited by Harry Hornby to take a seat on the board, becoming one of the first former players to become a director at Odsal.

Two years later, in 1957, Frank became vice-chairman when Cyril Bunney took over as chairman and took on the responsibility of being Northern's representative on the Rugby League Council, the game's governing body.

On December 5 Harry Hornby, the man behind the rise of Bradford Northern and the success of Odsal Stadium, severed all connections with the business; five weeks later, on Friday January 17, 1958, Frank Whitcombe died at home from pneumonia. He was 44.

The shock at his premature departure rocked the rugby league world, the city of Bradford and the whole of Yorkshire and South Wales; tributes were many and heartfelt.

George Thompson, a journalist who knew Frank well, compiled this farewell: "Frank Whitcombe might easily have gone as team manager of the party which is to tour Australia at the end of this season.

"He intended to be present at the Council meeting in Leeds and, had it been decided to make the appointment immediately, he would have submitted his name as an applicant. Early this week, at Bradford Northern's board meeting, he was hesitant about making the application, partly because he had only recently been appointed to the Council.

"Later that evening, when four of us were talking over the issue with him, he suddenly pulled a letter out of his pocket and, turning to secretary Eric England, said: 'Here is my application; send it in.' We went home together and Frank spoke mostly on two subjects: his tour chances and the necessity to find some new players at Odsal before the Challenge Cup began.

"We talked again on Wednesday about his tour chances but the following day he was ill with a cold and stayed in bed, sending his apologies for his absence to the Council.

"At the meeting Gideon Shaw, the chairman of the selection committee, said on hearing of Frank's application: 'Who better? He has been out there, he knows the game thoroughly, he can handle players and knows how to make them do their job. I'm delighted he is putting in; he is the man for me'.

"Besides having a great career as a footballer, Frank was a wonderful personality off the field. That is why he was such a character, happy-go-lucky but shrewd in many ways with his wife Doris in the pub business.

"The tales he could tell made many of Northern's board meetings twice as long as they should have been but nobody worried about that; many knew him only as a rugby player, few as a long-distance lorry driver on the trunk roads during the war.

"Two would-be thieves of his lorry while Frank was having a cup of tea will remember him. It was dark outside the café when Frank heard a lorry engine starting up. He went outside and saw a man in the driving seat of his vehicle. Frank grabbed him, pulled him out of the seat and one full-blooded punch was sufficient. He then went for the other man and again one punch dealt with him.

"Frank told me, 'I left them there on the ground, out to the world. They were asking for it'.

"Several times, though, having had to drive to London after an early morning start, he only just got back to Bradford in time to play. Three or four times he was running late after driving through London during the Blitz but always the cry in the Odsal dressing room was, 'Don't worry, Frank will get through'.

"Once he arrived only 10 minutes before kick-off. His playing togs were ready, he had got through again and there was a laugh for his team-mates when he said, 'I'll bet I've given Uncle Harry (Harry Hornby) the jitters'.

"That was Frank, always the joker and the ideal fellow, as a player or director, to have on the football coach. One of the biggest cheers the lads ever gave him was when he took over the driving of the coach to the Wembley final against Leeds. He did so with the comment: 'He's alright as a driver but Uncle Harry must have told him to go slow to cut down on our drinking time'.

"Frank never minded taking a punch from the opposition; the other fellow soon learned, as one in particular did in a Wembley final after one of Northern's smaller players had been injured. Frank fathered those smaller lads but with the game over he would often have a pint with the other fellow and joke about what the latter had received.

"Frank is a massive loss to his family, to his thousands of friends and to Bradford Northern. We shall all remember him by those words I often heard him say: 'You never know m'lad. You never know'.

Everyone in rugby league had their sad say. Cyril Bunney, Northern's new chairman, said: "I don't know what to think. This is a terrible blow. He will be a tremendous loss to his family and to his friends at Odsal. No man is irreplaceable but he was as near to me as possible in all the help and guidance he has given to me and to Bradford Northern. His loyalty knew no bounds; this season alone he has travelled thousands of miles at his own expense looking at players for Odsal."

From Charles Horsfall, the chairman of the Council, came this: "What bad luck for his family and Bradford Northern in the help he was giving in re-building the club. He was always a great sportsman and could take it and give it with a smile in addition to being a wonderful forward."

Bill Fallowfield, the secretary of the RFL, said: "What a pity. I liked Frank immensely. He was the kind of man the game can ill afford to lose. He had only been a member of the Rugby League Council a short time but his knowledge and genuine love of the game would have been most helpful."

Dai Rees, Northern's guiding light through the glory years, added: "Frank Whitcombe had a great part in putting Bradford Northern on the rugby league map. The names of Frank Whitcombe and Odsal are synonymous. He was one of the game's greatest personalities. Genial Frank has gone but his name will live on at Odsal."

Jim Sullivan wrote in his *News of the World* column: "The game has lost two great personalities by the death of Frank Whitcombe of Bradford Northern and Walter Mooney of Leigh, both of whom toured Australia.

"Frank, whom the London press termed the 'Man Mountain' after his Lance Todd trophy winning performance for Bradford Northern against Wigan in 1948, first played for Broughton Rangers after leaving Cardiff. I begged Wigan officials to sign him, but he never arrived at Central Park.

"Frank loved his rugby and had been mentioned as a possibility of being one of the managers of the forthcoming Australian Tour."

Frank's great friend Trevor Foster gave his own, brief tribute: "Frank Whitcombe was the outstanding prop forward of his generation alongside Ken Gee, the Wigan legend."

Arthur Clues, the Australian forward who had seen both sides of Frank, said: "Many is the tussle I've had with Frank but off the field we were the greatest of pals. I reckon he is one of the best front-row forwards for his size ever to play football."

The renowned journalist George Thompson paid tribute to Frank, from his time in rugby union, when he wrote: "Before the war, Frank was stationed at Aldershot, under the command of Colonel Charles 'Jock' Hartley OBE, who was a senior Vice President of the Rugby Football Union and, during the war, Director of the Army Sports Board. When I was in the Colonel's London Office during the war he asked me whether I knew anything about a rugby player called Frank Whitcombe and expressed the opinion that he was the best forward he had ever seen playing in the

Army. The Colonel apparently idolised Frank, until he joined the Rugby League".

Writing in the Daily Herald, Alan Cave commented: "Frank Whitcombe, Bradford Northern's heavy weight forward has gone, it is hard to realise that this hearty young man, after all he was only 44, has suddenly been taken from our midst".

"This mountain of a man was a rugby artist; his playing weight in Bradford Northern's glorious cup days of the late 40s was eighteen and a half stones. Yet he was as nimble as a ballet dancer, no prop forward of his bulk could be imagined to distribute the ball like Frank Whitcombe did, he was amazing".

"Swift as a half back and almost impossible to effectively tackle, because 'smiling Frank' nearly always got in his pass. Hooking must have been a real pleasure with the massive Whitcombe on one side as Vic Darlison, the Odsal hooker in those great Bradford years, will admit".

"Frank Whitcombe was always so quick on the break and many's the man who has been unexpectedly grabbed by Whitcombe, who so suddenly wheeled round and collared him; he was half a pack by himself and a wonderful inspiration".

"Frank was manager Dai Rees' secret weapon in the last of Northern's three successive Wembleys in 1949, when after the big fellow had missed earlier rounds, he 'unexpectedly' brought him on for the final against Halifax, as the man to upset so many of Halifax's plans. Of course Dai Rees had it planned all along and Northern won the cup".

"When his playing days were over Frank Whitcombe turned to the administrative side and with every promise of success, his old Odsal team pals will miss Frank very much, so shall we all".

On Saturday January 18, Bradford Northern visited Doncaster at Bentley Road where there was a minute's silence in tribute to Frank Whitcombe and the Northern players wore black arm-bands.

Three weeks after Frank's death Trevor Foster was elected on to the Northern board as his friend's successor.

Frank's funeral service was held at St Luke's Church in East Morton, near Keighley, on January 22 and internment was at Morton Banks Cemetery.

He had played in five Challenge Cup finals for Bradford Northern and the only other players to share that record were Ernest Ward, Donald Ward, Vic Darlison and Eric Batten; all four attended the funeral, as did many former players and supporters.

The coffin was borne by Malcolm Davies (Cardiff and Bradford Northern), Trevor Foster (Newport and Bradford Northern), Phil Crabtree

Thirsty Work! Frank Whitcombe behind the bar where he had on display the Yorkshire League trophy and his 1946 tour cap.

(Bradford Northern), Stanley Rees (son of Dai Rees), Bob Smith (Bradford Northern) and Brian Radford(Aberavon and Bradford Northern).

Much is made of the team-spirit which helped Bradford Northern become the club they did and one consequence of Frank's death underlines that strength. After the funeral, Trevor Foster approached Doris Whitcombe and her family and offered to help out for a few weeks at the Airedale Heifer near Keighley, the last public house Frank and Doris had run together. Trevor volunteered to pull a few pints and collect empty glasses.

Twenty years later he was still working at the Heifer on busy Saturday nights, proving once again that friendships made in sport often last longer than playing careers; that loyalty is a lasting condition of the mind and body.

23

THE WHITCOMBE SPORTING DYNASTY

As would be expected of two young Whitcombes, Frank's sons Brian and Frank junior, who had enjoyed such a rugby education when Bradford Northern players would stay at their house over weekends, were keen to be involved in the oval ball game.

Frank junior began his organised sporting life as a left-back playing football for Grange Boys Grammar School and Brian and Frank took their first steps in rugby league with the Sedbergh Boys Club based near their home in Bradford.

But in August 1952, the boys were taken by their father to Lidget Green, the ground of Bradford RFC, where they were joined by the sons of three other rugby league internationals, Sandy Orford, George Bennett and Ken Jubb.

Bradford's victorious team at Gloucester, during their 1954 Easter Tour, with 17 year-old Frank Whitcombe junior fourth from right in the back row.

Under the tutelage of David Firth, a great rugby man and then the wise captain of Bradford's second XV, the Whitcombes developed rapidly and Frank became one of the youngest to play for the first team when he made four appearances at prop at the age of 16 in the 1952-3 season.

The following season Frank established himself as a first XV prop and he played in a memorable 8-3 victory over Gloucester at the forbidding Kingsholm ground on April 19 1954 when he was just 17.

Such was his progress he was called up by Yorkshire for their pre-County Championship trials the following autumn and performed well enough to earn selection to face Ulster, the county's traditional season-opening match, in which the opposition invariably included their Irish internationals. He was Bradford's 136th player to be selected for Yorkshire.

The following week he played against Northern Command and made his County Championship debut against Cumberland and Westmorland as an 18-year-old. In that season Bradford would supply six players to the

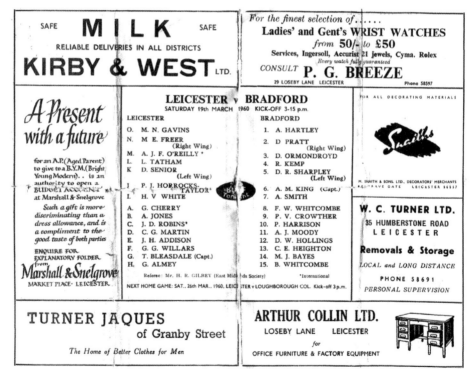

LEICESTER v **BRADFORD**
SATURDAY 19th MARCH 1960 KICK-OFF 3-15 p.m.

LEICESTER		BRADFORD	
O.	M. N. GAVINS	1.	A. HARTLEY
N.	M E. FREER	2.	D PRATT
	(Right Wing)		(Right Wing)
M.	A. J. F. O'REILLY *	3.	D. ORMONDROYD
L.	L. TATHAM	4.	R. KEMP
K	D. SENIOR	5.	D. R. SHARPLEY
	(Left Wing)		(Left Wing)
J	P. J. HORROCKS-TAYLOR*	6.	A. M. KING (Capt.)
I.	H. V. WHITE	7.	A. SMITH
A.	G. CHERRY	8.	F. W. WHITCOMBE
B.	A. JONES	9.	P. V. CROWTHER
C.	J. D. ROBINS*	10.	P. HARRISON
D.	C. G. MARTIN	11.	A. J. MOODY
E.	J. H. ADDISON	12.	D. W. HOLLINGS
F.	G. G. WILLARS	13.	C. E. HEIGHTON
G.	T. BLEASDALE (Capt.)	14.	M. J. BAYES
H.	G. ALMEY	15.	B. WHITCOMBE

Referee: Mr. H. R. GILBEY (East Midlands Society)   *International
NEXT HOME GAME: SAT., 26th MAR., 1960. LEICESTER v LOUGHBOROUGH COL. Kick-off 3 p.m.

Frank and Brian Whitcombe both played for Bradford against Leicester Tigers at Welford Road on March 19, 1960. In the Leicester team were future Tiger coaches 'Chalkie' White and Graham Williars. The final season in which Leicester Tigers wore letters on their jerseys, in preference to numbers, was 1997-8.

Yorkshire team: Colin Heighton, Peter Hodgson, Tommy Ramsden, Rod Turner, David Howard and the young Whitcombe.

Conscription would stay in force in Britain until 1960 with all able-bodied young men required to spend two years in uniform as they completed National Service.

As a result of this, rugby in the Services enjoyed a hugely successful period, with each branch desperate to have the best players – all service men played as amateurs so rugby league stars could play alongside union men – in their ranks.

The great Alex Murphy was capped by the RAF during his National Service and formed a formidable half-back partnership with Mickey Booth from Gloucester as his scrum-half. Years later Murphy attended the RAFRU 90th anniversary dinner and wrote an article for the menu: "It almost didn't happen. I had been contacted by the top brass at RAF Haydock regarding

Frank Whitcombe junior proudly wears his Yorkshire county cap and jersey.

my forthcoming National Service and when I received a notification to go for a test in Liverpool along I trotted, did my aptitude test and was told to report to Catterick.

"The following night I was in bed and there was a thunderous knock at the front door. I went downstairs to find Joe Nolan, the chief at RAF Haydock, standing there. 'Why didn't you contact me before you went for your test,' he barked. 'If you end up in the Army I'll be in big trouble'

"How it happened I will never know but I joined the RAF and it turned out to be two of the most enjoyable years of my life. I reported to RAF Cardington for a two-week stint and on my second day in the service played in an Inter-Command match for Technical Training Command, beating Transport Command 23-0.

"I only spent a week at RAF Cardington as I had special permission to play for St Helens in a Cup game, which we won, then moved on to RAF Bridgenorth for six weeks of square-bashing before a posting to RAF Haydock just 10 miles from home.

"We played RAF matches every Wednesday and I was allowed to play for Saints at weekends as long as there was no clash of fixtures. On one occasion Saints had a home Challenge Cup match but the RAF had an Inter-Services game at the same time. How was I going to get out of it?

"In the Wednesday game, I was advised not to play my usual game of running with the ball and instead to play a rugby union stand-off's game of booting the ball into touch every time it was passed to me by the scrum half.

I did this up to half-time, when we were losing, and before I had reached the dressing room I was called to one side by Bill Thompson – who was the officer in charge of the team – and warned that he had realised what I was doing and that if I did not turn the match round in the second half I would be posted to RAF Gan in the Indian Ocean.

"This was a direct threat from the RAFRU chairman Group Captain Cameron. Anyway, we won and I was allowed to play for Saints but got sent off so it had all been for nothing. After that all went well.

"I played against Welsh rugby union clubs and travelled to France to play; the only team I was not allowed to play against were the Springboks as they said I was a professional. I was privileged to play in an Inter-Services final against the Army, which we won, and still have the linesman's flag which was presented to me as man-of-the-match.

"I was released to go on the Ashes-winning Great Britain rugby league tour of Australia and New Zealand in 1962. I was injured in the final Test against Australia and I returned home early to England.

"With not much of my National Service left I thought I would be released early but no such luck. I was so important at RAF Haydock that I was promoted to be in charge of the greenhouse where my tomatoes became legendary, especially in St Helens market!"

Brian Whitcombe spent his National Service years in the Royal Artillery which, alongside Bradford prop Peter Harrison, he played for the Gunners Club.

Former Wakefield RFC and Yorkshire centre John Kay served in the 1st Battalion the Yorkshire and Lancashire Regiment; he remembers the quality of rugby players during the days of National Service: 'Major Crow' Fraser, along with his secretary Major Adams, at 1st Training Regiment, Royal Signals, trawled through all the intakes of recruits every six weeks and cherry-picked as many top rugby players of either code as they could.

"As a result 1TR RS were the pre-eminent Army side and won the Army Cup many times and provided the bulk of the players for the full Army XV as well as Northern Command. Fixtures were often arranged between the Northern Division County Championship teams and the Army's Northern Command as warm-up games for both."

"Frank Whitcombe Jnr, a current Yorkshire player, was taken for 1TR RS and another Yorkshire player there was Phil Horrocks-Taylor, a future England and British Lions fly-half, who recalled his rugby at Catterick: "At various stages many top rugby players such as England rugby union internationals Nim Hall and Peter Jackson, Great Britain centre Brian Gabbitas and Scotland's full-back Ken Scotland served in 1TR RS."

National Service brought two young Cardiff rugby players to Catterick who would make a huge impact on rugby league. First came future Great Britain captain Clive Sullivan, who turned professional with Hull FC, while Royal Signals rugby was the beginning of a glorious career for Billy Boston.

He remembers: "I signed for Wigan when I was doing my National Service at Catterick after winning the Army Cup final against the Welsh Guards at Aldershot. Wigan kept it quiet for me. They had showed me a suitcase containing £1,500 in £5 notes; my mother jokingly asked for £3,000, to which the Wigan chairman instantly agreed. At home neither Cardiff RFC nor Wales had shown any interest in me."

After just six week in uniform Frank Whitcombe Jnr was picked to play for the Army against Cumberland and Westmoreland at Cockermouth. Following on from his father, at this time vice-chairman of Bradford Northern, the young Whitcombe, at 21, weighed 15st.

That invitation was quickly followed by two more, one to play for the Army against Oxford University at Iffley Road on January 23 1958, the other to join former Yorkshire and England scrum-half Denis Shuttleworth in the Army team to face Gloucester at Kingsholm two days later. Young Whitcombe seemed certain to win his first Army cap before long.

But such dreams were not to last. Frank Snr's death on January 17 meant that Frank Jnr was unable to play in either game as he was needed to help run the family business and was discharged from the Army on compassionate grounds.

Frank junior married Mollie Cockcroft in Keighley on January 24 1961; it was a marriage between two rugby families. Mollie's father Tommy had played on the wing for Keighley RLFC during the Thirties and her brother Billy would follow in father's footsteps, a tall, elusive wing whose most notable achievement was to score one of Keighley's two tries against Wigan at Central Park in the John Player trophy in December 1973, Keighley's only success on that ground in their history.

Tommy Cockcroft and his wife Eileen ran the bar at Keighley RLFC's Lawkholme Lane ground for many years.

By this time, young Frank was a fixture in a Yorkshire team which was beginning to have the look of possible County Champions for the first time since 1953.

In the freezing winter of 1962-3 all sport was badly affected and rugby's traditional fixture programme was no exception. It was normal that the County Championship was concluded well before the start of the Five Nations' Championship in late January but in that bitter season 12 weeks were lost and Yorkshire's crucial Northern Group play-off game against Lancashire was long delayed.

John Kaye remembers that match going ahead at Twickenham after the great rivals had finished level following the group matches. "The game was played under wet conditions although I don't think it was actually raining. A strong wind was blowing over the open South Terrace straight up the pitch.

"Yorkshire faced the wind in the first half, which ended at 3-3. John Brash had opened the scoring for Yorkshire before Keith Bearne levelled the scores for Lancashire. In the second half, Ian Gibson scored a try for Yorkshire when he intercepted a pass, behind the try-line, from Lancashire's stand-off Tom Brophy. All Ian had to do was catch the ball and touch down.

"He scored not too far from the posts but in the strong wind the conversion attempt was blown wide."

Frank Whitcombe Jnr's performance in the match was mentioned by Monty Griffiths in the *South Wales Echo*: "In the Yorkshire XV, which won the Battle of the Roses at Twickenham on Saturday was a Welsh prop from Bradford, Frank Whitcombe junior.

Frank Whitcombe (second from left) goes in search of the ball in Yorkshire's playoff game against Lancashire at Twickenham, March 9 1963.

"I add the word junior because his late father, Frank Whitcombe senior, was one of the greatest Welsh rugby league forwards of all time. For a good many years now the younger Whitcombe has been recognised as one of the best in the North. One wonders whether he could have gone further still if his skills could have been displayed to the selectors with a club nearer to Wales."

Formidable scrummaging was not the only thing young Frank Whitcombe had in common with his father; he was also renowned for looking after his team-mates. Peter Crowther, who would play a record number of 414 first XV games at hooker for Bradford, remembers: "I made my debut for Bradford at Sale the week after playing for Yorkshire Schools against Wales Schools at Otley.

The Yorkshire team for the County Championship final, April 27 1963.
Back Row L-R: Ian King (Yorkshire touch judge), John Kaye (Wakefield), Rodney Childs (Halifax), Richard Bell (Halifax), John Waind (Wakefield), Mike Bayes (Bradford), Ian Gibson (Leicester Tigers), Frank Whitcombe (Bradford), Richard Baldwin (Harrogate), Peter Johnson (Headingley).
Front Row L-R: David Bell (Hull & East Riding), Mike Campbell-Lamerton (Halifax), Frank Malir (Yorkshire Rep RFU Committee), Colin Heighton (Sheffield), Mike Byrne (Yorkshire president), Phil Horrocks-Taylor (Leicester Tigers), John Brash (Middlesbrough), David Senior (Leicester Tigers).

"Sale's hooker was the former England captain Eric Evans, a real hard man, but Frank looked after me like an uncle. A few weeks later we played a Yorkshire club with a formidable reputation and their prop said to me in the first scrum 'which side of your jaw do you want breaking?' Three scrums later the would-be hit man was flattened in a scrum. He did not make any more threats."

Next for Yorkshire was an 8-3 semi-final win against Hampshire at Headingley on April 3. Frank Davies wrote in the *Daily Mail*: "What a magnificent example was set by the Scottish giant Mike Campbell-Lamerton who used every ounce of his 17st in the scrums, line-outs and loose.

"How he and his lock partner John Waind, those chunky props Rodney Childs and Frank Whitcombe and hooker Roger Baldwin found the stamina to shove like tanks and chase round in the loose like greyhounds I don't know."

Victory took Yorkshire to a final against reigning champions Warwickshire, who were appearing in their sixth successive final, at their fortress of Coundon Road, Coventry, on April 27, before a tightly packed crowd of 15,000.

Again, John Kaye remembers: "The significant part of the game was the last five minutes. Yorkshire were leading 10-8, David Senior having scored a try under the posts, running over Cook, the Warwickshire full-back, as though he wasn't there.

"I can see that try with my mind's eye as though it was yesterday but can't for the life of me visualise the other one (it was scored by John Brash). David Bell must have converted both of them to give us 10 points.

"With about five minutes to go, about 40 yards from their line on our left John Waind, who was up against two international second-rows in Tom Pargetter and John Owen, won the ball at a line-out with a clean, two-handed catch.

"He burst clear, straight past their scrum-half George Cole and only had full-back Cook to beat but Peter Jackson, the multi-capped England wing, was giving chase. Nowadays John would have taken the ball into contact with Cook and waited for support but he was wary of being caught and tackled by Jackson and having to release the ball on the ground.

"In the event he decided to kick ahead, not a common skill among second-row forwards, and the ball skewed off his boot and into touch about 10 yards from the Warwickshire goal-line, giving them a defensive line-out.

"Incredibly we won the ball again and it was given back to our scrum-half Peter Johnston. In those days you could still kick to touch on the full and that is what Johnston should have done to keep us camped on their line.

"Instead he tried to open up play and from there it all went downhill. He threw the most awful pass behind Phil Horrocks-Taylor and Peter Robbins, Warwickshire's England flanker, hacked the ball upfield. The ball flew to our right wing Richard Bell, who had ample time to fall on the ball, secure it and kick to touch.

"Instead he tried to pick it up but only succeeded in fumbling it back towards our line, not just once but three times. I was screaming at him to fall on the ball but he probably couldn't hear. Eventually the ball bobbled and bounced up straight into the hands of Frame, who set off for our line.

"Phil Horrocks-Taylor, Ian Gibson and myself, having had to turn and chase, were way behind but David Senior covered across from the left wing and tackled Frame just short of the line. There was a photograph in the next issue of *Rugby World* quite clearly showing Frame with his face pressed into the ground with Senior on top of him and with the ball in the crook of his arm, grounded a good two feet short of the line.

"The referee, M. King of Surrey, a portly military gentleman, was way behind play and didn't see Frame make a double movement to put the ball over the line, which should have meant a penalty to Yorkshire. The ball then squirted out of Frame's control but back out of the in-goal area and I tried to gather it, knocking it back into the in-goal area as I did so but, of course, I couldn't touch it down as that would have conceded a five-yard scrum.

"I then gathered it and kicked it to touch but the referee decided I had knocked on and awarded Warwickshire a scrum on our line which they pushed over for the winning try; Cole converted to give them a lead of 13-10.

"At that late stage we still had an outside chance to rescue the game when I gathered a loose ball on our right-hand touchline just inside their half and saw Senior clear over on the left. Unfortunately my cross-kick bounced away from him and the chance was lost and with it went the game and the County Championship.

"There was small consolation for me as this was my third County Championship game that season which meant I qualified for my County cap but had we won I would have also qualified for a County blazer, the normal requirement being 10 games, which I missed by one. Mentally scarred for life!

"I visited Richard Bell at his restaurant in Filey a few times and he definitely blamed himself for not securing that loose ball when he had the chance."

Frank Whitcombe Jnr had made a sufficient impression during Yorkshire's run to the County Championship final to have persuaded the England selectors to include him in their plans for their final trial match before their meeting with the All Blacks on January 4 1964.

He was a reserve for the Probables v Possibles game but that was not good enough for one observer, Pat Marshall, of the *Daily Mail*: "Hard men, fit men, strong men; that is the crying need for English rugby. Without them the All Blacks will crush England as surely as they crushed Western Counties on Saturday.

"I would hazard a guess that those two tough Yorkshire props Rodney Childs and Frank Whitcombe would massacre the front row chosen to represent the Possibles."

The 1963-4 tour of the British Isles and France by the seventh All Blacks, under the leadership of prop forward Wilson Whineray, was a special time for rugby as the 36-game itinerary took the tourists to all corners of the land, giving the opportunity to players of pitting themselves against the acknowledged world champions and giving thousands of rugby followers the chance to see the famous All Blacks – and their threatening Haka war dance.

A team representing the North Eastern Counties – Yorkshire, Northumberland and Durham – was chosen to face the All Blacks on January 11 1964 and such was the interest in the match no club ground could cater for the numbers of spectators expected.

So, with the co-operation of the Yorkshire Agricultural Society, it was decided to play the fixture at the Great Yorkshire Showground in Harrogate and the decision was justified as the sold-out stand and packed bankings around the pitch illustrated.

Ralph Caulton played for the All Blacks at Harrogate.

Frank Whitcombe junior played in many big matches in his rugby career but this was the biggest by far. His immediate opponent was Wilson Whineray, the All Blacks' captain, and his fellow prop was Rodney Childs from Halifax. Twenty-nine years earlier Frank's father and Arthur Childs, from Abertillery, had packed down together in a trial match for the Welsh national team.

Playing for the All Blacks that day in 1964 was winger Ralph Caulton, who made 50 appearances for the New Zealanders, 16 of them Test matches, between 1959 and 1964. He was the 600th man to earn selection for the All Blacks and scored 31 tries, eight of which were in international matches.

He would say half a century later: "It is my pleasure to supply details of the visit of the 1963-4

All Blacks to Harrogate. I played in that game but I have had to refer to some old clippings and my own tour diary to take me back in time.

"We stayed at Ilkley, at the Craiglands Hotel, arriving there on the Thursday January 9. On the Friday we were taken to Beverley, the headquarters of the RAF fighter base at Leconfield. We had lunch in the Officers' Mess then watched a flying display consisting of two Hawker Hunters, one Spitfire and three Lightnings. Air Marshall Gus Walker flew in at 3pm to have afternoon tea with us.

Ralph Caulton in Wellington, in 2015.

"On Saturday we left by coach for Harrogate, taking an hour to get to the Showground. It was overcast and quite windy and the 'locals' started well, having 11 points on the board in as many minutes.

"We knew that although we would have the wind behind us in the second half it was going to take some mighty effort to overhaul the lead the opposition had established. However, we managed to grind out enough points to win 17-11.

"Don Clarke was a great asset to our side with his strong punting and prolific goal-kicking but we were caught out now and again when his accuracy deserted him and the rest of the team had to dig deep to keep the points coming.

"Strangely, we left the ground almost immediately after the game, which was not normally the case, and the trip back to Ilkley took two hours due to the heavy traffic."

John Waind, the Wakefield and Yorkshire second-row forward, played for the North Eastern Counties that day when he was instructed to mark the legendary Colin Meads in the line-outs. His club-mate John Kaye watched the game from the stand and afterwards met-up with Waind for a drink.

"I saw John in the evening," recalls Kaye. "He had an even set of teeth before the game but afterwards the teeth on the right side of his mouth were 1mm longer than those on the left. He had a bruise which

The great New Zealand forward Colin Meads.

covered the whole right side of his face from the corner of his mouth to his ear, up to his eyebrow and down to his nose.

"I asked him who had hit him. 'Colin Meads,' he replied. How often, I said. "Just once,' he responded ruefully.

"What had you done, I enquired. 'I don't know,' said John, 'but I must have done something!"

Colin Meads would become one of four of the 1963-4 tourists to become Knights of the Realm, the others being Sir Brian Lochore, Sir John Graham and Sir Wilson Whineray, who, after the match, gave Frank his All Blacks tie in exchange for Frank's Yorkshire tie.

In the 1965-6 season, Bradford RFC celebrated their centenary whilst Frank Jnr was in his second year as captain of the first XV. The highlight of the year was the clubs' march to the Yorkshire Cup final in which they were to meet Harrogate at Otley's Cross Green ground.

The *Yorkshire Post* reported on the proceedings: "The team spirit which enabled Bradford to beat Harrogate 8-3 in the Yorkshire Cup final was

North Eastern Counties v New Zealand, January 11 1964.

North Eastern Counties
Back row L-R: J Donald, Frank Whitcombe Jnr, Tony Peart, John Waind, I Brown, Don Rutherford.
Middle L-R: M Forster, Roger Sangwin, J Rogan, Peter Johnston, J Ranson.
Front L-R: Rodney Childs, Mike Weston (captain), Colin Heighton, Stan Hodgson.

New Zealand
Back row L-R: McFarlane 'Mac' Herewini, Ralph Caulton, Brian Lochore, Paul Little, Colin Meads.
Middle L-R: Don Clarke, Keith Nelson, Jules Le Lievre, Ian Smith, Ken Gray.
Front L-R: Bruce Watt, Kevin Briscoe, Wilson Whineray (captain), John Graham, Dennis Young.

Frank Whitcombe Jnr captained Bradford RFC in 1964.
Back row L-R: Johnny Wild, Stan Hutchinson, David Holland, Richard Birkett, John Haslam, Brian Whitcombe, Peter Crowther, Tony Smith.
Front row L-R: Alistair Mackintosh, Geoff Blackburn, Roger Pickering, Frank Whitcombe Jnr (captain), Julian Holdsworth, Mike Watson, Geoff Cooke.

demonstrated when Mike Dixon and Frank Whitcombe went up together at the end of the match to receive the trophy.

"Whitcombe, the club's captain, had been out of action for a good part of the season through injury and during his absence Dixon had taken over the leadership. So well did Bradford play that when Whitcombe returned he insisted that Dixon should continue to lead the side and it was Dixon who led Bradford to their first Yorkshire Cup triumph for 41 years.

"With an equally sporting gesture Dixon insisted that Whitcombe should share with him the honour of receiving the Cup."

Frank Whitcombe was now heavily committed to helping his mother run the Airedale Heifer, on the main road between Bingley and Keighley and a popular pub of choice for many, not least sportsmen who would retire there for a drink after their game of rugby, football or cricket.

Rugby union then was an amateur game and with Bradford games as far away as London and the West Country, Frank was aware that his absence on Saturday evenings – the busiest time of the week in the Heifer – was not in the best interests of the business.

At the age of 30 and with several years still to play quality rugby ahead of him, he decided to leave Bradford, where he had appeared in 329 first-class matches, plus 31 for Yorkshire, and join the Keighley club, whose fixture list did not include long-haul journeys to the same extent as Bradford's.

Brother Brian, after 174 games for Bradford, also left Lidget Green and began a new playing career with Keighley. He and his wife Doreen would often be 'on duty' behind the bar with Frank and Mollie, the formidable Doris Whitcombe and the loyal Trevor Foster when the regulars packed the Airedale Heifer. Brian is still a prominent figure at Keighley and rarely misses a first XV game.

But before saying farewell to Bradford, Frank had spotted a young forward who, he thought, had the potential to become a good player. Jim Golby was the son of Joe Golby, an outstanding rugby league player during Frank senior's career at Odsal.

Joe, who won a Championship winner's medal with Wigan in 1934, had appeared for Bradford Northern as a guest player during the war, and

The Whitcombe family home for over 25 years, The Airedale Heifer Inn, Keighley.

Jim would go on to become captain of Bradford, playing 318 games for the club and becoming a Yorkshire County player.

Jim Golby recalls: "I first met Frank Whitcombe at a pre-season trial game at Bradford Salem RUFC; I was playing with Salem during my holidays from college.

"After the game Frank came over to me in the dressing room and asked if I was interested in playing rugby at a higher level. I told him I was still at college and was expected to play for them during term time so he gave me a telephone number to contact should circumstances change.

"They did and in November 1966 I made contact with Bradford RFC and was selected to play for the Vandals – the second XV. I played two games with the Vandals then was selected make my first XV debut against Nottingham at Lidget Green.

"Frank had been left out of the team for that game but was called in at the last minute as one of the props was injured. He gave a master-class that day; I remember it vividly. However, he had decided by then to join

The Keighley team before their first game in the Wartime Emergency League against Huddersfield on 30 September 1939.
Back row L-R: Arthur Thurling, Jim Traill, Len Mason, Jack Bleazard, George Harris, Unsworth*, Jim Gill, Norman Foster. Front row L-R: Poole*, Les Sowden, Don Phelps, Tom Cockcroft, Tom Bancroft. (* trialists, full names unknown)

Billy Cockcroft gets his pass away for Keighley against Bramley, on Boxing Day 1973.

Keighley – I think he played for them the following week – and he was a major loss to Bradford but a great gain for Keighley."

Frank was made captain of Keighley for the 1967-8 season and held the position for four seasons after which he took up the vice-captaincy to support the club's new leader Kevin McGee. He later led the second team and played a major role in bringing through young players who would become the backbone of the first XV.

His ability to encourage youngsters was given a new dimension when he took over the running of the Colts XV, a position he held, with great support from wife Mollie, for 15 years, educating many under-18s not only in rugby but also in growing up. He became a life member of the club – as did Mollie – and the club's stand at their Utley ground is named in Frank's honour.

Frank and Mollie had four children Sara, Emma, who would play hockey for Bradford Schools and retain a true devotion to rugby union and Simon, who died tragically young, but it was Martin, the eldest, who carried on the Whitcombe rugby dynasty.

He grew up watching his father and Uncle Brian playing for Keighley and on winter Sundays would accompany his grandfather Tommy Cockcroft to watch his uncle, Billy Cockcroft at the Lawkholme Lane ground.

Martin would help the groundsman, Billy Watson, collect the corner flags and clean up the changing rooms after matches, listening all the time to Billy, a man steeped in rugby league. He had played at hooker for Huddersfield in the 1934-5 Challenge Cup final and was capped by England against Australia while playing for Keighley.

Martin's rugby education was furthered during games of touch-and-pass on the lawn behind the Airedale Heifer with his father, Uncle Brian, Trevor Foster and another former rugby league star Ken Davies.

Billy Watson wearing his England jersey.

He was enrolled at Keighley RUFC at an early age and progressed through the Bantams and Colts sections of the club, latterly under the guidance of Terry O'Brien, a Welshman from Mountain Ash, who had turned professional with Keighley.

At Bingley Grammar School – where Willie Davies had once taught – he was coached by Mike Atkinson, a former winger with the Bingley club, and such was his progress he was capped four times at prop by England Schools 19-Group in the 1979-80 Five Nations' tournament.

When it was time to leave school he decided to join the RAF. In February 1981, while still training as a Physical Training Instructor at RAF Cosford, he won the first of his 14 RAF caps when the Air Force were beaten by the Royal Navy 15-12 at Twickenham.

Martin's rank at that time was Aircraftsman and Dave Smith, the secretary of the RAFRU observed: "Martin became one of the very few to be capped while at the lowest rank in the RAF. Paul Bate, the Rosslyn Park full-back, had been capped by the RAF in 1978 and in 1981 Martin Whitcombe became the last AC to be capped. It will probably never happen again."

ACs were known in the RAF as "Erks" and there had earlier been several outstanding 'Erks' capped by the RAF, among them: 1952 – Jim Greenwood (Scotland and British Lions); 1955 – Mick Sullivan (Great Britain RL); 1957 – Don Rutherford (England and British Lions) and Jim Challinor (Great Britain RL); 1959 – Austin Rhodes (Great Britain RL); 1961 – Alex Murphy (Great Britain RL and an inaugural inductee into the RL Hall of Fame); 1966 – Billy Steele (Scotland and British Lions).

Air Force rugby gave Martin Whitcombe his first taste of the senior game and his next step, taken in July 1981, came when he was posted to RAF North Luffenham where he met his wife Carron and accepted an invitation to join Leicester Tigers.

'Chalkie' White, the club's hugely-influential coach, picked him to make his first appearance against their great Midlands rivals Northampton at Franklin Gardens and he made his home debut the following week against Swansea when he scored a try. Later in the season he was capped by Leicestershire in the County Championship.

In those days the RAF had an annual Friday night fixture with Leicester at Welford Road and Martin clearly remembers one of those games. " I was playing for my employer – the RAF – and my good friend Steve Kenney was playing for the Tigers.

"Steve was the ultimate club player, making over 360 appearances for the Tigers, and the only time I saw him lose his temper was with me.

"After I had trodden on his hand for the third time he picked up a clod of turf and hurled it at me, much to the amusement of the other players. He missed me so grabbed more mud and grass and finally connected. Despite the encouragement of my team mates, who were all laughing, I could not get angry with him.

Leicester Tigers, Dean Richards and Martin Whitcombe. Coach, Chalkie White was not afraid to play young forwards in his team. (Photos: Neville Chadwick)

icester Tigers players Ian Smith (left) and Steve Kenney look on as Martin Whitcombe is about tackle Jim Calder (Barbarians), December 22 1983.

"We walked off the field at the end, me with my arm round Steve's shoulders, him still complaining. Today we always have a laugh over the incident whenever we meet up."

Martin's first experience of playing against an international team came, on December 29 1981, when he played for Combined Services against Tony Shaw's Australian Wallabies at Aldershot Military Stadium.

Playing for Leicester also gave the young Whitcombe his first taste of playing abroad. He played in both games against Zimbabwe on the club's 1982 tour; winning 22-18 in Bulawayo and drawing 15-15 in Harare then two years later he played against the Arabian Gulf in Bahrain and the Southern Gulf in Dubai.

On May 10 1985 during Leicester's tour of France – this was the era before front-row replacements were allowed – Whitcombe played most of a bruising game against Olympique Chambérien with a broken fibula. Leicester lost 32-6.

Steve Kenney (left) is in support of Martin Whitcombe; Leicester Tigers against the Barbarians at Welford Road, December 22 1983.

Martin Whitcombe then joined Bedford, who were captained by former Leicester full-back Andy Key, for the 1986-7 season and played against Kenya in Nairobi, a game which formed part of Bedford's centenary celebrations.

He played in the winning County Championship team with Yorkshire in 1986-7, earning their first title in 33 years, and gained national recognition when he was selected to play for the Rest in the England final trial at Twickenham on January 3 1987.

While playing rugby for Durban High School Old Boys in South Africa, Ian Macintosh, the Natal Sharks coach, selected young Whitcombe to play in the 1987-8 Currie Cup and on 23 July he made his debut against Transvaal at Kings Park, Durban. In his day job, Whitcombe was working with Zulu civilians to rebuild infrastructure destroyed by local clashes between the African National Congress and the Inkatha Freedom Party in South Africa's townships during the Apartheid era. Here he saw many scenes of violence, and on one occasion, witnessed a 'neck-lacing'.

Firstly he worked in the township of KwaMashu, 20 miles north of Durban, in the workers hostels in 'A' section and later 'L' section, and helped rebuild school security fences. He also worked at Ntuzuma, Umlazi and Imbali, 15 miles from Pietermaritzburg

McIntosh, a future Springbok coach, said of Martin in his autobiography *Mac: The Face of Rugby*. "I can recall my first away trip as Natal coach and the painful tradition which precedes the flight home. Natal teams, down the years, have developed the quaint habit of beating the bottom, three times, of every new player moments before he boards the plane. The routine is carried out on the airport apron while wide-eyed passengers look on.

"The instrument of torture has changed over the years from the touch-judges flag to a cane but only players with 35 caps or more are permitted to wield the rod. Some see the initiation as barbaric but even experienced international players, Oliver Roumat, Tom Lawton and England loose-forward Chris Butcher thought it was a wonderful tradition once they had taken the rap.

Martin Whitcombe opens the scoring for Yorkshire in the 1987 County Championship semi final against the North Midlands.

"The tradition caused a fair amount of consternation amongst some overseas players who joined Natal. Take the England B prop Martin Whitcombe. Tony Watson took the first swing and Martin let out a roar and immediately turned and sought retribution.

"Fortunately for Tony, it was a prop in pursuit of a winger and not the other way around and he made his escape. Martin puffed when the chase was called off: 'If you did that in England, you would start a bloody war'.

"Natal signed some marvellous overseas players and personalities - the Frenchmen Oliver Roumat and Thierry Lacroix, Wallabies David Knox and Tom Lawton, New Zealanders John Plumtree, Murray Mexted and Murray Pierce, and Englishmen Martin Whitcombe and Chris Butcher.

"Whitcombe was a real character. On one occasion I was driving him and Butcher to a game.

"'Do you miss Zimbabwe?' Chris asked me. 'Yes, at times' I replied, 'I do miss the fishing trips.'

Martin Whitcombe (third right) prepares to pack down against Heinrich Rodgers (No 1), Springbok hooker Harry Roberts looks on. North of England against South Africa, Elland Road, Leeds, November 10 1992.

'I also miss fish 'n' chips!' came Martin's laconic response from the back seat."

Martin fondly remembers his time in South Africa: "To have the opportunity to take the field alongside great players like Rudi Visage and Hugh Reece-Edwards, and to play against the likes of Danie Gerber, Franz Erasmus and Jannie Breedt was a rare experience for an English player at that time. Those players were, in my opinion, truly world class but due to the international boycott of South Africa's apartheid regime, they didn't get the opportunity to show their skills on the global stage."

Martin also paid the price for his playing exploits in South Africa. In June 1989, he and Peter Winterbottom were due to tour Zimbabwe with Yorkshire, but due to their breaching of the Gleneagles Agreement by playing in South Africa both were declared undesirable aliens – *persona non gratia* – by Robert Mugabe's ZANU PF government. As a result the tour was cancelled.

Back in England there then came a move to Sale FC, where Martin was captain from 1992-3 and played in the team which won the Courage League One title in 1993-4. For the Northern Division he played against Australia and South Africa and for the last three years of his career he joined Phil Davies at Leeds

Off the field, the Whitcombe family received a letter from Stuart Duffy, the Bradford Bulls' media manager, informing them that a panel consisting of rugby league writers Nigel Askham and Brian Smith, Jack Bates, a long-serving director at Odsal, Charlie Ebbage, who made his first visit to Odsal in 1938, and Trevor Foster, who had given 60 years of loyal service to the club, had selected their 'Millennium Masters' of the finest players to have worn the Bradford jersey.

Martin Whitcombe and Andy Macfarlane with the Courage League One Championship trophy

Tour manager Fran Cotton with Sale & North of England players, L-R: Andy Macfarlane, Jim Mallinder and Martin Whitcombe, following the North's 8-8 draw with Namibia in Windhoek, August 1992.

Their team was: Keith Mumby; Eric Batten, Ernest Ward, Paul Newlove, Jack McLean; Willie Davies, Tommy Smales; Frank Whitcombe, James Lowes, Jimmy Thompson, Jeff Grayshon, Trevor Foster, Ellery Hanley. Replacements: Henry Paul, Robbie Paul, Karl Fairbank, Ken Traill.

Those players were remembered when their names were read out at half-time during a Bradford Bulls' match at Odsal on Friday September 8 2000.

At the time of writing this book, in 2016, Frank Whitcombe senior's great-grandchildren, Natasha and James Whitcombe, were studying at Bradford's Woodhouse Grove School and showing great promise at netball and rugby union, respectively.

They play on an area called the 'Grainge Pitch', named in honour of former Bradford Northern and England winger Leslie Grainge, a former pupil at Woodhouse Grove, who scored a try for Northern on December 26 1938, in a 25-7 victory over Bramley, the day Frank Whitcombe made his debut.

Standing in front of the 'Grainge Pitch' at Woodhouse Grove School is from (from left) Roger Howard (director of sport), Natasha Whitcombe, James Whitcombe, Kerren Jennings (head of girls PE) and Keith Jones (senior master).

Appendix - 1

THE RUGBY CAREER OF FRANK WHITCOMBE

A RUGBY UNION

Representative matches

1935 May 4	Rest 5 v 13 Wales	Cardiff Arms Park
1935 March 2	Army 11 v 8 Royal Navy	Twickenham
1935 March 23	Army 3 v 6 Royal Air Force	Twickenham
1935 April 27	Final of the Middlesex Sevens	Twickenham

B RUGBY LEAGUE

Club Career

1935-1938 Broughton Rangers - played 123; tries 11; goal: 1
1938-1949 Bradford Northern - played 331; tries: 35; goal: 1

Rugby League Challenge Cup Final

Frank Whitcombe played in five Rugby League Challenge Cup finals, winning on three occasions.

1943-44
Bradford Northern's 8-3 aggregate victory over Wigan in the 1943-44 Challenge Cup final, the 0-3 defeat at Central Park, Wigan, on Saturday April 15 1944, and the 8-0 victory at Odsal Stadium, Bradford, on Saturday April 22 1944, Whitcombe scoring the decisive try in the game.

1944-45
Bradford Northern's 9-13 aggregate defeat by Huddersfield in the 1944-45 Challenge Cup final, the 4-7 defeat at Fartown Ground, Huddersfield, on April 28 1945, and the 5-6 defeat at Odsal Stadium on May 5 1945, three days before the Second World War ended.

1946–47:

Bradford Northern's 8–4 victory over Leeds in the 1946–47 Challenge Cup final at Wembley Stadium, on May 3 1947.

1947–48:

Bradford Northern's 3–8 defeat by Wigan in the 1947–48 Challenge Cup final, at Wembley Stadium, on May 1 1948, when Frank was awarded the Lance Todd trophy. He was the first player from a losing team to receive the award, as well as being the first forward and the oldest player to be a Lance Todd trophy recipient. This was the first rugby league final attended by a reigning monarch, King George VI.

1948–49:

Bradford Northern's 12–0 victory over Halifax in the 1948–49 Challenge Cup final at Wembley Stadium, on May 7 1949, the first Challenge Cup final to be 'sold out' the crowd was 95,050 spectators.

On Saturday April 30 1949 Bradford Northern played Whitehaven RLFC. Harry Hornby, the managing director of Bradford Northern, had a bronze medal struck by Edouard Fraisse of Paris to commemorate Whitcombe's achievement of winning the Lance Todd trophy the previous year and for his services to rugby league football. This was presented to him after the match.

Rugby League Championship

Frank Whitcombe played in five Rugby League Championship play-off finals, winning on three occasions.

1939-40 v Swinton. Won. Played in both legs. Away-leg won 21–13, home-leg won 16–9. Whitcombe scoring a try in each game.

1940-41 v Wigan. Won. Played in both legs. Away-leg won 17–6, home-leg won 28–9.

1941-42 v Dewsbury. Lost 0-13.

1944-45 v Halifax. Won. Away-leg lost 9–2, home-leg won 24–11.

1947-48 v Warrington. Lost 5–15.

County Cup final appearances

Frank Whitcombe played in four rugby league Yorkshire Cup finals, winning all four matches.

1940–41 v Dewsbury, on Saturday April 5 1941, at Fartown Ground, Huddersfield. Bradford Northern won the 1941 Yorkshire Cup (Spring) final 15–5.

1941–42 v Halifax, on Saturday December 6 1941, at Fartown Ground, Huddersfield. Bradford Northern won the 1941 Yorkshire Cup (Autumn) final 24–0.

1945–46 v Wakefield Trinity, on Saturday November 3 1945, at Thrum Hall, Halifax. Bradford Northern won the 1945 Yorkshire Cup final 5–2. Try scored by F Whitcombe.

1948–49 v Castleford, on Saturday 30 October 1948, at Headingley Stadium, Leeds. Bradford Northern won the 1948 Yorkshire Cup Final 18–9.

Yorkshire League

Yorkshire League Winners 1939–40
Yorkshire League Winners 1940–41
Yorkshire League Winners 1947–48

Representative matches

1940 (March 23)	Yorkshire XIII 13 v 10 Lancashire XIII	Craven Park, Barrow
1940 (May 4)	Tour Probables 29 v 21 1936 Tourists	The Willows, Salford
1942 (March 28)	Yorkshire 13 v 2 Lancashire	Crown Flatt, Dewsbury
1946 (January 6)	Rugby League XIII 19 v 6 France XIII	Parc des Princes, Paris

International Games for Wales: 1938 to 1948

1938 (November 5)	Wales 17 v 9 England Att.15,000	Stebonheath Park, Llanelli
1939 (April 16)	Wales 10 v 16 France Att. 25,000	Stade Chaban-Delmas, Bordeaux
1939 (December 23)	Wales 16 v 3 England Att. 15,257	Odsal Stadium, Bradford
1940 (November 9)	Wales 5 v 8 England Att. 5,000	The Watersheddings, Oldham
1941 (October 18)	Wales 9 v 9 England Att. 4,339	Odsal Stadium, Bradford
1943 (February 27)	Wales 9 v 15 England Att. 17,000	Central Park, Wigan
1944 (February 26)	Wales 9 v 9 England Att. 16,028	Central Park, Wigan
1945 (November 24)	Wales 11 v 3 England Att. 30,000	St. Helen's, Swansea
1946 (March 24)	Wales 7 v 19 France Att. 18,000	Stade Chaban-Delmas, Bordeaux
1946 (October 12)	Wales 13 v 10 England Att. 20,213	Station Road, Swinton
1946 (November 16)	Wales 5 v 19 England Att. 25,000	St. Helen's, Swansea
1947 (January 18)	Wales 5 v 14 France Att. 24,500	Stade Vélodrome, Marseille

1948 (March 20)	Wales 12 v 20 France Att. 12,032	St. Helen's, Swansea
1948 (November 20)	Wales 5 v 12 Australia Att. 9,224	St. Helen's, Swansea

Games for Great Britain: 1946 - Australia

May 29	Great Britain 45 v 12 Southern Tablelands	Manuka Oval, Canberra
June 1	Great Britain 14 v 10 New South Wales	SGC, Sydney
June 2	Great Britain 12 v 15 South Coast Division (try: Whitcombe)	Wollongong
June 8	Great Britain 21 v 7 New South Wales	SGC, Sydney
June 12	Great Britain 33 v 2 Western Districts	Orange
June 15	Great Britain 13 v 18 Newcastle	Newcastle Sports Ground
June 17	Great Britain 8 v 8 Australia (try: Whitcombe)	SGC, Sydney
June 19	Great Britain 61 v 5 Northern New South Wales	No 1 Oval, Tamworth
June 22	Great Britain 24 v 25 Queensland	Cricket Ground, Brisbane
June 27	Great Britain 35 v 12 Central Queensland (try: Whitcombe)	Rockhampton
June 30	Great Britain 55 v 16 North Queensland	Townsville
July 6	Great Britain 14 v 5 Australia	Exhibition Ground, Brisbane
July 9	Great Britain 21 v 15 Brisbane	Cricket Ground, Brisbane
July 11	Great Britain 29 v 12 Ipswich	Ipswich
July 16	Great Britain 53 v 8 North Coast	Grafton

Games for Great Britain: 1946 – New Zealand

July 29	Great Britain 8 v 17 West Coast	Victoria Park, Greymouth
August 3	Great Britain 9 v 7 Auckland	Carlaw Park, Auckland
August 7	Great Britain 42 v 12 South Auckland	Davies Park, Huntley
August 12	Great Britain 22 v 9 Auckland	Carlaw Park, Auckland

Testimonial match

Frank Whitcombe's Testimonial match for Bradford Northern was on April 10 1948, at Odsal, against Wakefield Trinity.

Bradford Northern against Leeds at Headingley, Frank Whitcombe (centre) gets his pass away to Willie Davies; (far right) Northern's Barry Tyler looks on.

Appendix - 2

'AUSTRALASIAN TOUR 1946'

THE REPORT OF THE RUGBY LEAGUE COUNCIL

PRIVATE AND CONFIDENTIAL

AUSTRALASIAN TOUR 1946

To the Chairman and Members
        of the Rugby League Council.

Gentlemen,

        After due consideration, and in the light of experience
gained, I submit this report regarding primilary the business
side of the Tour.

        The Touring Party departed from Devonport on
Wednesday, April 3rd, in H.M.S. Aircraft Carrier "Indomitable",
commanded by Captain Andrews. Our accommodation and food were
satisfactory, being berthed in cabins and dormitories respectively. Mr. Crockford, your Managers and members of the Press
dined in the Ward Room and the players in the Warrant Officers'
Mess. Subsequently the players had a mess allocated to them
exclusively. The voyage to Freemantle was uneventful and
Captain Andrews granted every facility at his disposal for our
benefit and comfort.

        Prior to arrival in Freemantle, the Captain raised
the question of playing a game there, and to this suggestion
we readily agreed. This match duly took place on April 30th
and was attended by His Worship the Mayor of Freemantle and
Chief Citizens. The former graciously gave a civic welcome
to our party on arrival in Australia. A collection taken at
the game realised £44, this being augmented by a donation of
£10.10. 0d. from the Rugby League and the proceeds devoted to
Naval Charities. The match was refereed by Mr. E. Waring.

        On the following day we learned that H.M.S.
"Victorious" had sustained damage in the Australian Bight
during passage from Australia with passengers for England, and
that until repairs had been completed her departure would be
delayed. Subsequently it was decided by the Authorities to
disembark all passengers from the H.M.S. "Indomitable" and
transfer them to Leenwin, a naval depot near Freemantle, and
embark the H.M.S. "Victorious" passengers on H.M.S. "Indomitable"
to proceed to England.

        Our accommodation and food at Leenwin were satisfactory.
The Commander of this naval depot placed all foilities for
training at our disposal.

        We left Leenwin on Tuesday, May 7th, and I was noti-
fied that we would be conveyed to Sydney by troop train. There
were no facilities for sleeping on this train, which was under
military control. Prior to departure a knife, fork, spoon
and military blanket were issued to each person. We were
ordered to keep our compartments clean and tidy. There were
morning inspections by the Officer in Charge, and it is worthy
of note that our party was congratulated by him upon the
cleanliness of our quarters. The meals en route were usually
served alongside the railway at various points and eaten whilst
sitting on the lines or sand, whilst the presence of flies did
not add to the comfort of the situation. The food was served
from boilers in front of which we were required to parade. As
we approached Adelaide meals were taken in canteens at various
points. The food was fairly good in quality but lacking in
quantity, and all found it necessary to make purchases to
supplement that provided. An allocation of money was given
to somewhat meet this extra unavoidable expense.

        I would here observe that every endeavour had been
made to make the journey between Freemantle and Sydney by air
and I received every possible assistance from the Board of
Control, with whom I was in constant communication. The
conditions to Melbourne were certainly grim, and considerable
discomfort and inconvenience were experienced by all. From

-2-

Melbourne to Sydney sleeping coaches were provided and Sydney safely reached at 1.10 p.m. on Sunday, May 12th.

We were met by Members of the Australian Board of Control and New South Wales League, with Mr. Sharp, Secretary. A very sincere and hearty welcome was extended to us. During our stay in Sydney we were housed in the Olympic Hotel, Moor Park, Paddington, and found it very satisfactory, the Manageress, Mrs. Mason, giving us every consideration.

On arrival my first concern was the completion and confirmation of the fixture list in Australia, the New Zealand Tour, and booking at the earliest possible moment our return passage to England.

On May 13th I had an interview with Mr. Sharp and discussed with him at some length the foregoing important subjects.

Wednesday, May 15th, the Australian Board of Control extended an official welcome in the form of a dinner.

Thursday, May 16th, we were received by the Premier, Mr. McKell, at the Treasury, who welcomed us to Australia and hoped that our stay would be beneficial, and promised all facilities and so enable the tour to be successful.

In the evening Mr. Crockford, Mr. Popplewell and myself met the New South Wales and Queensland Leagues. The matters as per Councils instructions were frankly discussed, and consisted of the ban on players transfers and interpre- tation of rules. With regard to the ban on players, I elicited from Mr. H. Hegg, Chairman, that it was possible for players to be taken from Queensland Clubs to New South Wales Clubs and vice versa. With this admission I pointed out it could not be argued with any degree of conviction that a satisfactory solution of this contentious matter could be reached. Further discussion was therefore deferred, pending a settlement of policy between New South Wales and Queensland Leagues. In answer to a further question and to clarify the position, Mr. Hegg stated that all games would be played according to the interpretation of rules in England. Several of these rules were discussed, namely, play the ball 10 yards rule, forward pass and putting the ball in scrum. It was agreed to witness the match on Saturday, May 18th, between New South Wales and Queensland, referee Mr. McMahon. This game was attended, and during same some free kicks were given for forward passes, the 10 yards radius rule was not operated, but the whole width of the field. Play the ball was crude and not in accordance with the rule, and similarly putting the ball in the scrum. At the conclusion of the game the referee, Mr. McMahon, approached Mr. Popplewell and enquired if he was satisfied with the interpretation of the rules, and Mr. Popplewell replied "Yes". I immediately strongly protested against this agreement, especially in view of the fact that Mr. Popplewell and myself had not compared notes before expressing any opinion. I also called the attention of members of the Australian Board of Control on many subsequent occasions, but the interpretation of rules foreign to those in England continued throughout the tour, not only in Australia but also in New Zealand. I am convinced these rulings had detrimental effect on the players and on numerous occasions players have protested against what to my mind was a gross injustice after assurances had been given that the English rulings would operate. It was perfectly obvious that no consideration was given to my protests judged by the continuance of this handicap. I might here mention that, in the final match against Auckland, New Zealand, so incensed were the players regarding rulings foreign to them that there was a probability of the second half not being played unless matters could be adjusted. Previous to the interval I had a conversation with Mr. Redwood, Chairman of the New Zealand

...ague, with a result that the referee gave decisions more in keeping with our interpretation. Further reference to this important matter will be made under observations.

On Friday, May 17th, a civic reception was given by the Lord Mayor of Sydney supported by the Minister of Education, Admiral Westwood and Chief Citizens, approximately 300 persons attended.

Sunday, May 19th, we were the guests of the Board of Control, a motor tour having been arranged by them to Palm Beach. Unfortunately it rained heavily all day. This was our first experience of rain, but, nevertheless, an enjoyable time was spent. The first match of the tour was played at Junee on Wednesday, May 22nd.

I would here state that owing to not being in possession of the selected team I was unable to forward same to the Junee Honorary Secretary. This was a source of embarrassment to me, as also on two subsequent occasions.

Many applications for matches had been received by Mr. Sharp, and after consideration we agreed to play at Canberra, with a guarantee of £100. This extra fixture was strongly supported by the Board of Control. His Royal Highness, The Cuke of Gloucester, to whom the players were introduced, attended this game. Previous to the match The Prime Minister, Mr. Chifley received us at Parliament House, accompanied by Mr. Johnston, Minister of the Interior.

On June 3rd and 4th, at the invitation of the Australian Government, we visited Jenolan Caves. This was a welcome diversion and thoroughly enjoyed by all. Mr. R. Savage representing the Government also attended, together with Mr. H. Hegg, who also received an invitation to be present. On June 6th I called the attention of Mr. Popplewell to what, in my opinion, to the effect that too much attention was being given to social activities and insufficient time to the requirements of the tour, adding that the players had not produced the form which gained them selection in the touring side. Subsequently a curfew was instituted, but as far as I could perceive, was not enforced even the first night it was supposed to be in operation.

An invitation was received from the Referees Society, for the Managers to attend their meeting on Wednesday, June 5th. This was attended by Mr. Popplewell, I was not present, and I am not therefore in a position to give a report of the proceedings.

Owing to the position of affairs regarding the carrying out of arrangements, and the necessity to give details of the travelling in Queensland, a meeting with the players was held in the Hotel Daniels, Brisbane. The above mentioned matters were discussed and instructions given at the conclusion of this meeting. F. McCue asked if it was a fact that other players had been consulted regarding the selection of teams, as the truth of this was gaining ground amongst the players, and consequently causing grave concern. An admission of this fact was given. In view of the serious position that was formed, I closed the discussion and gave an undertaking to mention this matter later, which promise I now fulfil. The travelling arrangements in Queensland owing to the internal position, were also very trying.

In fairness, however, to the Queensland League, it must be stated that the matter was beyond their control, and I hasten to gratefully acknowledge the ready assistance they gave to make our journeys as comfortable as conditions would permit, and acknowledge with gratitude the valuable assistance rendered by Mr. V. Jensen and Mr. E. Simmons of the Queensland League. Throughout our journeys in Queensland Mr. Jenson travelled with us and shared all the difficulties and inconveniences, and was

-4-

always ready to assist. The position then existing will, no doubt, be better appreciated that in order to enable our journey to be continued our coach was attached to a goods train. This journey usually occupies seven hours, the goods train took twelve hours, and again no sleeping carriages could be provided. Travel by train was daily becoming more difficult to arrange. A number of trains ceased to run and the service was cut to a minimum, raising steam was by wood. Undoubtedly this state of affairs was affecting the temperament of all concerned, and after due consideration it was decided to travel by air on every available opportunity. The immediate effect of this decision was noticed in the changed demeanour of the players. On one occasion in Queensland it was found desirable to transfer the players from an hotel to alternative accommodation.

On July 7th at the invitation of the Legislative Assembly we had a motor trip to Southport, accompanied by Mr. Bruce, Minister of Works and Housing, Mr. Brassington, Speaker of the House and Mr. Keyatta, a member of the Legislative Assembly. Next day, July 8th, at the invitation of Mr. Brassington, we visited the Houses of Parliament, and also attended a civic welcome by the Lord Mayor of Brisbane.

On July 17th the Board of Control and the New South Wales Leagues gave the Touring Party a farewell dinner. Mr. Popplewell was not present.

I conveyed the thanks of the Rugby League Council and our own for the very kind hospitality and ever ready assistance and consideration extended to us throughout the tour, and a sincere desire that the good feeling now existing may long continue and the Rugby League game prosper.

On July 18th the Ashes Cup was presented to Mr. Popplewell by the Chairman of Tattersalls Club.

NEW ZEALAND TOUR

Difficulties regarding transport from Australia were experienced, and it was not possible to make the journey by sea; air travel having to be undertaken. This was successfully accomplished in three parties, at a cost of £30 per passenger. The three parties left Sydney on July 22nd, 23rd and 24th respectively. Previous to our departure from Australia the New Zealand League were somewhat perturbed by our not readily agreeing to visit New Zealand. I assured them that we had every intention of fulfilling our obligations but until we had an assurance that our return passage to England had been arranged, I could not agree to tour New Zealand, especially as I was in possession of the information regarding unsuitable sailings for England from Australia in the immediate future, and further, that the party desired to leave New Zealand at the earliest possible date after August 10th. Immediately I learned passage had been booked on the 'Rangitiki', I cabled, by return, acceptance of fixture list and gave the date of arrival in New Zealand. Prior to this assurance of booking our return, I had a month previously provisionally fixed all arrangements to make the crossing of the Tasman by air, and to forward the heavy luggage by a small cargo steamer, which arrangement was duly carried out.

On arrival in New Zealand we were received by Mr. Redwood, Chairman of the League, and other members of his Committee. On Thursday, August 8th, we were received at Parliament House by Mr. Fraser, Prime Minister of New Zealand, and Members of Parliament.

On August 8th, Mr. Crockford, Mr. Popplewell and myself had a meeting with the Committee of the New Zealand League, and the following is a report of the proceedings.

-5-

RE MEETING WITH THE NEW ZEALAND LEAGUE

At this Meeting the New Zealand League was represented by Messrs. Redwood (Chairman), Dobbe, Fergusson, Asher, Swift, Philburn, Tremain, Bennet and Carlaw.   The British representatives being Messrs. Crockford, Popplewell and Gabbatt.

Mr. Redwood welcomed your representatives and spoke of the serious concern the New Zealand League held regarding players leaving to play for English Clubs.   They were finding difficulty to retain players to compete against England and Australia, and it is not therefore in the interest of goodwill. He hoped this Conference would consist of free and frank discussion.

Mr. Crockford much appreciated our welcome and stated the Rugby League Council are anxious to help New Zealand and assist in protecting her players.

Mr. Popplewell also voiced thanks for the reception, and stated should the Rugby League Council extend an invitation to New Zealand he would, for one, welcome a team to England and support a visit.   He also considered protection of players necessary.

Various views were expressed regarding this vital matter, and New Zealand are anxious that a transfer fee shall be brought into operation at the earliest possible moment. They are not at the moment concerned about an agreement with Australia.   Fear was expressed that if some arrangement was not forthcoming the game will go out.   This was the opinion of Mr. Carlaw, the Honorary Secretary, who suggested a fee of £500.   He was anxious that England should know that New Zealand were optimistic regarding the standard of management and the future.

It was finally resolved to suggest that for each player transferred from New Zealand the sum of £300 be paid to the League.

The question of a proposed tour to England was discussed, the cost of which was estimated at £9000.   The balance in hand at the conclusion of the English Tour was estimated at £3,000.   The transport accommodation etc. was mentioned.   Mr. Crockford and Mr. Popplewell mentioned Harrogate as likely headquarters during their stay in England.

Other matters under discussion were interpretation of rules such as, pass forward, play the ball, putting the ball in scrum and the replacement of injured players up to half time.

Whilst in New Zealand the opportunity was taken of visiting Rotoura - I understand this has been done on previous tours.   The visit was highly interesting and enjoyed by the whole of the party.   During our stay a visit was made to a Maori School where the children rendered action songs, which were much appreciated.   We discussed various suggestions to make our visit in a tangible form and after consideration decided to purchase a rose bowl for the girls and a cup for the boys, to be awarded annually to the best girl and boy athlete.   The Maori adviser, Madame Renee and Mr. Alexander, Head Master, readily agreed to the proposal, and expressed their sincere thanks and appreciation.   The trophies were duly obtained and inscribed "British Rugby League Touring Team 1946" with further inscription setting forth the conditions of holding same.   The total cost was £6.17. 0d.

On Thursday, August 8th, a letter was received from the players asking that their percentage of bonus should be considered, with a view to increasing same.   I duly forwarded this letter to Mr. Fallowfield and will offer comments when same is discussed.   It was agreed to play an extra match

-6-

against Auckland.   This was duly played on August 12th and was a financial success.

On Wednesday, August 14th, we sailed from Wellington on board the H.M.S. "Rangitiki".   Before leaving Auckland Mr. Redwood, Mr. Carlaw and other members, hoped we would have a safe journey home and carry away happy recollections of our visit to New Zealand.   We assured them of our grateful thanks for their many kindnesses and trusted their efforts on behalf of the Rugby League would be successful.

Throughout our stay in New Zealand the hotel accommodation was good.

During the voyage to Panama, it was learned that the "Rangitiki" would call at New York and probably stay three days.

The question of playing a match there was raised, and I understand that certain players approached Mr. Popplewell with a view to a game being arranged.   I am informed he told the deputation that he was not in favour of playing a match, owing to the players not being fit, and he was afraid the prestige of the game would suffer accordingly.   Subsequently Mr. Risman and Mr. Kitching interviewed me and I referred them to Mr. Popplewell, who later informed me he had an open mind on the matter.   In the meantime I cabled Mr. Fallowfield informing him of our intentions and received a favourable reply with safeguards as to financial terms and date of arrival in England, which were carefully noted.   I subsequently interviewed Capt. Holland of the "Rangitiki" with a view to ascertaining, if possible, the length of stay in New York.   He said he would prefer a joint meeting with your Managers, Mr. Crockford, members of the Press and Mr. H. Sunderland, to talk the matter over.   I pointed out to him that the information I desired did not concern anybody but the Managers, who desired some information of the approximate stay in New York.   He was very keen to have a joint meeting and in deference to his wishes I notified the people he desired to be present.   This meeting was duly held and all the before mentioned people attended.   The Captain stated our stay in New York would be approximately 30 hours.   He also stated the grounds would be very hard, and the temperature about 90°. A question was also asked if he, the Captain, considered a football match could be played, I interjected that this point was no concern of his.   Looking back on the sequence of events, I am of the opinion that this project had been previously discussed with the Captain.

Later the ship, owing to the strike of dock workers on the wharfs at New York, was diverted to Halifax.   This information was cabled to Mr. Fallowfield.

Before leaving this subject I desire to place on record my sincere thanks to Mr. H. Sunderland and Mr. E. Waring for the very valuable assistance in the provisional arrangements, by their contacting various people in New York.

We arrived at Panama on Monday, September 2nd and entered the canal on Tuesday, September 3rd, arriving the same day at Christabel, where a few hours shore leave was given, the first for three weeks.

Curacao was reached on September 7th, where leave was granted until 3.0 p.m. and at 4.15 left for New York, but, as previously reported, we were diverted to Halifax.   Had New York been visited I had contacted Messrs. Thos. Cook & Sons, with a view to a motor tour of the city being arranged. On Thursday, September 12th, the "Rangatiki" berthed at Halifax, and a full day was spent on shore.   Our departure from Halifax took place at 12.20 a.m., Saturday, September 14th.

-7-

Tilbury was reached on Sunday, September 22nd at
10.0 p.m. and we were welcomed by Mr. Hughes, Chairman, Mr.
Lockwood, Mr. Anderton, Mr. Hornby and Mr. Fallowfield, on Monday,
September 23rd.

I desire to place on record appreciation of the arrangements made for our comfort and convenience on arrival at Tilbury
and departure to our homes.

We appreciated the Councils desire to mark our
arrival by a dinner but this, by mutual consent was deferred.

OBSERVATIONS

I received a letter from Mr. Fallowfield complaining,
in my view rather harshly, of weekly reports not being forwarded
to the Council. This letter was handed to Mr. Popplewell who
informed me that to his knowledge no such reports had been
furnished during the previous tour. I would also add that
previous to departure I was not informed that weekly reports
were required. Following this letter, cables stating, when
available, gate receipts and attendances were sent, and also
each week a report on activities, etc. We appreciated the
congratulatory cables from Mr. Hughes and Mr. Fallowfield upon
the winning of the Ashes.

Standard of Play in Australia and New Zealand

The standard of play, in my opinion, is not of the pre-
war quality, and the Authorities concerned are alive to this fact.

I had many confidential talks with members of the
Australian Board of Control, and New South Wales and Queensland
League, and I found a sincere desire at the earliest possible
moment to attain the pre-war standard of football. In all
conferences and talks a very healthy co-operative spirit was
evident, and I suggest that the present time is most opportune
for the placing on a sound and lasting basis a mutual agreement
on two outstanding problems, namely, interpretation of rules
and ban on players. The refereeing was not of a high standard.

Australian Press

Certain members of the Australian Press on several
occasions caused concern amongst the players by the publishing
of alleged remarks they had made during interviews. This also
applied to your Managers. Eventually at a meeting the players
were directed to refrain from making statements, in view of the
distortion placed upon their remarks.

From my personal observation I am of the opinion that
the hospitality given to sections of the team by members of the
Australian Press was not in the best interests of the players
concerned.

I feel it is only fitting that I should refer to one
member of the British Press, whom the Council gave permission to
accompany the touring party. It will be remembered, no doubt,
my attitude with regard to Mr. Eddie Waring of the "Sunday
Pictorial', and my observations regarding him at the final
meeting of the Tour Sub-Committee. I therefore took the earliest
possible opportunity of making my acquaintance with Mr. Waring
and discussed with him various policies that I was determined to
pursue throughout the Tour, and it gives me the greatest possible
pleasure to be in a position to report that I received from him
every possible assistance and co-operation; at all times, for
which I am most grateful.

In the very near future the Council will be called
upon to decide as to the next visit of a team from the Antipodes.

-8-

It will be remembered that New Zealand in 1939 sent over a team to England, and this tour, owing to the outbreak of war, was cancelled. They are anxious to again tour England and so is Australia. Of the comparative playing strength of either country I favour, at the moment, Australia.

New Zealand are well aware of their limitations, judged by the fact that they are hoping to recruit more capable players in the event of their touring England.

The following is an extract from the financial returns :-

Financial Particulars :

Total Gate Monies Received :-

		£. s. d.
Australia	...	49,937. 6. 8.
New Zealand	...	9,300. 6. 7.
		£59,237.13. 3.

Tax :-

Australia	...	11,710.13. 6.
New Zealand	...	1,214.11.10.
		£12,925. 5. 4.

Nett Gate :-

Australia	...	38,226.13. 2.
New Zealand	...	8,085.14. 9.
		£46,312. 7.11.

England's Share (Australia) ...	...	22,931. 2. 6.
" " (New Zealand) ...	...	4,851.14. 3.
		£27,782.16. 9.

Australia's Share	...	15,295.10. 8.

New Zealand's Share	...	3,234. 0. 6.

I would not like to close this Report without taking the opportunity of putting on record sincere thanks to my employers, the Barrow-in-Furness Corporation, who, without hesitation, gave me leave of absence to undertake the position of Business Manager in connection with this tour.

In conclusion I desire to record my thanks for having been privileged to be Business Manager of the 1946 British Rugby League Touring Team.

Tom Gabbatt

BUSINESS MANAGER,
Australasian Tour, 1946.

2nd October, 1946.

ADDENDUM TO REPORT

ANALYSIS OF GATE RECEIPTS ENGLISH TOUR OF AUSTRALIA 1946

FIXTURE	PLACE	DATE	GROSS GATE £. s. d.	LESS TAX £. s. d.	NET GATE £. s. d.	ENGLAND'S SHARE £. s. d.	HOME SHARE £. s. d.
Southern Division N.S.W.	JUNEE	May 22nd	649.2.9	146.14.9	502.8.0	301.9.5	200.18.7
Canberra	CANBERRA	" 29th	445.19.6	111.10.0	334.9.6	200.0.0	134.1.6
New South Wales	SYDNEY	Jun.1st	6012.9.0	1426.18.10	4585.10.2	2751.6.0	1834.4.2
South Coast Divis.N.S.W.	WOLLONGONG	" 2nd	1330.2.10	318.8.5	1011.14.5	607.0.6	404.13.11
New South Wales	SYDNEY	" 8th	5249.0.3	1242.13.0	4006.7.3	2403.16.4	1602.10.11
Western Division N.S.W.	ORANGE	" 12th	958.2.3	214.17.5	743.4.10	445.18.11	297.5.11
Newcastle	NEWCASTLE	" 15th	2437.0.10	586.2.8	1850.18.2	1110.10.9	740.7.5
AUSTRALIA 1st TEST	SYDNEY	" 17th	10106.3.11	2373.4.9	7732.19.2	4639.15.2	3093.3.8
Northern Division	TAMWORTH	" 19th	804.6.0	175.11.6	628.14.6	377.4.6	251.10.0
Queensland	BRISBANE	" 22nd	2914.9.6	688.14.11	2225.14.7	1335.8.9	890.5.10
Wide Bay	BUNDABERG	" 25th	663.19.0	148.8.6	515.10.6	309.0.0	206.10.6
Central Queensland	ROCKHAMPTON	" 27th	718.0.2	168.18.6	549.1.8	329.9.0	219.12.8
North Queensland	TOWNSVILLE	" 30th	1298.0.5	296.8.5	1001.12.0	600.19.3	400.12.9
Mackay	MACKAY	Jul. 2nd	568.15.6	123.1.8	445.13.10	267.8.3	178.5.7
AUSTRALIA 2nd TEST	BRISBANE	" 6th	6009.16.4	1405.11.10	4604.4.6	2762.10.9	1841.13.9
Brisbane	BRISBANE	" 9th	2257.15.6	529.0.2	1728.15.4	1037.5.2	691.10.2
Ipswich	IPSWICH	" 11th	803.11.3	186.17.8	616.13.7	370.0.2	246.13.5
Toowoomba	TOOWOOMBA	" 13th	1281.17.1	285.10.5	996.6.8	592.16.0	403.10.8
North Coast Division	GRAFTON	" 16th	966.18.9	233.2.11	733.15.10	441.0.0	292.15.10
AUSTRALIA 3rd TEST	SYDNEY	" 20th	4461.15.10	1048.17.2	3412.18.8	2047.15.3	1365.3.5
			49937.6.8	11710.13.6	38226.13.2	22931.2.6	15295.10.8

ANALYSIS OF GATE RECEIPTS ENGLISH TOUR OF NEW ZEALAND 1946

FIXTURE	PLACE	DATE	GROSS GATE	LESS TAX	NET GATE	ENGLAND'S SHARE	HOME SHARE
			£. s. d.	£. s. d.	£. s. d.	£. s. d.	£. s. d.
South Island	CHRISTCHURCH	July 27th	1265. 4. 6.	156. 6. 7.	1108.17.11.	665.11. 4.	443. 6. 7.
Maoris	WELLINGTON	" 31st	1134. 0. 0.	142. 0. 0.	992. 0. 0.	595. 4. 0.	396.16. 0.
South Auckland	HUNTLEY	Aug. 7th	424. 2. 0.	52.10.10.	371.11. 2.	222.18. 8.	148.12. 6.
West Coast	GREYMOUTH	July 29th	535.14. 0.	54. 2. 0.	481.12. 0.	289. 0. 0.	192.12. 0.
Auckland	AUCKLAND	Aug. 3rd	2319.15. 1.	291. 0.11.	2028.14. 2.	1217. 4. 6.	811. 9. 8.
New Zealand	AUCKLAND	" 10th	2086.11. 6.	313. 1.10.	1773. 9. 8.	1064. 1. 9.	709. 7.11.
Auckland	AUCKLAND	" 12th	1534.19. 6.	205. 9. 8.	1329. 9.10.	797.14. 0.	531.15.10.
			9300. 6. 7.	1214.11.10.	8085.14. 9.	4851.14. 3.	3234. 0. 6.

-2-

BIBLIOGRAPHY

Whitcombe Family Archive

Four Scrap books belonging to Frank Whitcombe.

The photographs in this book are from six photograph albums which belonged to Frank Whitcombe and the Whitcombe family archive.

Trevor Foster's contributions to this book came from recorded statement's about his rugby career and experiences made by him during his life time to his son Simon Foster.

Books

Bradford Northern The History 1863-1989 by Nigel Williams: self published, 1989.

The Compete History of Bradford Northern Rugby League Football Club by Cedric Ludlum: MQ Printing Ltd., 1989.

Come on Northern - The Fall and Rise of Bradford Northern RLFC 1954 to 1965 by Trevor Delany: London League Publications Ltd., 2012.

Bumper - The Life and Times of Frank Bumper Farrell by Larry Writer: Hatchette, 2011.

The History of Army Rugby by John McLaren: The Army RFU, 1986.

Port Vale Personalities: A Biographical Dictionary of Players, Officials and Supporters by Jeff Kent: Witan Books. 1996.

The History of Royal Air Force Rugby by John Mace: Royal Air Force Rugby Union, 2000.

Willie by Mike Gardener: Dixon Printing Co., 1994.

Rugby League in Manchester by Graham Morris: Tempus Publishing, 2003.

Rugby League Records 1895-1979 edited by Irvin Saxton.

Lionel Cooper Souvenir Brochure compiled by A N Gaulton, 1955.

History of Rugby League Booklets 1939-1945.

England Expects Rugby Football League Tour Brochure by Stanley Chadwick 1946.

Eddie Waring – the Great Ones and Other Writings by Tony Waring: Scratching Shed Publishing Ltd., 2010.

Dragon in Exile-The Centenary History of London Welsh RFC by Paul Beken & Stephen Jones: Springwood Books Ltd., 1985.

Hero - Rugby Leagues' Greatest Award Winners by Graham Morris: Vertical Editions, 2005.

Bradford RFC Rugby Centenary Book 1866-1966: Bradford RFC, 1966.

Willie Away - Wilson Whineray's All Blacks Of 1963-64 by Terry McLean: Herbert Jenkins, 1964.

Yorkshire Rugby Union - Official Handbook 1975-6 by Phil Gaunt.
The Official History of Leicester Football Club by Stuart Farmer & David Hands:
    Rugby Development 2014.
Mac - The Face of Rugby by John Bishop: Don Nelson Publishers, 2000.
Natal 100 - The Centenary of Natal Rugby Union by Reg Sweet: Natal Rugby
    Union, 1990.

Newspapers

Auckland Sporting times
Canberra Times
Courier Mail
Daily Advertiser
Daily Herald
Daily Mail
Die Burger
Evening Chronicle
Eastern Counties Advertiser
France Soir
Gloucester Citizen
Hull Daily Mail
Leicester Mercury
Molong Express
Natal Mercury
News of the World
Rugby League Parade
Rugby League Gazette
Rugby League Review
Rugby World
South Wales Echo
Sunday Despatch
Sunday Mail
Sunday Pictorial
Sunderland Echo
Sydney Morning Herald
Telegraph and Argus
The Times
Western Daily Press
Western Morning News
Yorkshire Evening Post
Yorkshire Observer Budget
Yorkshire Observer
Yorkshire Post

ST DAVID'S PRESS

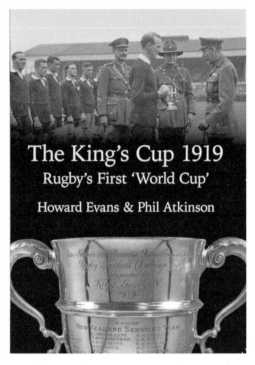

The King's Cup 1919
Rugby's First 'World Cup'
Howard Evans & Phil Atkinson

'An intriguing retelling of a significant but largely forgotten chapter of rugby union history, superbly illustrated.'
Huw Richards, author of '*A Game for Hooligans: The History of Rugby Union*'

'Howard is an authority on rugby's history'
Andy Howell, Rugby Correspondent, *Western Mail*

The world of rugby union celebrated the 8th Rugby World Cup in 2015, but a tournament held in 1919, The King's Cup, can rightly claim to be rugby's first competitive 'World Cup'.

Meticulously compiled by Howard Evans and Phil Atkinson, ***The King's Cup 1919*** is the first book to tell the full story of rugby's first 'World Cup' and is essential reading for all rugby enthusiasts and military historians.

With over 140 photos and illustrations, and chapters focusing on the competing teams, the players, and every game in the tournament, the authors have provided a comprehensive and attractive record of a long-forgotten but historically important competition of which most rugby supporters are completely unaware.

978 1 902719 443 – £14.99 – 192pp – 140 illustrations/photographs